ALSO BY HUNTER S. THOMPSON

HEY RUBE

BLOOD SPORT, THE BUSH DOCTRINE, AND THE DOWNWARD SPIRAL OF DUMBNESS

MODERN HISTORY FROM THE SPORTS DESK

Hunter S. Thompson

SIMON & SCHUSTER • NEW YORK
LONDON   TORONTO   SYDNEY

SIMON & SCHUSTER
Rockefeller Center
1230 Avenue of the Americas
New York, NY 10020

For information about special discounts for bulk purchases,
please contact Simon & Schuster Special Sales at
1-800-456-6798 or business@simonandschuster.com

DESIGNED BY DANA SLOAN

Manufactured in the United States of America

10 9 8 7 6 5 4 3 2 1

Library of Congress Cataloging-in-Publication Data

Thompson, Hunter S.
  Hey Rube / Hunter S. Thompson.
      p.   cm.
    1. Sports—United States.   2. Newspapers—Sections,
columns, etc.—Sports.   I. Title.

GV583.T56 2004
796'.0973—dc22   2004052110

ISBN 0-684-87319-2

To George Plimpton and Warren Zevon,
who are no longer with us. . . .
And to David Rosenthal, who is.

Now it is not good for the Christian's health to hustle
the Aryan brown,
For the Christian riles, and the Aryan smiles and
he weareth the Christian down;
And the end of the fight is a tombstone white with the name
of the late deceased,
And the epitaph drear: "A Fool lies here who tried
to hustle the East."

—Rudyard Kipling, "The Naulahka"

Those who have had a chance for four years and could not
produce peace should not be given another chance.

—Richard Nixon, October 9, 1968

Contents

PART TWO

PART THREE

Foreword

The first time I met Hunter was in October of 1973 at the California Street mansion home of Jann Wenner, founder of *Rolling Stone* magazine, where I had just been hired to be the managing editor. Jann accurately predicted that Hunter and I would bond over sports. (It was Jann's last accurate prediction.) As I walked into the living room, Hunter was watching the *Monday Night Football* Buffalo Bills–Pittsburgh Steelers game. Within fifteen minutes we had devised a game of chance: Hunter would have the left side of the screen, the light jerseys, the even-numbered uniforms, and all the Caucasian players. I would have the right side of the TV, the dark jerseys, the odd numbers, and all of the non-Caucasian combatants. Add up the points scored for each of our "teams," and the loser would buy the winner a bottle of Wild Turkey, Hunter's preferred adult beverage of the day.

What we had not foreseen was that the critical points that would determine the outcome would be scored by Franco Harris. And, of course, the deciding factor was whether Franco Harris, the son of a mixed marriage, was on the Caucasian or non-Caucasian side of the ledger. Into the room walked George Plimpton, world renowned sports author *(Paper Lion)*, world-class intellectual (Harvard), and diplomat extraordinaire. Hunter and I quickly agreed that George would make the ideal arbiter. No sooner had we posed the issue when George, as only George could, poured forth his ruling with the expertise of Hippocrates and the authority of a Supreme Court justice. Did we get an earful of recessive genes! Hunter listened attentively and watched with bemused amazement until George declared Hunter the loser, at which time Hunter furiously grabbed a full bottle of the host's very own Wild Turkey, guzzled half of it, stole the keys to the host's white Mercedes Benz, and pulled out of the driveway, foot to the accelerator, waving the Wild Turkey out the window and screaming, "Vermin, scum, rat eaters!" Why do sports and HST go together? Because Hunter likes to lose his temper over grave matters.

Dr. Hunter "Sports" Thompson. That's how I have come to know the Prince of Gonzo. Competitor, sportsman, strategist, champion of the teams that win him wagers. Hunter? Sports?—Why?

Because sports brings out his giddiness. The trademark "Ho, hos," the whimsical smile, and the worship of mischief are all elements of HST's literary persona that easily and conveniently attach themselves to sports.

Because Hunter's ultimate goal is to be named the Prime Minister of Fun, and sports is his Proud Highway.

Because Hunter loves anarchy, domination, power, wealth, dynasty, revenge, and failure. Mood swings are a staple of the Gonzo lifestyle.

Because sports is full of rebels and rascals, Hunter's closest friends.

Because Hunter is genetically predisposed toward uncertainty, adventure, and risk.

And because sports, for Hunter, are a serious subject to be enjoyed to the fullest and consumed in copious amounts.

Hunter visited Washington in the fall of 1978 and invited me to a Sunday football feast at his Hyatt Regency hotel suite. Before the first kickoff, Hunter, the always gracious host, ordered room service for the game. "I'd like a fifth of Chivas Regal, three six-packs of Heineken, a half dozen bloody marys, and everything chocolate on the menu." I was the only other person in the room and informed my host that I was on a diet that precluded sweets and alcohol. One hour later, two waiters delivered the order with looks only cameras could capture. The chocolate tray included a German chocolate cake, a vat of Breyer's chocolate ice cream, a half dozen chocolate cupcakes, a plate of chocolate cookies, one chocolate sundae, two chocolate cream pies, and a buffet of various chocolate pastries. And of course, the requisite postprandial chocolate bonbons.

Hunter was ready for some football.

Normally, Hunter ingests his sports from his command

post on an elevated swivel chair in his Owl Farm kitchen next to the leather refrigerator. From his catbird seat, Hunter operates the satellite dish, monitors the phone lines, and directs his domestic staff. Throughout the evening, he regularly hurls creative epithets at the TV screen and digests whatever nourishment gets him through the night to sunrise.

But the real showpiece at action central is the conversation—in the room and on the phone—a steady stream that flows seamlessly from sports to politics and politics to sports. The tone, on the other hand, scrambles the brain pan.

Rage—a Dubya press conference response; the missed layup.

Passion—making the case for John Kerry; stomping on Al Davis.

Calm reserve—the facts about development on Woody Creek political environmental issues; breaking news about Shaq's ailing knees before a critical game.

Doom—Bin Laden's strategy; the fear of another fixed game—remember B.C. in *Good Fellas*.

Advocacy—Free Lisl Auman; cheer the beloved Indianapolis Colts to the Super Bowl.

Woofing—Pity the fools who expose their political leanings or favorite teams. They quickly become victims of the Gonzo stiletto.

Elation—Hunter toasts to the victors, thumps his desk at the mention of great wisdom, cheers for the winning wagers, justice, and fun. Good times.

The conversation cruises comfortably in tone and topic until it's time for Hunter to go to work writing, sometime around two or three in the morning. The voices of sports and politics come from Nicholson, Douglas Brinkley, Depp, Del Toro, Irsay, the Sheriff, Ed Bradley, et al. The price of entry is knowledge, expertise, and outrageous thinking. Enter at your own risk. And it's not an either/or proposition. It's politics and sports. Hunter will remind you that boxing is a sport and can be a factor in political strategy.

In 1983, as March Madness was about to begin, Hunter

found himself in Manhattan again among "the fools and the brackets" as part of the emerging culture of "the sports dumb." The NCAA tournament was moving along, and Pepperdine was putting the finishing touches on a middle-of-the-road North Carolina State team late on a Friday night. When North Carolina State started fouling to catch up, Hunter quietly murmured, "I'll take North Carolina State to win the whole damn thing. I like Valvano. He seems to know what he's doing."

So it was a natural in 2000 when espn.com launched an adventurous initiative called *Page 2* that I called Hunter and asked if he wanted to take a page from his past and become a sports writer again. Thus began his weekly "Hey, Rube" column that challenged many conventions known to sports, the Internet, writing, and editing.

—*John A. Walsh*

ADDRESS REPLY
ATTN: Base Staff Personnel Officer
        Personnel Report: A/2C Hunter S. Thompson   23 Aug 57

1. A/2C Hunter S. Thompson, AF 15546879, has worked in the Internal Information Section, OIS, for nearly one year. During this time he has done some outstanding sports writing, but ignored APGC-OIS policy.

2. Airman Thompson possesses outstanding talent in writing. He has imagination, good use of English, and can express his thoughts in a manner that makes interesting reading.

3. However, in spite of frequent counseling with explanation of the reasons for the conservative policy on an AF Base newspaper, Airman Thompson has consistently written controversial material and leans so strongly to critical editorializing that it was necessary to require that all his writing be thoroughly edited before release.

4. The first article that called attention to the writing noted above was a story very critical of Base Special Services. Others that were stopped before they were printed were pieces that severely criticized Arthur Godfrey and Ted Williams that Airman Thompson extracted from national media releases and added his flair for the inuendo and exaggeration.

5. This Airman has indicated poor judgement from other standpoints by releasing Air Force information to the Playground News himself, with no consideration for other papers in the area, or the fact that only <u>official</u> releases, carefully censored by competent OIS staff members, are allowed.

6. In summary, this Airman, although talented, will not be guided by policy or personal advice and guidance. Sometimes his rebel and superior attitude seems to rub off on other airmen staff members. He has little consideration for military bearing or dress and seems to dislike the service and want out as soon as possible.

7. Consequently, it is requested that Airman Thompson be assigned to other duties immediately, and it is recommended that he be earnestly considered under the early release program.

8. It is also requested that Airman Thompson be officially advised that he is to do no writing of any kind for internal or external publication unless such writing is edited by the OIS staff, and that he is not to accept outside employment with any of the local media.

W.S. EVANS, Colonel, USAF
Chief, Office of Information
Services

Author's Note

It is no accident that this column is titled *Hey, Rube*. That is what's called my "Standing Head" in the arcane jargon of Journalism, and it will not change anytime soon. "Hey, Rube" is an old-timey phrase, coined in the merciless culture of the Traveling Carnival gangs that roamed from town to town in the early 20th century. Every stop on the circuit was just another chance to fleece another crowd of free-spending Rubes—Suckers, Hicks, Yokels, Johns, Fish, Marks, Bums, Losers, Day traders in Portland, fools who buy diamonds from gypsies, and anyone over the age of nine in this country who still believes in his heart that all cops are honest and would never lie in a courtroom.

These people are everywhere. They are Legion, soon to be a majority, and 10,000 more are being born every day. It was P. T. Barnum, the Circus man, who explained the real secret of his vast commercial success by repeating his now-famous motto, "There's a sucker born every minute," in this country, and *his* job was to keep them amused. Which he did—with a zeal that has never been equaled in the history of American show business.

Barnum knew what people wanted: Freaks, Clowns, and Wild Animals. The Barnum & Bailey Circus came to town only once a year, and those days were marked as sacred holidays on the John Deere calendars of every Rube in America. . . . Those dates were Special; many schools closed when the Circus came to town, and not every student returned when the public frenzy was over. "Running away with the Circus" was the dream of every schoolboy and the nightmare of every mother with a bored and beautiful daughter.

Pearl Harbor was 60 years ago, before we had TV and computers to keep us totally informed. When half the U.S. Navy was destroyed by Japanese bombs, at least we knew who did it and where they lived, and that news was spread all over the world in a matter of minutes, with eyewitness accounts and photos of burning battleships.

What has gone wrong with our communication system since then? Why are we more ignorant and less informed today than we were in 1941?

That is an eerie question, eh?

You bet it is. If World War III can start in a vacuum of silence and stonewalling by the White House, we are doomed like rats in a maze of fear. We are slaves to mendacity and hostile disinformation. Bread and circuses were not enough to sustain the Roman Empire and they will not be enough for the United States of America.

How long, O lord, how long? This blizzard of shame is getting a little *old*, isn't it? Just how low do we have to fall before the voters catch on?

Indeed. How many times can a man be robbed—on the same street, by the same people—before they call him a Rube? Bob Dylan said that, in a tattered old song called "Blowin' in the Wind." Read it and weep, you poor bastards—because Dylan was yesterday, and George Bush is *now*.

That is a morbid observation, at best, and we are all stuck with it. The 2004 presidential election will be a matter of life or death for the whole nation. We are sick today and we will be even sicker tomorrow if this wretched half-bright swine of a president gets re-elected in November. Take my word for it. *Mahalo.*

It was not at all clear to me when I first started writing this *Hey, Rube* column just before the 2000 presidential election that it was actually a week-to-week calendar / record / diary of what it was like to be alive and suffering in the first disastrous days of the George W. Bush administration.

That is a long sentence for a short thought, but I won't hang around and worry about it. We have bigger things to brood on and enormous reasons for wallowing in terminal craziness until we finally hit bottom.

Who knows *why* it happened? But there is no doubt about *what* it was: the suicidal *collapse* of the American empire in the *final year* of the American century.

The Empire collapsed for the same corrupt and greedy reasons that plagued and destroyed so many other empires in the long curve of history.

The Roman Empire lasted more or less 900 years—which is 888 years longer than Adolf Hitler's "Thousand-Year Reich." They both imploded because of internal corruption and a pampered, decadent citizenry. They were weak because they no longer used their muscles or their brains. After only 500 years, they were all either pimps or whores.

But so what? If you have lemons, make lemonade. That is ancient Hawaiian Wisdom—and that is what I have tried to do here. So buckle up and prepare to look into your own rearview mirror and see how it happened, as seen through the innocent eyes of a sportswriter.

PART ONE

WE IS THE MOST IMPORTANT WORD IN POLITICS. . . . SWINE OF THE WEEK. . . . A MILE WIDE AND AN INCH DEEP. . . . YEAR OF THE DOOMED ELECTION. . . . END OF THE AMERICAN CENTURY. . . .

The New Dumb

Something is happening here
But you don't know what it is
Do you, Mister Jones?
　　　　　　　—BOB DYLAN

No sir, not a chance. Mr. Jones does not even pretend to know what's happening in America Right now, and neither does anyone else.

We have seen weird Times in this country before, but the year 2000 is beginning to look super weird. This time there really is nobody flying the plane. . . . We are living in dangerously weird times now. Smart people just shrug and admit they're dazed and confused. The only ones left with any confidence at all are the New Dumb. It is the beginning of the end of our world as we knew it. Doom is the operative ethic.

The autumn months are never a calm time in America. Back to Work, Back to Football Practice, etc. . . . Autumn is a very Traditional period, a time of strong Rituals and the celebrating of strange annual holidays like Halloween and Satanism and the fateful Harvest Moon, which can have ominous implications for some people.

Autumn is always a time of Fear and Greed and Hoarding for the winter coming on. Debt collectors are active on old people and fleece the weak and helpless. They want to lay in enough cash to weather the known horrors of January and February. There is always a rash of kidnapping and abductions of schoolchildren in the football months. Preteens of both sexes are traditionally seized and grabbed off the streets by gangs of organized perverts who traditionally give them as Christmas gifts to each other to be personal sex slaves and playthings.

Most of these things are obviously Wrong and Evil and Ugly—but at least they are Traditional. They will happen. Your driveway will ice over, your furnace will blow up, and you will be rammed in traffic by an uninsured driver in a stolen car.

But what the hell? That's why we have Insurance, eh? And the Inevitability of these nightmares is what makes them so re-assuring. Life will go on, for good or ill. But some things are for-ever, right? The structure may be a *little* Crooked, but the foundations are still strong and unshakable.

Ho ho. Think again, buster. Look around you. There is an eerie sense of Panic in the air, a silent Fear and uncertainty that comes with once-reliable faiths and truths and solid Institu-tions that are no longer safe to believe in. . . . There is a Presi-dential Election, right on schedule, but somehow there is no President. A new Congress is elected, like always, but some-how there is no real Congress at all—not as we knew it, any-way, and whatever passes for Congress will be as helpless and weak as whoever has to pass for the "New President."

In the world of sports, it is like playing a Super Bowl that goes into 19 scoreless Overtimes and never actually Ends . . . or four LA Lakers stars being murdered in different cities on the same day. Guaranteed Fear and Loathing. Abandon all hope. Prepare for the Weirdness. Get familiar with Cannibalism.

Good luck,
DOC
—*November 20, 2000*

The Fix Is In

Luck is a very thin wire between survival and disaster, and not many people can keep their balance on it.
I have never believed much in luck, and my sense of humor has

tended to walk on the dark side. Muhammad Ali, one of my very few heroes, once took the time to explain to me that "there are no jokes. The truth is the funniest joke of all."

Ho ho. It takes a special kind of mind-set to believe that & still have smart people call you Funny. I have never quite understood it.

—HUNTER S. THOMPSON, *Fear and Loathing in America*

This eerie Presidential election has been a painful experience for Gamblers. Almost everybody Lost. The many, many Losers don't feel the pain yet, because they are still in Shock & Denial. There are rumors in Washington that Gore's most trusted advisors have sealed him off so completely that he still firmly believes he Won. . . . Which is True, on some scorecards, but so what? Those cards don't count. . . . George Bush is our President now, and you better start getting used to it. He didn't actually steal the White House from Al Gore, he just brutally Wrested it away from him in the darkness of one swampy Florida night. Gore got mugged, and the local Cops don't give a damn.

Ho ho ho. Where the fuck did he think he was—in some friendly Civics class? Hell no, he was in Florida, arguably the most vicious & corrupt state in the Union. . . . Not only that, but he was brazenly *invading* Florida, trying to steal it from right under the noses of the whole Bush family. It was a bold move & brilliantly done, in some ways—but then so was Lee's brave decision to invade the North & attack Gettysburg.

Gore was Doomed in Florida, and he knew it about halfway through Election Night. The TV wizards had already given the state & its 25 precious Electoral Votes to Gore, which gave him an early lead & caused wild rejoicing in Democratic headquarters all over the country.

My own immediate reaction was bafflement & surprise, and I think I almost believed it. . . . But not really. The more I brooded on it, the more I was troubled by waves of Queasiness & shudders of gnawing doubt. I felt nervous & vaguely confused, as if I had just heard a dog speak perfect English for 30 or 40 seconds. That will get your attention, for sure. . . . Some people get permanently destabilized by it: Nothing they see with their own eyes will ever look quite the same to them again. As in "I know that the object I'm looking at is an Egg—but I also know that if it talks to me like a person, it is not an Egg."

There was an exact moment, in fact, when I knew Al Gore would *Never* be President of the United States, no matter what the TV networks said—and that moment was when the whole Bush family suddenly appeared on TV and openly scoffed at the idea of Gore's winning Florida. It was Nonsense, said the Candidate, Utter nonsense. . . . Anybody who believed he'd lost Florida was a Fool. The Media, all of them, were Liars & Dunces or treacherous whores trying to sabotage his victory. They were strong words and people said he was Bluffing. But I knew better. Of course Bush would win Florida. Losing was out of the question. Here was the whole bloody Family laughing & hooting & sneering at the dumbness of the whole world on National TV.

The old man was the real tip-off. The leer on his face was almost frightening. It was like looking into the eyes of a tall hyena with a living sheep in its mouth. The sheep's fate was sealed, and so was Al Gore's. . . . Everything since then has been political flotsam & gibberish.

The whole Presidential election, in fact, was rigged and fixed from the start. It was a gigantic Media Event, scripted & staged for TV. It happens every four years, at an ever-increasing cost, & 90 percent of the money always goes for TV commercials. Of course, nobody would give a damn except politics is beginning to smell like professional football, Dank & Nasty. And that's a problem that could haunt America a lot longer than four years, folks.

I am watching more NFL football this year but enjoying it less and less. There is something wrong with the game, something vital is missing, but I can't quite say what it is. No weekend goes by without at least one wild & exciting game, plus one or two shocking upsets—but somehow they all seem vaguely meaningless, like watered-down wine or weak whiskey.

I thought I had solved all my problems when I found a way to watch every game, every Sunday, all at once or separately. I had everything, right at my fingertips. I missed nothing. My friends called me "toggle-boy" because of my expertise with the channel switcher. They dropped by every Sunday to drink & mooch & gamble. It was like an impossible dream come true. Fred Exley would have loved it.

But still there was something wrong. Even reading the Sports section began to give me a queasy feeling. I came to secretly dread the coming of Sunday, although I never admitted that to anybody. It was too weird.

Only after long brooding & extended medical analysis did I discover the obvious answer. It is the dangerous thinning of the NFL talent pool, a problem not totally unknown to the world of presidential politics. There are too many teams and not enough quality players. The League is destroying quarterbacks faster than colleges can churn them out. Every pro team *must* have two quarterbacks, because one of them is certain to get crippled or mashed by some steroid-crazed monster who weighs 388 pounds and runs faster than Deion Sanders and is desperate to hurt people. He will lose his job if he doesn't, and his obvious target is the Quarterback.

There may be Parity in the NFL these days, but it is the same kind of parity that you find at bush league Racetracks and Arena Football League games. The next MVP of the Super Bowl is just as likely to have been a full-time grocery store bagger last year as a Heisman Trophy winner. The teams change names & locations every year. Even winning coaches go crazy with angst or get fired on the whim of a new owner. Players come & go like substitute teachers or half-bright fashion models. Some beat their wives in public, and others get arrested for Murder. But the games go on like clockwork and the money keeps pouring in. . . . Most stadiums are sold out every Sunday. But only rich people can afford to attend the games in person. It's not much different from getting involved in National Politics.

—*November 27, 2000*

Welcome to
Generation Z

I have been overwhelmed by the massive response to my sheepish confession, last week, that my lifelong passion for the ceremonial watching of pro Football on TV is not quite as keen this year as it has been. At first I felt vaguely ashamed to admit this, especially in print—but within hours of the thing's (delayed) appearance on Page 2, I was deluged with messages from people who Agreed with me and said they'd been feeling guilty about it but were afraid to say the words.

The NFL's TV ratings seem to be dropping about 10 percent a year for at least the last five, which has not deterred the networks from paying more and more for broadcast rights and charging more and more for Super Bowl commercials. They figure they are breeding a whole new Generation of football fans by getting the teenage beer drunkards hooked early—and after that they will be loyal lifetime rabid fans, just like me.

Ho ho. I have no more loyalty to Pro football than I do to the Democratic Party. And neither do these whooping babbling nerds that appear in Beer commercials. They would barely even notice if the Green Bay Packers were bought by Arabs and moved to Palm Beach. Or Kuwait.

This kind of faithless fan base is a disaster waiting to happen. Like they say in Politics, "It's a mile wide and an inch deep."

Jesus, and we wonder why the Election turned out so weird. The Pollsters knew *nothing*, because the people they talked to lied to them. Nobody wants to talk to a fucking Pollster, anyway. They are Vermin. And they are getting paid to harass you with questions, but you're not getting a dime for it. You're not even getting on TV.

It was obvious from the start of this doomed 2000 election that nobody in America except a few Rich people gave a hoot in hell about who won—but why should they have to admit it in public and look Dumb? . . . No, they would Lie & Lie & Lie—and then they would flip a coin. Why not? It's fair, and nobody will ever know, for sure anyway.

That's why this goddamn useless Election ended in a Tie. A million consecutive coin flips will give you a 50-50 split every time. . . . Which raises the sickening question of What are the NFL's real TV ratings each week? What if half the people watching the games out of habit don't really give a flying fuck who wins the game? That would be the end of Pro Football as we know it—No ratings, no commercials, no TV, & no money. You will be forced to watch Wrestling, Figure Skating, & Golf on Sunday afternoons. Good luck.

December is always a good month for Rich people. It is a time for profit taking & gross displays of wealth, for giving huge Rubies & Diamonds to each other at bogus Charity Balls, & for seeing themselves on the covers of their own magazines. . . . The year 2000 will be branded in history as "the year of the Doomed Election," which caused Millions of Americans to question themselves & suffer Loss of Self-Esteem for seemingly unexplainable reasons.

The beginning of the new century will also be marked in history as the quasi-official birth of what will come to be known as Generation Z. . . . Never mind the gibberish of Mystics & Astrologers; this is the Generation that was *born* into the Richest Economy in the history of the world. They were born rich & Powerful, the certified Aristocrats of a new & Amazing century.

The American nation is more Dominant now than primitive American leaders like Harry Truman & Richard Nixon ever dreamed of. We *are* Number One. Nobody argues. We have dollars, we have bombs, & we have the Will to use them.

Let's get back to Generation Z & its Lush & Extravagant birthright in this year of Our Lord 2000. . . . It may be a Mixed blessing to be hatched at the top of the Heap. Indeed. The Stock Market might crash, crazed Muslim terrorists might put Nerve Gas or Anthrax in your drinking water, Your daughter might get Rabies or turn into a famous Porno slut with two Junkie boyfriends who will Hack into your secret Computer Code & loot your Bank Accounts. . . . But these are Uptown Problems, for sure, compared to being born in a Great Depression or forced to join a Hitler Youth Brigade at the end of WW2. Nobody is ever going to feel sorry for the gilded little sots of Generation Z.

SWINE OF THE WEEK

Swine of the Week is always a difficult choice, but this first one is an obvious No-Brainer for lame-duck VP Al Gore Jr. & his whole lame family, formerly of Tennessee & Washington, DC, & soon to be listed prominently as "Homeless/No Known Address." Gore will be remembered as the Hapless, worm-eaten Dunce who fumbled the White House away to a gang of sleazy Oilmongers from Texas who promised nothing for sure except a collapsing Market & heavy punishment for any degenerate fool who indulges in Oral Sex on U.S. government property. Al Gore defied all known Trends, Odds, & laws of Probability by running for President as co-architect of the greatest prosperity in American history & still Losing.

The chance of that happening is as close to a Mathematical Impossibility as the chance of a Presidential Election ending in a Tie—or, for that matter, a sitting President & Leader of the

Free World getting thrown out of office for enjoying the mouth of a woman. . . . Jesus, and we rave & rant about the Taliban for making their women wear veils.

Sodomy is still a felony crime in the state of Virginia, which includes all the leafy, high-dollar suburbs just across the Potomac River from Washington. This is where poor Marv Albert got busted for allowing his love-bites to get out of control. His passion was too pure, they said, so they took him off NBA games for a while. . . . Georgia is another state where you can still go to prison for Sodomy, even when enjoyed in the privacy of your own bedroom.

—*December 4, 2000*

The White House Disease

The incredible dumbness of Sportswriters is a subject I thought I'd exhausted a long time ago—but let's hit it one more time, just for the fun of it. . . . I have described them as "a rude & brainless subculture of fascist drunks" and "a gang of vicious monkeys jacking off in a zoo cage" and "more disgusting by nature than maggots oozing out of the carcass of a dead animal. . . ."

But they keep coming back for more, like pimps & real estate agents, & on days like this I run out of patience. . . . I have explained many times that I am, by Profession, a Gambler—not some jock-sniffing nerd or a hired human squawk box with the brain of a one-celled animal. No. That would be your average career sportswriter—and, more specifically, a full-time Baseball writer.

Okay, how's that for Rudeness? I can Play in this league. I

don't like it, but when my own editors at ESPN start asking me to get outraged about the Huge Salaries being paid these days to Baseball Pitchers—instead of the truly Insane high-stakes Gambling that is going on right now in our national Political Arena—I know how Thomas Jefferson felt when he said, "I fear for the fate of my country when I reflect that God is Just."

As for Pitchers, they are as useless as tits on a boar hog & should all be put to sleep. Baseball's only hope for survival is the elimination of the "pitcher" position completely. See below.

The cure for White House Disease is not so simple. It is like a combination of Blue balls & malaria, an interminable Fever that is always Incurable & often Fatal. The symptoms are blindness, freezing, sweating, weeping, & delusions of suffering beyond Death.

Let's face it: The only true Blood Sport in this country is high-end Politics. You can dabble in Sports or the Stock Markets, but when you start lusting after the White House, The Joke is Over. These are the real Gamblers, & there is nothing they won't do to win.

Nothing involving jockstraps or sports bras will ever come close to it for drama, violence, savagery, & overweaning lust for the spoils of victory. . . . The Presidency of the United States is the richest & most powerful prize in the history of the World. The difference between winning the Super Bowl & winning the White House is the difference between a Goldfish & a vault full of Gold bars.

The very heart of the American electoral system now seems to be cracking. . . . This is like a Super Bowl that goes into 99 scoreless overtimes, or a night when the sun never sets. Even Congress is preparing for Trench Warfare: the GOP leadership is now daring Clinton to try to pass a Spending Bill before the year ends. Blocking the bill would paralyze the Nation & prevent all payments for anything by the Federal Government. The moment is reminiscent of Political events that occurred just before the start of the Civil War. . . . Beware. There may be no Super Bowl this year.

It is no accident that this vicious mess has come to a head in Florida. I know the state well. Florida has been very good to me in many wild & beautiful ways that still make my whole body hum when I think about them.... I know Tallahassee & I know Palm Beach. I have run amok in Naples & suffered terrible boat crashes in the waters off Miami & the treacherous channels of Key West.... I have run aground at midnight on sandbars far out in the ocean; I have lost control of my boat in many posh marinas & been rescued at sea by the Coast Guard so often that they came to recognize my voice on the shortwave radio. I have known great happiness in Florida & I still have a certain love for it.

But I also know it to be the most corrupt & profoundly degenerate state in the Union. So many of its elected officials are so openly For Sale that politics in Florida is more like an auction than a democratic process. Its Congressmen have been jailed for Felony Fraud, & its Senators have routinely committed more heinous crimes than Richard Nixon was ever accused of.... More murders & rapes go unreported in Florida each year than in Corsica & Sicily combined. The state has no Income Tax & essentially no Law. Its cities are ruled by Depraved sots and its Universities are snake pits of cheating & random sex in Public. The libraries are filled with Beer Drunkards looking for Skull sessions & beautiful girls who are proud & Eager to oblige them. Oral sex is more common on the streets of Miami in the daylight hours than anywhere else in America.

Rude people will now & then ask me why I think I know so much about Politics & I tell them it's because I'm Smart.... But that is a lie: the real reason is that I'm an incurable Gambling addict.

The gambling habit is no different from any other acquired addiction (Crack, Nicotine, Flogging, Lying, etc.) in that there are always two (2) very different types of addicts: the User & the Binger. The binge gambler is doomed from the start & so is a binge Flogger, like the infamous Marquis de Sade. . . . The Marquis was a Multi-Addict, & he took his flogging vice too far.

It was not the Vice but the Binge that destroyed him. The history of the Time suggests that if de Sade had learned Moderation—if he could have kept his brutal Floggings down to one or two a week, even three—the cops might have left him alone. But *no*, the Marquis wouldn't listen, so his legacy was to go down as the most Vicious Pervert in history.

Al Gore will not be so lucky. At least people are still interested in de Sade's crazed excesses, but nobody will ever care about the fate of Al Gore. He will forever be known as "the Loser" of the doomed 2000 Election. He was Wrong from the Start, & he will be happy to get out of Electoral politics, & Bush is an Unhappy winner. He will be beaten like a rat in a wastebasket & he will age 14 years in the next Four.

The Bush family has already Corrupted the Presidency & the U.S. Supreme Court. Millions of Americans will never again be Confident that their vote will be counted in any election.

It is not just the state of Florida & its whole voting Process that got exposed as Corrupt & Fraudulent in the past 30 days. The ugly truth is that this same horrible mess could have happened in *any* other place, from Bangor to Honolulu—and the result would have been the same. . . . All we need now is the squalid Spectacle of Jeb Bush on TV, saying, "I am Not a Crook."

—*December 2, 2000*

New Rules for Baseball

Hi, folks. My name is Thompson, and I don't have much space for this high-speed presentation, so let's get started and see how tight we can make it. . . . My job is to devise a whole new set of rules and concepts to shorten the time it takes to play a game of Major League Baseball, or any other kind.

This is a major responsibility and I am keenly aware of the angst and bitter squabbling that will erupt when somebody tries to screw with the National Pastime. . . . But it must be done, and if I don't do it, somebody else will. So here's the plan.

Eliminate the Pitcher: This will knock at least one hour off the length of a game, which is now up to 3:42. One World Series Game took five hours and twenty minutes, which is unacceptable to everybody except the Pitchers. Yes. . . . So we will ELIMINATE THE PITCHER, and he won't be missed. Pitchers, as a group, are pampered little swine with too much money and no real effect on the game except to drag it out and interrupt the action.

Limit All Games to Three (3) Hours: Like football and basketball and hockey, the Baseball game will end at a fixed time. THE SCORE, at that moment, WILL BE FINAL, based on an accumulation of TOTAL BASES gained in 3 hours.

All Base Runners May Run to Any Base (but not backwards): First to Third, Second to Home, etc. And with NO PITCHER in the game, this frantic scrambling across the infield will be Feasible and tempting.

ALL "PITCHING," by the way, will be done by a fine-tuned PITCHING MACHINE that pops up out of the mound, delivers a remote-controlled "pitch" at the batter, and then drops back out of sight to free up the whole infield for running. . . . If a batter hits a home run with the bases loaded, for instance, his team will score 16 total bases (or 16 points). But, if it's 3 up and 3 down in an inning, that team will score Zero points.

Think of 22–5, perhaps, or 88–55. Yes sir, we will have Huge scores and constant speedy action for 3 straight hours.

The heroes of the game will be the CATCHERS, not Pitchers. The CATCHER will dominate the game and be the highest-paid player. . . . With no Pitcher and no Mound to disrupt the flow, runners on base will be moving at the crack of the bat, and it will be the CATCHER'S job to shut them down or pick them off whenever possible. Foot speed and a bazooka throwing arm will be paramount. . . . There will be no more of this bullshit about Bull pens and Managers scratching their heads on TV for hours on end, no more lame pickoff throws to first, no more waving of signs and agonized close-ups while pop fouls bounce off the roof. . . .

No, there will be no such thing as a base on balls. Each batter will get five "pitches" from the robot—only FIVE (5)—and if he doesn't get a hit by then, he is Out. . . . And the CATCHER will control the kind of drop or curve or speed he wants the machine to throw. And it will obey. Those goddamn pitching machines can put a Slider past you at 98 miles an hour five times in a row, with no problem. They can throw hideous wavering knuckleballs and half-moon curves—all depending on and according to what the CATCHER wants to dial up on his remote control unit. He can even order that the batter be whacked in the ribs by a 102 mph fastball, although that will cost his team two (2) bases, instead of one. And you won't want to have some poor Cuban drilled in the ribs when you're nursing a 31–30 lead.

Okay, folks, that's it for now. I am already late and I have written too many words—but the Concept is sound, I think, and there is a clear and desperate Need for it. . . .

Everybody agrees that Baseball games Must be shortened, but nobody is really Working on it. . . . And meanwhile, the games get longer and longer. The good old "meat in the seats" argument won't work after midnight, when the seats are mainly Empty, and TV networks get nasty when they start having to refund money to advertisers when the ratings sink lower and lower. Pro wrestling and golf are bigger draws than baseball games. . . . I have not been to a live baseball game in 20 years, and I hope I Never see another one. Not even the New Rules would drag me back to the Ballpark—but I am a Doctor of Wisdom, a professional man, and some of my friends in the Business have asked me to have a look at this problem, which I have, and this is my solution, for good or ill.

Next spring ESPN will put my theories to the test by sponsoring a series of "New Rules" baseball games in New York, Chicago, Omaha, and Seattle, among others. . . . Tickets will be sold and big-time sports talent will be employed. The success or failure of these Games will determine the fate of Baseball in America.

Purists will bitch and whine, but so what? Purists will Always bitch and whine. That is their function. *Res Ipsa Loquitur.*

—November 6, 2000

Get Ready for Sainthood

Okay. That horrible farce is Over now. We can Relax and get back to sports. So let's get back to Al Gore for a minute. He says he "will spend some time in Tennessee, mending fences" in his home state, where his neighbors didn't vote for him. . . . Ho ho. I would feel very nervous if I lived down the road from the Old Gore place in Carthage right now.

When hill people start talking about "mending fences" just after suffering a brutal public beating, they are not thinking about pounding nails into wooden posts. They are already cooking up a hell broth of vengeance and punishment down there tonight.

When the Boss gets home for the holidays, it will be more savage than the Hatfields & McCoys. Some of his neighbors are already Doomed, and others will flee the state in a long caravan going south to Florida for Xmas. Many will have dead animals stuffed down their chimneys or get burned out by mysterious fires. Thousands of government jobs will be terminated & fancy farms will go on the block for a dime on the dollar. . . . That is how big-time Politics works, in Tennessee or anywhere else. When you Cross a still-powerful Loser, you'd better run when you see him coming.

The Xmas season is always a good time to say you're leaving town, then change your mind and sneak back home like a burglar.

Yes sir, it's time for the NFL play-offs & a frenzy of football action. . . . No more of that rotten Politics. We can afford to turn our backs on these swine for a moment. They will be too busy Looting & Bribing their new Connections in Washington to have time for stabbing people in the back. They love the Christmas spirit & they don't want to ruin it. The stabbing will start in January, when it will become like the Night of the Long Knives.

Meanwhile, I have a Serious problem with the Play-offs. My Boys have Failed miserably—the 49ers were beaten like chickens right in front of our eyes all year long. . . . It was humiliating. . . . I have been addicted to the 49ers for 25 years, through thick & thin. I sat through hailstorms on the wet planks of Kezar Stadium when John Brodie was getting sacked & stomped like a bird every Sunday.

I drank beer with Dave Wilcox* at the Stadium Bar & Grill on Stanyan Street, right across from the Park & the Police station. I would chain my red motorcycle to a standpipe at Kezar during games or at night after Antiwar rallies.

So when the Good Years came, I figured we deserved them. I was Proud to live & die with the 49ers. I had tasted the sour wine of Defeat, so when Joe Montana showed up, & then Ronnie Lott & Jerry Rice, I saw it as a triumph of Good Karma. My friends agreed. When our Boys finally beat Dallas, we felt we were part of a New Master Race, & we behaved accordingly. We were winners. All roads led to San Francisco. And why not? It was the Cradle of Civilization. To be a Winner in San Francisco was to be a winner all over the World.

Ah—but that is another story & we don't have time for it now. The real story is about how the Fate of some greedy half-bright Sports Team can drastically affect the Fate(s) of its Loyal lifetime Fans, including You.

And me. And Jack Nicholson. . . . Fred Exley got mixed up with Frank Gifford, & look what happened to him. In Jack's case, it was the Lakers who made him what he is today. In my case, it was the Forty-Niners & San Francisco that determined my Fate in life. I might have become a shepherd, or Night Manager of the famous O'Farrell Theatre, if not for Joe Montana & Bill Walsh—just as Jack might be an aging pimp in Nevada today if not for Magic Johnson.

And so much for all that. I still need a team for the Playoffs. . . . As a gambler, I'm better off without one, but as an Addict I must have a team—so I have chosen the New Orleans Saints. Why not? They are 16–1 long shots to win the Super Bowl, and they still have to beat St. Louis to win the NFC West. . . . Unless Tampa Bay beats the Rams tonight, which I am betting will not happen. So the Saints game on Xmas Eve should be a humdinger. I make it New Orleans by 3 or 4.

Ed. Note: These are only the Doctor's predictions. He is not taking bets on the World Wide Web.

Why am I betting that St. Louis will beat Tampa tonight & thus remain tied with NO atop the NFC West?

Because Kurt Warner will not throw *four* interceptions against the Bucs' defense—which is what Miami's Jay Fiedler did when Miami lost by three points to TB last week in a monsoon rain that slowed all movement by about 50 percent.

Only a 200-foot Tsunami in the Gulf of Florida will prevent the Rams' racehorse-fast receivers from getting open against Tampa Bay, and Warner will hit them in the hands nine times out of 10—which means that the Bucs' only chance here will be if Warren Sapp cripples Warner early in the game.

Meanwhile, the games will go on like always. The Rams will lose the Xmas Eve showdown in New Orleans. They will be sent off to play on the road & get croaked in the snow by some goofy team like the Giants.

* *Dave Wilcox is not a Hall of Fame linebacker for nothing. He played like a wolverine on speed & had the full-field vision of a Human fly. But off the field he was a quiet man who wore Levi's & Pendleton shirts & enjoyed a cool beer now & then. He was a farm boy from Oregon & he had little patience with pushy strangers. . . . I lived a few blocks from Kezar at the time, and I often ran into Dave & other 49er players in our neighborhood bar. It was called the Stadium Club, as I recall, and one rainy afternoon I was in there with a friend of mine, an Ivy League lawyer who had just scored some Acid in Golden Gate Park. He was also a rabid 49er fan, so when he saw Wilcox at the bar, he eagerly sat down & started babbling at him about Football & Jesus & how "God put us here on this earth for purely Experimental reasons."*

I tried to ignore him & so did the players—but when the lawyer finally intruded too far into Wilcox's Personal Space, the linebacker turned quickly on

*his stool, seized the lawyer by his striped necktie, & jerked his head straight
down in a way that caused the lawyer's Chin to smack down on the bar with a
terrible noise that still makes me shudder when I remember it. . . . The bar-
room fell silent & so did the lawyer, who staggered outside & spit little chips of
bloody teeth all over the sidewalk. He could barely talk because he had bitten
off a piece of his own tongue, which he picked up & took with him to the Emergency Room. . . . The incident made me so nervous that I never went into the
Stadium Club again, but I still admire Dave Wilcox, & the lawyer still talks
with a Lisp.*

—December 18, 2000

The Xmas Vice

Gambling is a dangerous vice, but millions of people are
hooked on it and many will suffer grievously before this holiday
season is over. The traditional "Christmas spirit" runs completely against the grain of the natural laws of Gambling,
which have nothing to do with silly human weaknesses like
Generosity or Kindness or Carelessness.

If Santa Claus had a gambling habit, he would have been
dead a long time ago. . . . There are a lot of criminal psychos between here & the North Pole, and they would show no mercy
on a goofy old man who gets loaded one night a year and drives
around through strange neighborhoods with a truckload of
jewelry & furs & gold Rolex watches.

What if the Hell's Angels got their hands on him? They
would set him on fire & stuff him headfirst down a smoking
chimney. . . . Which is not much different from how Professional gamblers treat their victims at Xmas time—which is
also the end of the football season & the start of the Playoff

frenzy that will build & grow & throb like a Shark's heart for 33 more days until Super Bowl Sunday.

Yes sir, this is Harvest time for the Bookies, and Fleecing time for Rubes. When a gambler looks down on a hotel lobby crowded with whooping football Fans, he sees a flock of bleating Sheep—dumb beasts, ready for fleecing & slaughtering. It makes him crazy with hunger. He throws back his head & howls like a Jackal in heat.

There are thousands of wild whores on the streets of Nashville tonight, and not all of them are women. Many are politicians working the crowd out of habit—or pansexual pimps in high drag.... A huge football crowd has swarmed into town for the Tennessee-Dallas game & the downtown hotels are booked wall to wall with gamblers, wild rubes, and whores who dearly love Football—Especially the hometown Titans, who may soon be the champions of the World.

They are on their way to the Super Bowl & so are the gamblers & the whores & the mass of foul scum they bring with them.... A Winning Team on the road to the Super Bowl is like a traveling circus that picks up more & more fleas at every stop along the way & finally deposits the whole load on an innocent city like Tampa.

Hell, what's a few million diseased fleas, compared to the Billion dollars or so that will pour into the local economy along with the Big Game? Any big city in America would cough up many millions to get the NFL to even consider putting the Super Bowl in their town, and never mind the fleas.

Nashville, in fact, was once the Syphilis capital of America. During the Civil War the Yankees called it the City of 10,000 Whores because of the rampant disease that plagued the Union Army as more & more Southern women turned to prostitution as the Confederacy began losing the War—75 percent of them terminally infected with Syphilis, which made soldiers unable to fight.

Al Gore is not from Nashville, & he is probably not a real Football Fan either. Gore will watch the game at home tonight, in Carthage, while he jabbers to his wife about Santa Claus & Whiskey & why his own goddamn state voted heavily against him for President. . . . Hell, Adelphia Coliseum will hold far, far more people tonight than Gore would have needed to win Florida. There are high school games on the outskirts of Nashville that draw 10,000 fans.

Yeah, suck on that for a while, Bubba. If your Family Dog got loose tonight, it would draw a bigger crowd than you pulled in Palm Beach. . . . Shame on you, Al. They chopped you up like a worm.

The Tennessee Titans will beat the jabbering slime out of the Dallas Cowboys tonight. They will whip them like baby mules & embarrass the whole state of Texas. . . . But not for long, and not enough to make George Bush cry.

(Which one, you ask? Hell, it hardly matters, does it? They all spring from the same root, and they all have the same greedy instincts. The only time they cry is when they lose money—and that won't happen tonight. The Cowboys are 14-point under-dogs, but the real spread is more like 33.)

It is not sane to give away 33 points in the playoffs, or even in the Super Bowl—although I did once, and I won. . . . It was my finest day in the gambling business. The Broncos were play-ing the 49ers in Super Bowl XXIV & the closing spread was 11, which I gave without hesitation in a crowded Aspen bar. . . . It is always a huge advantage, when fleecing people in public, to bet against rabid fans on their own turf. You want to do it in a loud, mocking voice that grates on the nerves of everybody within hearing range, so even your Friends will be infuriated & start betting rashly.

On this day the 49ers scored twice before the Broncos even got the ball. The crowd went into a funk, and bettors among them were happy to take 22 points, at only 2–1 odds. Nobody wants to Quit & slink away this early in the Big Game.

By the middle of the second quarter the score was some-

30–3. And the homeboys were getting desperate. ...es had long since gone from hundreds of dollars into thousands—so when I offered to give 33 points at 5–1 payoff odds, they eagerly gobbled it up. Hell, they were six points ahead & the Broncos were bound to score soon. Ho ho. The final score was 55–10. It was my finest day in the gambling business.

—*December 25, 2000*

The Curse of Musburger

The start of a new year is always a good time to watch football and settle old scores, so let's get to it. I have some serious grudges to grind at the end of a foul year like 2000. It was not so much a bad year as a deeply Wrong one—but to make a list of reasons why it was Wrong would torture us all & only double the suffering.

I have old scores to even with all manner of people: Brent Musburger, Lyle Lovett, Lawyers, foreigners, Pit bulls, Russian Pimps, and the whole Los Angeles Police Department. There are rotten people everywhere.

My grudge against Brent Musburger has been smoking on a personal back burner for many years—since the early 1980s, in fact, when Brent was covering the NBA finals for CBS-TV, and it involves the word "downtown."

That is when Musburger changed the language of sports-writing forever when he came up with the ignorant notion that any basketball player firing off a long three-point shot is shooting from "downtown." (Celtics announcer Johnny Most might have coined the "downtown" trademark in the 1960s, but it was Musburger who beat it to death.)

I still hear in my dreams the wild stupid gibberish coming out of that yo-yo's mouth every time Nate McMillan or Dennis Johnson drilled one of those long flat three-pointers.

"All the way from downtown," Brent would scream, "another one from Downtown!"

It drove me mad then, & it still does every time one of those fools blurts it out. It was quickly picked up and adopted by a whole generation of half-bright TV commentators every night of the bloody season. It has become part of the Lexicon now, & it will not be easy to correct. . . . In gyms & Coliseums all over America (even in Greece or Korea), wherever basketball as we know it is played, there will be some howling Jackass braying "From downtown! Another three-pointer! Is this a great country, or what?"

It is the Curse of Musburger, another dumb and relentless squawk from the world of baseball writers.

"Going downtown" has more than one meaning—from going to work at 66 Wall Street in New York to anal rape in Alcatraz—but it always means going to a busy place, for good or ill. The *Random House Historical Dictionary of American Slang* says it's "where the action is"—a noisy, crowded place with many intersections & tall buildings & freaky-looking strangers.

Indeed we all know that place. We see it every night on ESPN & on the hardwood at Boston Garden. . . . It's that violent little place just under the glass on a big-time Basketball court where tall brutes slam each other around like crazed fish. They call it "Rebounding."

Downtown is where you score—not somewhere out in the wilderness, where people are far apart & not much happens. You don't fire a long jump shot from Downtown, you fire it into Downtown. The Real definition of "Taking it downtown" is to suddenly drive to the basket & into a cluster of 7-footers who seem to have you sealed out—like Allen Iverson launching himself at Robinson & Duncan & dunking it over them. To think Otherwise would be to think like a Baseball Writer, or like Brent Musburger.

He is a creepy bugger, for sure. I saw him whooping it up in the Superdome last week. He was hanging with some kids at the Saints-Rams game, acting like Mr. Rogers.

Which is not a bad thing, necessarily, but it will get on your nerves in a hurry if you're drunk. The last time I saw Brent socially was in the dinner lounge at Caesar's Palace in Vegas. I was dining with my old friend Jimmy the Greek & some women who said they were traveling with (famous fight promoter) Bob Arum, when Musburger came up to our table & started abusing the Greek in a loud voice about something Jimmy had said on the air about him. . . . We had a very prominent table, as the Greek always did, so I had him thrown out.

"What's wrong with that bum?" Jimmy asked. "He acts this way every time he gets around the Champ. I should have him killed."

He signaled for the maitre d', but one of the women stopped him. Later that night a man was stabbed to death in the parking lot by a Sonny Liston fan.

The real definition of "downtown," back then, was wherever Muhammad Ali was at the time—which is still true: I saw him with the Mayor in Times Square on New Year's Eve. The Champ always draws a crowd.

—*January 1, 2001*

Cruel Twist in the Coaching Business

My mood is foul tonight, so I will try to keep this short. I must keep this short, in fact, because I can barely see the page I'm working on. My left eye is swollen shut and my mouth is so crooked that I lisp & spit when I talk. My phone rings constantly, but I can't answer it & football games are meaningless.

On Friday (or maybe it was Thursday or Saturday) I was bitten on the cheek by a Brown Recluse spider & my face swelled up like a Blowfish. My eyes are like slits and my nose has disappeared. . . . I am Diss-Figured, in a word, and my sense of humor is cruel.

This is an ugly way to live, but at least it has given me time to brood & bitch & fondle my crystal ball for the Meaning of Life in this rotten little year 2001.

The rest of the year will be marked by three distinct trends—or Drifts, or Developments, Plagues, Fads, Fashions, & certainly inescapable Realities: *huge tits, thin wallets,* and *enormous fear* of *bill collectors.* . . . These will be the Primary Drive Energies behind everything else that happens in 2001. This is all Ye know & all Ye need to know.

People scoff at the notion that naked women will soon be delivering the news on TV—but it is True, and it will happen very soon, for good or ill. Naked women Already deliver almost everything Else on TV, from sitcoms in prime-time Miller Lite & Magnavox ads & goofy little orgies on the Playboy channel at dawn, so why should the News or the Weather or Sports-Center be any different?

You don't need a crystal ball or the bite of a poison spider to see these things coming. All you have to do is read the newspapers or watch the TV News to see the stock markets staggering and the current craze for quick-fix "breast enhancements" swirling all around us on every street corner. . . . The boobs of Britney Spears are the hottest topic in Web chat rooms all over the world. The Implant industry is cranking up for a record-setting year, & the Santa Claus factory will look a lot different next Christmas than it ever has in the past: no more of those stupid little toys or bikes or Barbie dolls.

No. The gift that every high school girl in America will be demanding this year is a top-of-the-line Boob Job, and millions will get their wish. It is no longer considered lewd or sleazy to give your 12-year-old daughter a hot-looking set of torpedo tits for Christmas.

They are not cheap yet: $5000 or so is said to be Reasonable in the soccer mom set—which it is, compared to a new BMW convertible or chain of perfect diamonds—and if you don't give her new boobs for Xmas you will Never hear the end of it. You will be Blamed, from now on, for every Wrong thing that happens in her life—from bad grades & pimples to evil boyfriends & nervous breakdowns & Failed marriages & finally, Insane Asylums. . . .

It is already a truism in high schools that Big Boobs are absolutely Necessary if a girl wants to be successful in this world, and Huge Tits can make you a Billionaire. Look at Anna Nicole Smith on the cover of Playboy—all she needed to pocket a quick $450,000,000 was one (1) smart idea & a gigantic pair of knockers. Is this a Great Country, or what?

Okay, okay, that's it for boob jobs. Let's get back to the Stock Market & the coming Crash. There will be a definite shrinkage of the Money Supply, and that is always bad news for the Disposable Income crowd. Lifestyles will be greatly diminished & many unpayable debts will be run up on Canceled credit cards. Half the people you know will declare Bankruptcy or turn to Prostitution for rent money. That is what they mean by "Crash."

Life will get meaner & dumber, and greedheads like Alex Rodriguez & Shaq & the hideous Daniel Snyder will have to drive around town in Armored cars. The crime rate will sky-rocket & violent burglaries will be commonplace. . . . The parking lot at Yankee Stadium will become a savage No Man's Land, like it was in the Good Old days of the Seventies. A nice club seat at Mile High Stadium will cost Ten dollars & Fifty cents, & Junk Sex will be available Night & Day at every Quick-Mart.

Major sports markets will go belly up, & high-end teams like the Forty-Niners & the Celtics will wallow and crash into Bankruptcy. "Fans" will prey on each other like vultures in public Restrooms at the Garden & the Superdome. Your home will be Burglarized & you will suspect your Neighbors of doing it. Sales of canned Dog food will soar, water will cost more than gasoline, & Airports will be like War Zones.

(Whoops! Get a grip on yourself, Doc. This is supposed to be a harmless little Sports column. Let's not scare the children so soon after Xmas.)

Okay, I told you I was in a foul head—so we'll save that riff on Fear & Failure & Off-Duty Cops working as Armed Debt Collectors for next week. My face is swelling again & I have to call the Nurse. Later.

—*January 8, 2001*

The NFL Sucks
. . . Another
League Bites
the Dust . . .
Rich Kids
with Weapons

The NFL sucks. . . . That is a nasty way to open a column, but after watching another one of these putrid play-off games, I have nothing else to say. It is embarrassing to have to admit that I've been taking the NFL seriously all these years.

Waking up to watch the Giants-Vikings game on Sunday was like rolling out of bed & stepping into a pile of steaming animal dung. The score at halftime was 34–0, & the Vikings had two first downs. Neither Moss nor Carter had caught a single pass & the Giants led 386–45 in total yards. The game was over, all bets were off, & the crowd in my kitchen was sullen. They had come here to watch football, not a road-paving operation.

The Oakland bettors had given six points, so their game was over by halftime. The Raiders were clearly doomed. . . . Fortunately I had bet against them, just as I bet against Minnesota in the first game—although my personal preference was strongly for both Oakland & the Vikings.

That is Fan-thinking, & I have learned from painful experience that it is almost always the Wrong way to bet. I learned this the Hard way, by consistently betting money—even serious money—against the Dallas Cowboys because I Hated them. I consistently Lost my bets. Those wretched bastards beat me nine times out of ten. They were a very Good football team, & the 49ers were Not.

It was that simple, but it was more than a year before I

learned to swallow my pride & my natural home team passion
& bet like a smart boy on the Enemy & make money instead of
having fun & losing it. Once I started betting *on* the Cowboys, I
went on a winning streak that lasted for 10 years. It was a crucial lesson to learn.

The Sheriff was one of those who got beaten like a gong
on both games. By halftime of the Oakland whipping he
was drinking heavily & rapping his knuckles on the bar whenever money changed hands, usually in My direction. At one
point he began raving & cursing about Al Gore, who will be
watching the game on TV about five miles from here in Snow-
mass. . . . It will be Gore's last ride in Air Force Two, & he is determined to make the most of it. His Secret Service handlers
have already requested/demanded more Special Protection
than he would need for a week in Miami Beach, & he also
wants armed guards to surround his wife & daughters 24
hours a day.

The Sheriff refused to have any part of it, because of the
huge Costs, & his rising anger drove women out of the room.
. . . Indeed, Al Gore & whatever remains of his family will
arrive here tomorrow for a weeklong winter vacation, & the
locals are getting edgy. . . . Presidential visits are fairly routine
in Aspen. The Clintons visited two or three times a year for
big-time Money-raising gigs, & Bush the Elder was here so
often that I came to be good friends with his Secret Service
agents.

They hung around the Woody Creek Tavern for weeks at a
time, protecting against assassins. . . . One summer the Whole
neighborhood was overrun by armed bodyguards from three
Nations. Bush traveled with a Presidential detail of 40 or 50;
Prime Minister Thatcher of England had another 45 or so; &
Prince Bandar of Saudi Arabia was here with his normal detail
of at least 30 personal assassins who never leave his side.

That is a lot of hired gunmen to bring into a rural community with a normal population of 300 cowboys & 50 confirmed
addicts. . . . The Prince lives here, of course, so we are used to

fast caravans of black Hummers & silver Mercedes 600s full of giggling naked children zooming around the Valley at all hours.

Why not? Prince Bandar is a good neighbor & I would never Dream of butting into his Personal life. He has lived right up the hill from me for ten or eleven years. I am wary of his Politics & no doubt he is wary of mine, but that is not a problem in this neighborhood. . . . I have lived across the street, as it were, from some of the worst Swine in America, & I have always assumed that at least eleven percent of all visitors to my house are carrying either concealed weapons or felony-dangerous drugs. (About three percent carry both—down from 44 percent in the Seventies & 20 percent in the Eighties, but most of those are dead now & the rest are in prison.)

"There is too much money out there," said the Sheriff, waving his arm in the general direction of Aspen. "The billionaires have run the Millionaires out of town, & the new crowd has no sense of humor. None at all. My deputies got a 911 call last night from a seven-year-old kid who wanted us to arrest his Nanny for being mean to him. It happens all the time." He made a quick chopping motion with his hand. "We had to Investigate it," he snarled. "It was utterly bogus. We should have drowned the little bastard."

In the old days I went to many games & personally "covered" nine or ten Super Bowls. I was a Sportswriter, among other things, & I enjoyed the games & the Gambling & the crazy dumb Excitement that goes along with the Spectacle. I liked hanging out with Paul Hornung & Jimmy the Greek & engaging in random violence here & there. It was fun.

It was not long before I learned that it was not even necessary to attend the games in person in order to Cover them & write excellent Super Bowl stories. . . . There is a relentless kind of Craziness that hovers in the air during Super Bowl week. You can get into serious trouble just for answering your Phone after midnight, or by simply opening your Hotel room door when somebody knocks on it. I once woke up in Reno with a strange woman about 15 hours after I attended the first half of a Denver-Washington game in San Diego.

It made perfect sense at the time, but I have never been able to explain it—not even to myself. It remains one of the darker adventures of my life & cost me about sixty thousand dollars at a time when I was stone broke. . . . It was a Crime of Passion, as I recall, & we will let it go at that.

On another occasion I was physically ejected from the Redskins Press box when I forgot to take my hat off for the National Anthem, & on another I got involved with the Bush family in Houston. I have flipped out in Miami & been kidnapped in New Orleans, all for just trying to do my job. The Super Bowl is always a high-risk Assignment for some people & I am definitely one of them.

As for this year in Tampa, the Game itself looks like a guaranteed Bummer. Baltimore will squeeze out a six-point victory over the Giants, but only about 2,000 people in America will care about it. Both the City & the Game will be neckdeep in wild whores & hustlers & Pimps from all over the world, & President Bush might even make an appearance at halftime. . . .

But I will not be there, & neither will Lyle Lovett nor Linda Lovelace nor eminent Lawyers like George Tobia & Gerald Goldstein, who are deeply diss-satisfied with pro Football.

And so am I, for that matter. The Play-offs have been a bleak anticlimax to a season that was once so full of promise. . . . The two Losing teams on Sunday scored a total of Six (6) points between them, & the outcomes were never in doubt. Gore's family will Lose all their bets & one of his daughters will manage to get busted for Drunk Driving. Many gamblers will not bet on the game at all, but the Bookies will win big, like always.

Before you even think about betting against the Smart money in Tampa, consider This: The over/under number for the Giants-Vikings game was 41$\frac{1}{2}$. The final score was 41–0.

—January 14, 2001

Slow Week for Sports, in Politics

Slow weeks are becoming more & more routine in the Sports business, just as they are in Politics—but last week was a clear victory for Politics, while Sports limped along like a crippled cat. . . . The hottest tickets of all were for the Inaugural Ball in Washington, where the new President's daughter flashed her boobs on worldwide TV & Bill Clinton slunk out of town like an unemployed Actor.

Meanwhile Super Bowl tickets went begging & the price of TV commercials for the Big Game sunk dangerously low. The over/under for Sunday's game was hovering around ten (10), & more & more people canceled their plane reservations to Tampa. . . . A combined score of 10 would be a new low for Action & another grim disgrace for the NFL. I have about six prime tickets for the game pinned on the lamp in front of me right now, & I can't even *give* them away. It's not just that people don't want to go to the game. They don't even want to be seen there.

I tried to give the tickets to my son, but he said he'd rather watch the spectacle over here at my house on TV. . . . When I offered them to Benicio Del Toro, he said the same thing. Ditto Keith Richards, who said he'd rather go to jail than fly to Tampa this weekend. . . . I had to send a set of $400 Club Seats back to my friend James Irsay of the Colts, whose generosity was wasted on me. Hell, I even have All-Access press credentials from ESPN that I won't use. I could be paid to go to this game, but. . . .

No. I have already adjusted my own line downward, from Six (6) to Three (3). Based on statements from both teams that they don't even plan to score points. . . . Diehard Giants fans are flocking to take the Three, as New York fans always will, rather than pass up a bet. One fool went so far as to insist on taking the Giants with no points at all. . . . Now that is a classic example of betting your Heart instead of your head. I would have given him 2–1 odds on that one, but he didn't even ask.

It is always had business to blindly follow the Conventional Wisdom on big-money events, so the smart way to bet this game is to go both ways & try for a winning Middle—as in Giving the Giants with no points & taking the Giants with Six. That way, a single Baltimore field goal will make you a winner on both ends. Good luck.

You will have to be working a genuinely Berserk gambling crowd to pull off a trick like this—but it happens, on some days, & the secret of making it happen is to invite the Right people to watch the game & bet with you. High on the Guest List should be hopeless Alcoholics with huge Egos & a weakness for Mob Hysteria in tense situations. These are the ones who will get Angry when their pregame bets start going wrong, and then they Double Up on every play in a desperate effort to catch up & win on some last-minute Fumble or shocking Interception. I have seen these loonies win on some days but not often. They are the spiritual descendants of legendary Old West gamblers who would bet the Ranch & even their Wives & Daughters on one final roll of the dice.

Bill Clinton is one of these people, and so is George W. Bush. They are both high-stakes gamblers, and in both cases it runs in the family. They are both proven Winners. Bush is Undefeated, but he is barely more than a Rookie in this league & his last win came against one of the weakest & dumbest candidates ever to run for President. Almost anybody could have beaten Al Gore in 2000, and Bush will not be that lucky next time. Even a blind pig finds an acorn now and then.

Clinton is a different animal. His record in major elections over 25 years of living in Public Housing is 8–1—two Presidencies, five Governorships, & one term as Attorney General of Arkansas—and he would still be President if not for the 22nd Amendment. . . . Clinton was a congenitally Lewd man who is evil in a way that seems Charming; Bush is a charming man who was born Evil. Clinton was born Poor & remains that way; Bush was born Rich & is now even richer.

They are both whores, because that is the nature of American Politics. They both have a designated Fool in the Family, because that is the nature of the Presidency. The fool is a necessary Lightning rod for criticism that would otherwise fall on the President & harm his approval ratings. Clinton had Roger, Carter had Billy, & LBJ had a brother so weird that he had to be locked in a White House attic for three years. There is always something queer in the closet.

With Bush it is going to be poor Jenna, the 19-year-old blonde who fell out of her dress while dancing with her father on their first official night in Washington. She is also a known sot & Night crawler who might go sideways at any moment. She is already painted as the Cross the Bush family has to bear.

Ho ho. There are no Accidents in the Bush family. Everything that happens to them is carefully scripted & accounted for: it is an old Family recipe that has worked for three generations & maybe more. Who knows?

The Key to it is not Luck but the Fix. The Fix must be in for anything to proceed properly. The Bush family Gunsels have understood all their lives that their main Job is to Reduce the Risk Factor to Zero. . . . It is a much-admired ability in politics, Business, Gunfighting, & even professional Sports. The Yankees don't win championships by being Lucky or by some crazed ability to "suck it up in the clutch." No. They win because they are from the Big Apple & they spend Big money for Big players & they have developed a keen taste for Habitual Domination. The Yankees put Meat in the Seats because they Expect to win, by any means necessary—and so does the Bush family of New England, Washington, & Texas. Young George spent more money on one day of his Inauguration Ceremonies than Richard Nixon did on his whole Campaign in 1972—and Nixon was crucified as a Criminal Spendthrift with the ethics of a snake.

Some people will tell you that Bill Clinton fits that description far better than Bush or Nixon—and they will not be entirely wrong. . . . Nixon stabbed his Enemies in the back, but Clinton did it to his Friends. His lust to inflict Punishment surpassed even Nixon's, and he put more people in prison than Caligula. He had his own brother locked up & he refused to pardon his old friend Webb Hubbell. . . . Richard Nixon was a criminally insane Monster; Bill Clinton is a black-hearted Swine of a friend.

Okay. That's it for now. More to come after that Orgy of ill-conceived gibberish that is the Super Bowl—where the best we can hope for, I think, is a 0–0 tie & four scoreless overtimes. Yes. That would make even nongamblers frantic for many hours from Coast to coast & trigger many Suicides. But so what? We are stuck with this game, so why not make it an Unforgettable Experience? One of my clearest memories in Sport is of being on a five-hour flight with Edward Bennett Williams while the agonizing Double Overtime Kansas City–Miami Play-off game was happening. There was no TV & we had to get a radio update from the cockpit every 20 or 30 seconds. The tension was Unbearable. People cried & howled all around us. The stewardess had to give us our own bottle of scotch to keep us from going Mad. . . . The only player's name I recall from that game is Ed Podolak, who told me later that he was going "in and out of consciousness" midway in the second overtime. "By then I hardly cared who Won or Lost," he said. "I thought of Fumbling deliberately just to get it over with."

—January 21, 2001

Lynching
in Denver

Peacocks don't move around much at night. They like a high place to roost, and they will usually find one before sundown. They know how many nocturnal beasts are down there looking for food—foxes, coyotes, wildcats, bloodthirsty dogs on the prowl—and the only thing that can get them when they're up high is one of those huge meat-eating owls with night vision that can swoop down & pounce on anything that moves, from a water rat to a healthy young sheep.

My own peacocks wander widely during the day, but at night they come back into their own warm cage. Every once in a while they will miss the curfew & decide to roost in a tree or on top of a telephone pole . . . and that is what happened last week while we were watching the Super Bowl. It was not a Lightning ball that blacked out my house but a male peacock that stepped on a power line & caused a short circuit that burned him to a cinder & blew half my Electrics.

The power came back, but the bird did not. It was fried like a ball of bacon. We couldn't even eat it. That tragedy occurred at halftime—so let the record stand corrected. Sorry.

Since then, I have consulted with many Lawyers on the Lisl Auman case—which gets uglier every time I look at it; 25,000 people have checked into her Web site since I mentioned it here two weeks ago. She is still in Prison, of course, but the massive Web response was extremely encouraging to her parents and her many supporters.

I don't do this very often—Never, in fact—but this case is such an outrage that it haunts me & gives me bad dreams at night. . . . I am not a Criminal Lawyer, but I have what they call "a very strong background" in the Criminal Justice System & many of my friends & associates are widely known as the best legal minds in that cruel & deadly business.

It is no place for amateurs, and even seasoned professionals can make mistakes that are often fatal. The System can grind up the Innocent as well as the Guilty, and that is what happened to 20-year-old Lisl Auman when the Denver District Attorney put her on trial for a murder he knew she didn't commit, then put her in prison for the rest of her Life Without Parole. . . .

In all my experience with Courts & Crimes & downright Evil behavior by the Law & the Sometimes criminal cops who enforce it, this is the Worst & most Reprehensible miscarriage of "Justice" I've ever encountered—and that covers a lot of rotten things, including a few close calls of my own. Which might easily have gone the other way if not for the help of some hammerhead Lawyers who came to my aid when I was in desperate trouble. (See *Songs of the Doomed*, Summit Books, 1990.)

I learned a lot about Karma in those moments, and that is what got me into the Lisl Auman case, and that is why I will stay in it until this brutal Wrong is Righted. . . . That is also why the first contribution to the Lisl Auman Defense Fund came from Gerald Lefcourt of New York, current President of the National Association of Criminal Defense Lawyers. "This is not going to be easy," he said with a wry smile. "But what the hell—count me in."

Indeed. It is no small trick to get a "Convicted cop-killer" out of prison—but it will be a little easier in this case because Lisl no more killed a cop than I did. She was handcuffed in the back seat of a Denver Police car when the cop was murdered in cold blood by a vicious skinhead who then shot himself in the head & left the DA with nobody to punish for the murder—except Lisl, who didn't even know the freak who pulled the trigger.

It is a long story & I can't explain it all now. But you can find it on the Web at Lisl.com.

And now back to Sports.

Hot damn, the Extreme Football League kicked off this week & drew a staggering 10.3 overnight Nielsen rating for NBC. It was a big hit with the teenage Nazi crowd, but the NFL tried to ignore it. Nobody called it Football, but so what?

It was good to see Jesse Ventura back on TV. I have great af-
fection for Jesse and I wish him well in anything he does. . . .
Which means, I guess, that I'm a charter XFL fan.

Why not? The first game on Saturday night was not bad.
The game itself sucked, but it was definitely good TV. The
Gov's commentary (with the play of Keith Elias) was the best
thing about the New York–Las Vegas game, a pitiful whipping
of the helpless NY/NJ Hitmen by the hometown Outlaws that
should have been a lot worse than the 19–0 final score. . . . The
cheerleaders were the stars of this game: they were not at all
the lewd & sluttish bimbos that we were led to expect, almost
promised, by NBC & the League. No. The Lewdness level var-
ied from team to team, but in the main they were Pretty girls,
Friendly girls, Sexy girls, but no lewder than the Dallas Cowboy girls or the Laker girls—at least not for now, but this is a
freewheeling League, for sure, and big changes can be made
very quickly. If the TV ratings start looking weak, the Lewdness level will be the first thing to change—if only because it
will be a lot easier to hire naked cheerleaders than to go out &
find better players.

They might Play for cheap in the XFL, but they won't play
Naked. That would make the game insanely dangerous & ugly.
The XFL girls, however, could turn the sidelines into a contin-
uous orgy weirder than anything on the stage at the infamous
O'Farrell Theatre in San Francisco, "the Carnegie Hall of Public
Sex in America."

The Brutality level in the two Saturday night games was no
worse than in any hard-hitting NFL game—but that too could
change if the ratings drop. But I doubt that will happen. We are
stuck with this fraud for a while. But it is a lot better than being
in Prison.

—February 5, 2001

Mad Cow Disease
Comes to the NBA

February is always a bad month for TV sports. Football is gone, basketball is plodding along in the annual midseason doldrums, and baseball is not even mentioned. It is a good time for building fires, reading books, watching movies, and cranking up random sex orgies with the neighbors.

Not even pigs will come out of their pens in February. They would rather stay inside & wallow around in their own excrement than venture out in the bitter cold for a breath of fresh air. . . . The human animal needs a Good Reason to get out of bed on a wretched morning in February. Nothing is moving out there on the icy streets except drunk drivers, desperate criminals, & people who don't have the imagination to call in sick for work. Hell, there are plenty of good reasons to wake up sick this time of year: the flu, Ague Fever, shin splints, Chicken pox, projectile vomiting, Rickets—even Black Hairy Tongue Disease, which is extremely contagious.

It is not enough to be merely in real pain or suffering from a Nervous Breakdown. That is not Contagious, and Contagious is what you need. It has to be something that even the Boss might catch & die from. Mad Cow Disease is big in the news right now, and people are deathly afraid of it. I have seen people go rigid with Fear at the sight of a brain-damaged cow with wild eyes staggering crazily around in circles with its legs caving in and its spine seizing up & its hooves lashing out in the air.

"Yes sir," I like to say to them, "and it's spreading to Humans now. One wrong hamburger is all it takes. There's *no cure*, and it spreads like wildfire. You can kill five or six people just by talking to them."

You won't have to worry about having to show up for work, once they hear you saying you have Mad Cow disease. It's a guaranteed excuse for not showing up at Work or anywhere else. And nobody is going to come around checking on you, either. Never in hell. You will be lucky if your neighbors don't nail your doors shut and burn your house down.

Luckily, I am not afflicted with Mad Cow—or any of the others, either, as far as I know. Knock on wood for that, eh? You bet. I am as healthy as I need to be, these days. But I am rarely without access to my trusty Pathologies text. It is a bulky book, very awkward to carry around, but I can open it to just about any page & find three good reasons for Not doing anything at all. Check it out.

I could not attend the XFL game in New Jersey last weekend, for instance, because I have better sense than to fly 2,000 miles in an airtight aluminum tube full of circulating germs, viruses, & deadly killer parasites from every country in the world. Even the pilots are Sick in most planes, and at least One passenger will be coughing up Ebola spittle or contaminating the Lavatories with some kind of lice & microscopic vermin. Only a fool would run that kind of risk for a stupid little football game.

Or a stupid Big basketball game, for that matter. God only knows what people who went to the NBA All-Star game in DC came down with. . . . The game itself was enough to make most people sick, and never mind that the final score was close. It was brazenly Fake basketball, far more bogus than anything the XFL put on TV. . . . At least the XFL players were making an honest effort on every play, and that is a hell of a lot more than can be said of the dismal NBA spectacle. For three Long quarters it was a goof-off mockery of itself. Only the final nine minutes were worth watching (only the last three, really), but by that time I had long since switched away to watch the news & 60 Minutes.

The Alan Iverson Show is not going to be enough to save the NBA from sinking out of sight in the TV ratings—not unless the doomed league can coax more than Nine minutes a game out of their insanely overpaid "stars." The fan base will continue to shrink, as more & more fans catch on to the morbid "fact" that the last nine minutes of Any NBA game are the only part of it worth watching. . . . Once the advertisers catch on, they will flee the scene like rats down a pipe into darkness. Not even the sleazemongers at Fox will pay big money to televise a dull & diminished NBA product.

I am more than just a Serious basketball fan. I am a lifelong Addict. I was addicted from birth, in fact, because I was born in Kentucky and I learned, early on, that Habitual Domination was a natural way of life. The first time I managed to pick up a basketball, I knew I was destined to lead the University of Kentucky to another National championship. . . . Even now, so many years later, I still believe Kentucky will go undefeated in March & win everything.

But that is another story, and we will save it for later. Meanwhile, I will be watching the ACC, Pac-10, and the SEC. That is where the basketball action is happening now—not in the NBA, where not much will happen until the Play-offs start in late April.

Okay.

HST

—*February 12, 2001*

Death in the Afternoon

The violent death of Dale Earnhardt hit the sport of professional auto racing harder than anything in memory since the assassination of John Kennedy. People who'd never even watched a NASCAR race were deeply disturbed by it, for reasons they couldn't quite explain. It seemed to send a message, an urgent warning signal that something with a meaning beyond the sum of its parts had gone Wrong & would go Wrong again if something big wasn't cured—not just in racing, but in the machinery of the American nation.

On the surface it was just another bad crash on a racetrack down in Redneck country. What the hell? It happens all the time. But this one had a resonance that echoed all over the U.S. It was the death of a national hero for no good reason at all— just an Occupational Hazard of the Speed business, shrug it off, forget it. But it was more than that. People noticed it, like they would definitely notice if Michael Jordan had been instantly killed by a brutal & deliberate foul to keep him from scoring in the final seconds of a close game.

Or if John Elway had been killed during a routine play in the last two minutes of a scoreless Super Bowl by a 300-pound blitzing linebacker who knew he would get a big Bonus for knocking a famous quarterback out of the game. Permanently. Dead from a broken neck.

Those ripples would have been noticed far beyond the city limits of Denver. And the killing of a hero like Elway could not have been shrugged off by somebody saying, "Sorry, but that's the way the game is played."

Well, no. That is Not the way the game is played—at least not for long, as anybody who watched the NFL last season can tell you. At least half of the league's star quarterbacks were injured by violent collisions. The Oakland Raiders alone crippled nine (9) opposing quarterbacks by themselves—so there was some kind of poetic justice in their being knocked out of the Super Bowl when the Ravens injured Rich Gannon.

Tony Siragusa's hit might have pleased the stupid bastards from the Backyard Wrestling crowd, but it also cost CBS about 15 percent of its TV audience for the Big Game. Millions of fans all over the country lost interest when the Raiders went down. Watching Ray Lewis play defense might have been interesting—but it was nothing like watching the highest-scoring Offense in the League going against a racehorse team like the Vikings. Savage Defense might be the way to win football games, but it is sure as hell not what puts Meat in the Seats—

no more than losing three of its star drivers in ten (10) months is going to make the NASCAR ratings skyrocket.

Or maybe, God help us, it Will. There is such an ever-growing appetite for Violence as Entertainment in this country—especially among those in the 18–35 demographic that TV is targeting—that something Dark & Disastrous is going to come of it. There is a good commercial reason why Fox just paid for TV rights to NASCAR, and it is exactly the same reason why every recently built racetrack from California to Maine is designed about 20 feet Wider than tracks were built in the old days, when it was physically impossible for more than three (3) cars to run side by side at 180 mph in the straightaway—the new & Wider tracks have created the bloodcurdling spectacle of four cars running fender to fender at top speed.

"It makes the racing vastly more Exciting," say the auto sport czars. "It dramatically raises the Potential Disaster factor & whips the fans into a frenzy." Right. Blood & guts, bread & Circuses, human brains all over the asphalt. The people of Rome demanded more & more Death & Cruelty on their Sunday afternoons at the Colosseum—until Nobody was left to Sacrifice. They ran out of Victims.

And so will the NFL, the NBA, and NASCAR. That is what makes people nervous about the meaning of Dale Earnhardt's death. It is the American Dream run amok. Watch it & weep.

—*February 20, 2001*

XFL, R.I.P.

I was going to write on the Meaning of Life this week, but I put it aside at the last moment when I got a tip that this might be the last chance I'll ever get to write anything except an Obituary for the XFL.

The doomed league's TV rating slipped another 25 points for the weekend—down 71 percent in the four quick weeks since Opening Day—and that steep a slide is fatal.

If the Dow Jones Index plunged that many points in four weeks, the sidewalks of Wall Street would be littered with the broken bodies of Stockbrokers. Five hundred people a day would be leaping to death off the Golden Gate Bridge.

The horrible reality of being suddenly stone broke and homeless is more than most people in this country can handle. They will literally seize up and go mad. Your everyday Nervous Breakdown is nothing compared to the hopeless Craziness of a man who woke up in the morning as a Prince and goes to bed as a Toad. That is a guaranteed overweening shock to the Central Nervous System: if you don't go insane from suddenly having to see everything in the world from a point only two inches high, your brain will surely be churned into cream by having to crawl, headfirst, with your eyes open, down a muddy hole in the ground just to have a place to sleep.

Nobody could handle a situation like That. It is Unacceptable. It is worse than any dream that ever happened in the worst and most tortured hallucinations ever suffered by the most pitiful LSD victim. . . . I spent a lot of time with Allen Ginsberg and I have swapped gruesome tales over whiskey at night with William Burroughs, and neither one of them ever even mentioned a vision so horrible as being instantly changed from a rich and powerful human like Donald Trump into a common leaping toad that might be swallowed alive by a snake at any moment.

Yet that is exactly what happens to people in this world who lose 71 percent of their customers in four weeks. They seize up and go crazy.

Out of personal loyalty to Jesse Ventura, I tried to watch the XFL "clash" on Saturday, but by halftime my heart was swollen by feelings of Hate and Despair. It was like watching a Festival of Shame taking place in a blinding rainstorm. Some fool from NBC appeared to have smeared Vaseline on the Camera lens to make it waterproof. It was like watching a game underwater and never really knowing the score.

A running back would appear on the screen for an instant, then disappear in a mass of mud-caked bodies. A long pass would vanish into a fog bank and never be seen again. There was no way to tell the officials from the players, except when a yellow flag was thrown and you could see who finally stooped down to pick it up.

The weird thing about the XFL is that nobody except Vince McMahon was anxious to see it born, and nobody except the cheerleaders will miss it when it's gone. There is no way to explain why it ever happened at all, except that some cluster of corporate thugs in the TV business figured they were in desperate need of a tax write-off. It was not even good entertainment, much less good football.

—February 26, 2001

The Most Horrible Curse in Sports

The world of sports has always been plagued by queer superstitions, but most of them are harmless. Nobody really cares if Derek Jeter wears the same moldy jockstrap for 39 straight days, just as long as the Yankees win games—Many games, in fact, including at least four in the World Series.

If I owned a baseball team, I would want Jeter in it. He is a certified Winner in more ways than that bitchy-rich shortstop from Texas will know for the next 10 years.

Jesus, what conceivable reason would a pampered whiner like A-Rod have for bad-mouthing Jeter in the national gossip press? His rant sounds like something Al Gore would say, or a swine like Jesse Helms. I have been planning to continue my personal "Swine of the Week" award for many months, so let's get it started right now and we'll give the second one to Alex Rodriguez. He talks like something out of a Roger Clinton cartoon.

The Clinton family is full of hard-core sports fans. His mother spent much of her time at the racetrack, and Roger was big on pro basketball—until, at least, he became persona non grata at Madison Square Garden. A CBS-TV camera caught him spitting beer on a man he was attacking from behind with an amateurish Stranglehold. He was quickly subdued by Secret Service agents, who led him away in a wristlock. Roger is a Monster, a mutant brute who should have been put to sleep a long time ago.

I mention this only because the Yankees are about to get a raucous new fan at the Stadium, and his name will be Roger Clinton, famous brother of incoming NY Mayor Bill Clinton, previously of Washington, DC. . . . That is the best early bet on the Political horizon right now, for good or ill. Clinton did not move to Harlem on some kind of Jazz-addled whim. No. He just counted the votes. The only thing that might stand in his way is that awkward little matter of Felony crime in Arkansas. Good luck. Clinton is already the Winter-book favorite to be the next Mayor of New York City.

Wow! The Big Apple press will love this one. It is like getting what you always wanted for Christmas—a guaranteed Nasty headline every day of the week. It is a Gossipmonger's dream.

Indeed, but we were talking about the so-called Jinx (or Curse) of *Sports Illustrated* and how deeply it is feared in the sports world. . . . Last week it struck Red Sox star hitter Nomar Garciaparra, whose wrist tendon split within hours after his cynically homoerotic image appeared on the cover of

SI. He will be out of action for the duration of Spring training, said his doctors. . . .

Well, okay—in the name of Fair Comment I will stay away from that one. But I hate to think what a veteran drillmaster like Pat Riley would say about it: under Riley's rules Nomar would find himself on the market within 48 hours.

That is how the meat market worked in the good old days when owners saw players more like Chattel slaves than employees—but even now when the pendulum has swung crazily in the other direction, Malingering is still dark poison for team morale. Like point shaving or getting repeatedly busted for wife beating, it has a long-term effect on the won-lost column, and that is bad for business.

Okay, that's about It for sports this time. But I have a flash of Good News from the Police Atrocity front, which is heating up in Denver. . . . Stand back! Good News is rare in the Criminal Justice System, but every once in a while you find it, and this is one of those times. To wit: the National Association of Criminal Defense Lawyers has formally entered the Appeals trial of young Lisl Auman—the girl who remains locked up in a cell at the Colorado State Prison for the Rest of Her Life with No Possibility of Parole for a bogus crime she was never even Accused of committing. She is a living victim of a cold-blooded political trial that will cast a long shadow on Denver for many years to come. Lisl is the only person ever convicted in the United States for Felony Murder who was in police custody when the crime happened.

The NACDL brings a heavyweight presence to this case that will quickly level the playing field. Nobody needs a public fight with a team of Elite warriors from the NACDL. It is like having to fight Joe Frazier every six months. There Will be terrible injuries, and there will be more than one trip to the Emergency Room this time. No more easy wins for the black hats. The worm is about to turn. That is also a good early bet. Take my word for it. And thanx again for your help.

—March 5, 2001

Urgent Warning to Gamblers: Beware the Ides of March

March is an ugly month for gamblers. It is a time of deep mud, foul treachery, and guaranteed personal failures. I have always hated March for personal reasons, but as a Gambler, I Really hate it.

Nothing good has Ever happened to me in March, and it has Never failed to bring horrible Fear, Grief, and extremely tangible Loss down on me—and I know in my heart that this year will be no different. I get the creeps every time I look at the calendar. . . . Big trouble, soon come.

Even Astrologers will tell you that March is a good time to lay low and beware of taking Risks. Disaster is Certain, because March is ruled by Mars, and that is Guaranteed trouble. The Sun is in Pisces, which is the worst time of Any year for making Decisions. They are sure to be made for reasons of Emotional disturbance rather than Logic or rational thought. That is the Law of the Universe.

And that brings Us, as Gambling people, to the terrible truth that March is also the month of the NCAA basketball tournament—and we know what That means for Gamblers, don't we? Yes sir. It is Extremely Dangerous territory for even the coolest and calmest Professional risk takers—much less for emotionally berserk Amateurs with "Home Team Fever." Those people are Doomed. That is a Mathematical Certainty, like a game of Musical Chairs with only One chair. You don't need a pencil to figure that one out.

Indeed. I have scars on my soul from past gambling disasters that will Never heal over. I still suffer hate and pain in my head every time I see the word "Duke" on a TV screen, and that rotten Thing happened nine years ago when that Swine Christian Laetner hit that impossible last-second shot against Kentucky. I still have a Memory Block about it—but as I recall, it was in the East Regional final that is still known as "the Best basketball game ever played." Jesus, it Was and remains the Worst Shock I've experienced in my Life.

March is a month without mercy for rabid basketball fans. There is no such thing as a "gentleman gambler" when the Big Dance rolls around. All sheep will be fleeced, all fools will be punished severely. . . . There are no Rules when the deal goes down in the final weeks of March. Even your good friends will turn into monsters. They will watch you intensely for any sign of emotional commitment to your bets, and then jump you like snakes on a toad. Loyalty is a fatal weakness in this business. It is an open invitation to a Beating.

I have been keenly aware of this problem for many years, and I am quick to take advantage when I see it in others. Any jackass who will bet his Heart instead of his Head on NCAA tournament games is either a brain-dead Sucker or temporarily Insane. That is a rule of Nature. And all Suckers are fair game, especially when they're crazy.

And that's about it for my Wisdom. I have preached it forever, yet for some sick reason I have never been able to cure myself of it, even when I know it brings pain.

Only two years ago, my good friend Ed Bradley walked into this house and beat me like a gong out of $4,000 on a Kentucky-Arizona game that suddenly went Wrong and bit me in the face. I was completely Humiliated, in front of my friends and family. They laughed like a gang of Hyenas.

I will never forget it—at least not until my people go up against Duke in two weeks. Hot damn! I can hardly wait. We will beat them like stinking animals. *Selah.*

—*March 12, 2001*

I Told You It Was Wrong

People mocked me when I picked Kentucky to go all the way in the NCAA finals this year. They said I was dumb, that I was doing exactly what I warned people Not to do, last week. I was betting my heart instead of my head—Homeboy Fever.

Well, maybe so. I am a Bluegrass boy, for sure, and the blood of Devil Anse Hatfield runs in my veins—but I don't hear any Fat ladies singing in my house tonight, no music has stopped where I dance. . . .

Betting on Kentucky has always been a white-knuckle proposition. The Holy Cross game on Thursday took three years off my life in ten minutes. Losing a 12-point lead when you've just doubled down is one of those things that I will Never learn to tolerate. It is like watching rats gnaw flesh off your body.

Every bastard in Boston was laughing at me when that happened. I could hear it all the way out here on the other side of the Continental Divide. . . . Ho ho. Remember that old sales pitch that said, "They laughed when I sat down to play the piano"? It was Liberace who said that, I think. He was selling quick-fix Music Lessons.

It was the same thing they said when Tayshaun Prince showed up in Lexington to play basketball. He was way too skinny, they said. He lacked the true grit of a winner. . . . But let me tell you something, Bubba—that boy Prince has the instincts of a flat-out professional assassin. He murdered Holy Cross in cold blood, and he did it again to Iowa. Prince is a Shootist. He can turn your nerves to jelly if you're Betting against him.

Ah, but dancing out loud is very bad Karma at this time of year. There are 16 teams still alive in this tournament, and every one of them is dangerous. Stanford survived by the skin of its teeth against lowly St. Joseph's, and Penn State's cruel bashing of North Carolina brought shame on the whole state.

My own real fear, right now, is that Kentucky might be so rabid for revenge against Duke that they will forget all about USC, which would be a fatal mistake. The Grim Reaper sits close to the floor in this tournament. A single missed free throw can be the difference between Life and Death. Ask that poor geek from Wisconsin how it feels. The next basketball game he plays will be in Korea.

And remember this, folks—I am a Hillbilly, and I don't always Bet the same way I talk. Good advice is one thing, but smart gambling is quite another. *Caveat Emptor.*

My topic next week will be "The Importance of a Good Education." But Kentucky has to beat USC first, and I want Duke to stay healthy long enough to get past UCLA. Once we get our hands on Duke, people will understand why it was Richard Nixon's favorite school.

—*March 19, 2001*

Where Were You When the Fun Stopped?

There are many harsh lessons to be learned from the gambling experience, but the harshest one of all is the difference between having Fun and being Smart. It is the difference between Winning and Losing, on most days, and the second half of the Maryland-Duke game on Saturday was a lesson for fun-loving Losers.

Saturday has never been kind or forgiving to these people. They are taught all their lives that Saturday night is when even fools can cut loose and take risks that would be out of the question on any other night: get drunk, shoot guns, dance naked in public parks, or even crouch in your basement and hack into the Pentagon database. . . .

If Sunday is the Lord's day, then Saturday belongs to the Devil. It is the only night of the week when he gives out Free passes to the Late Show at the Too Much Fun Club.

Not everybody believes this, of course, and the doubters are not without wisdom. It is no accident that the Dog-racing tracks do a booming business on Saturday or that people swarm into nightclubs and dance to a feverish beat. Why not? At least they'll have plenty of company. . . .

Indeed, even the Jails will be crowded, and the lines will be long at neighborhood check-cashing windows. Nobody feels guilty for things that happen on Saturday—not even the ones who fly off to Las Vegas and get married at Midnight by a Preacher who claims to be Elvis and fondles the bride while he talks. What the hell? It goes with the territory, these days. We are Modern people, and we like to do Modern things.

Ho ho. That is dangerous gibberish in some circles, and the Gambling fraternity is one of them. There is nothing Modern about doing dumb things for dumb reasons, and nothing new about the feelings of shame and disgrace that come down on people who think it is "Fun" to bet against Duke in a high-stakes basketball game that tips off on the last Saturday night of the season. Even when you're getting 5 points and your hot-shooting team jumps out to a 22-point lead before halftime, you're doomed. Take my word for it.

It was just about then, in fact, when the game shifted gears and I began feeling Fear in my heart. I looked around the room and saw gloom on the faces of those who were betting against me.

They laughed bitterly when I said I was nowhere near comfortable with my bet. "Those swine are still dangerous," I assured them. "This game is too weird to be true. We are seeing a false dawn, sure as hell."

They snickered. A few even paid up and left, unable to toler-ate the prospect of suffering for 20 more minutes in a trap with the corpse of Duke. One beating was Enough, they said, but two in a row would be utterly Unacceptable.

I shrugged and turned back to the game, but I set that money in a separate pile. There was no doubt in my mind that something horrible was going to happen, and it would happen very soon. Nothing in Nature was any more certain than that Duke would come out of its stupor and make a desperate run at me.

It had already started, and I shuddered when I saw the clock showing five or six minutes still left before halftime. That's impossible, I thought. The game should be over by now. The timekeeper must be on the Take. I slumped in my chair and squawked helplessly as I watched Maryland turning to jelly in a blizzard of dumb fouls and turnovers. My 22-point lead was getting chopped up like a pig falling into a meat grinder.

By halftime I'd abandoned all hope of winning—or even Losing by less than 5 points. I saw panic in the eyes of the Maryland guards as they brought the ball up the floor. Coach Williams was screaming desperately, but his wild cries fell on deaf ears. He knew he was beaten, and so did I.

The mood in my kitchen had changed drastically. They were still down by 16, but they sensed a wild turn of the tide. I saw smiles on their faces for the first time all afternoon. The Sheriff was feeling so bold that he offered to double his bet. Benicio Del Toro called in on the phone and also doubled down. I grimly accepted all offers, despite what I knew in my heart.

It was a matter of Honor, I felt, and also a deep-set Tradi-tion. . . . No bet goes unchallenged in This room.

Whoops! Have I forgotten to say that I'd already won all my bets on the Arizona–Michigan State game? Yes, I have—but things like that are easily lost in the horror of seeing a 27-point lead (with the spread) disappear right in front of your eyes. It seems impossible—especially for a very good team that has just beaten Stanford and Illinois—but Maryland was a special case this year, and only a fool would have bet real money on them to hold a big lead for more than 33 seconds against Duke in a serious game. They curled up like worms in a bonfire.

But so what? All that matters in the sports-gambling business is the score at the end of the day, and if you don't win Two out of Three, it is time to quit the business. They will call you a hopeless Loser and your wife will file for Divorce. Strange men in black suits will show up and kick down your door at night. That is the fate of Losers in this country.

—*April 2, 2001*

Running Away with the Circus

It is no accident that this column is titled *Hey Rube*. That is what's called my "Standing Head" in the arcane jargon of Journalism, and it will not change anytime soon. "Hey Rube" is an old-timey phrase, coined in the merciless culture of the Traveling Carnival gangs that roamed from town to town in the early 20th century. Every stop on the circuit was just another chance to fleece another crowd of free-spending Rubes—Suckers, Hicks, Yokels, Johns, Fish, Marks, Bums, Losers, Day traders in Portland, fools who buy diamonds from gypsies, and anyone over the age of nine in this country who still believes in his heart that all cops are honest and would never lie in a courtroom.

These people are everywhere. They are Legion, soon to be a

majority, and 10,000 more are being born every day. It was P. T. Barnum, the Circus man, who explained the real secret of his vast commercial success by repeating his now-famous motto, "There's a sucker born every minute," and his job was to keep the suckers amused. Which he did—with a zeal that has never been equaled in the history of American show business.

Barnum knew what people wanted: Freaks, Clowns, and Wild Animals. The Barnum & Bailey Circus only came to town once a year, and those days were marked as sacred holidays on the John Deere calendars of every Rube in America. . . . Those dates were Special; many schools closed when the Circus came to town, and not every student returned when the public frenzy was over. "Running away with the Circus" was the dream of every schoolboy, and the nightmare of every mother with a bored and beautiful daughter.

Ah, memories, memories. They are not always good for the brain—so let's get back to Rubes and the fact that I am still one of them on some days, and the final round of the Masters was one of those. I was lured, tricked, and then Fleeced without mercy by my trusted old friend John Walsh—now the Senior Vice President and Executive Editor of ESPN.com—who is also a lifelong Gambler.

I was not ashamed. The Fleecing Instinct is strong in the gambling fraternity. It is an irresistible urge, even for the few Rogues among us who call themselves "Gentleman Gamblers." My own firm rule is that I MUST WIN TWO OUT OF THREE. That is the Mandatory minimum for any gambler who plays with Real Money. Anything less is Unacceptable. If you can't win Two out of every Three things you bet on, it is time to quit the business. Gambling is an Acceptable Vice for most people, but a Fatal Addiction for others. . . . All medicines are deadly and dangerous, if taken repeatedly in large doses. A pound of pure Aspirin will kill a whole busload of young athletes. A craving for french-fried potatoes can make you swell up and stink like the rotting corpse of a whale.

These things are mathematically certain—just as sure as

the fate of fools who make too many bad bets with sports bookies or of those millions of hapless Rubes who got fleeced in the
Day-Trading racket. They got trapped in the flaming remains of
the Too Much Fun Club. They stayed too long at the party. They
knew it was dangerous, but they stayed anyway.

That is what happened to me last week. I bet against Duke
in the NCAA final, and I bet against Tiger Woods in the Masters. Both bets went wrong from the start, just as I knew they
would—even though I had Eight (8) large points against Duke
and a reasonable-looking 2-stroke edge against Woods. . . . Ho
ho. Never bet against the Smarter team in a major championship game. Especially when the point spread is so short as to
fall "within the margin of error."

Those are dangerous numbers. The Vegas line finally settled
on Duke (minus $4^{1}/_{2}$), and that was clearly not enough. Duke
could have flogged Arizona by 22, if necessary—but it was
Not, so they mercifully wasted the clock. I admired them for
it—just as I admired Tiger Woods for the graceful Dominance
he showed by staying just far enough ahead of his challengers
to keep his win safe, but still Interesting, in the Chinese sense
of the word, which is ominous.

"Interesting" is Fun, but it is the wrong way to bet, for any
gambler who wants to stay afloat in these times of Risk and
Confusion. The world is getting weirder and weirder. Huge
things are happening at speeds too high to measure, or even
fathom, in the brain of a normal human. We are like moths in a
blizzard.

—*April 9, 2001*

NBA and the Downward Spiral of Dumbness

A spiral that goes straight Down at unholy speed is called a Vortex, I think, and a spiral that whirls straight Up is called a Tornado. They might appear to be different, but among scholars of Physics and Quantum Science, they are both the same thing.

They can both kill you instantly. The only sure difference between being sucked down a bottomless sinkhole and getting sucked up in the air while strapped into your car and then dropped like a bomb on a schoolhouse 12 miles away is that your scrambled remains will be easily identified if you fall from the sky on a schoolhouse—your family will be disgraced and their auto insurance will be canceled for unexplained reasons.

"These things are always Genetic," they'll say. "And his Grandfather was hit by Lightning two or three times, and his Uncle got killed by a tractor. That whole Family is doomed, sure as hell."

The upside of being sucked like a roach down a hole in the earth is that your body will disappear forever. Any Coroner's Jury will have problems with That one. . . . "It was like he got flushed down a toilet," said one witness. "And that was the last time I saw him."

All spirals will get out of control now and then: witness the horrible fate of Dan Marino in his final game against Jacksonville. (He went 11 for 25, as I recall, with two interceptions and a fumble.) Not even Joe Montana was smart and sharp every Sunday.

But *wait!* Don't touch that dial! Stay tuned for the Point of this story—which is the downward Spiral of Dumbness that threatens to drag all of us down in the Mother of all killer whirlpools. It is the natural law of any Market economy that a rising tide lifts all boats (for 12 hours)—and unless the moon gets blown off its axis by some Pentagon dingbat who wants to "teach China a lesson," the same law applies with Low Tides.

It is the Freak tides that lead to disasters. And this eerie phenomenon of a guaranteed high-yield Economy that has made even Dumb people richer and richer for the last 20 years is a decidedly freakish tide. . . . It is also a law of nature that when too many dumb people get rich all at once, they will naturally rise to the top and be making more and more Executive decisions that will affect the lives of more and more people.

George W. Bush is an obvious example of the spiral of dumbness in action. But he is not alone. Other hideous examples are all around us from Mad Cow disease and the stock market plunge to the shutdown of Hollywood and the loss of TV from our lives. We live in times of diminishing expectations.

The golden success of the "Be Like Mike" league has gone up in a foul cloud of smoke. The game goes on, yet nobody has faith in its future. . . . The level of desperation has sunk to the spreading of shameless (grasping at) rumors of a "comeback" by Michael Jordan, which not even sportswriters pretend to take seriously.

It is far worse than dumb, for instance, to think for more than 10 seconds that a return to the days of Zone Defense will speed up the game or make it more exciting on TV. The Zone will add about as much speed and excitement to the NBA game as would the return of the dreaded Four-Corners offense or the elimination of the 3-point shot. Its return is the work of fools and bunglers who got caught in the Spiral of Dumbness.

—*April 16, 2001*

Bad Craziness
at Owl Farm

It was Saturday night in the mountains, and a heavy blizzard was falling. Six inches in six hours.

It happened so fast that my bright red, hot rod convertible was disappearing right in front of my eyes. The top was beginning to sag from the weight of the soggy spring snow. I knew it was futile to try to put it back in the barn. It would sink in the mush and be trapped in the blizzard all night. I must have been crazy to bring it out in the weather so soon.

But so what? I thought. The Shark has seen snow before. Let it Be. . . . I cranked up the fire and ate a few crab legs. I brought out a wad of small bills. The XFL championship game was about to start, and the last NBA play-off game of the day was about to end. The gambling would begin soon enough.

We had just settled down to drink whiskey and bet when the night was shattered and ripped by a sudden explosion just in front of the house—a crashing of metal and fire and wild screams of animals. I ran out on the porch with a shotgun and a huge police spotlight, just in time to be knocked back by another explosion and a wall of flame on the road. Chickens squawked and peacocks screeched in the treetops. It was like a bomb that had been dropped on a jungle. Flaming chickens fell out of the sky and hissed as they died in the snow. . . .

Then we saw a fiery human figure stagger into my driveway and fall in a heap on the ground. The Sheriff grabbed a fire extinguisher out of his car and quickly doused the burning man with a blast of steaming chemicals.

It was Cromwell, my neighbor from up the road. He'd been caught in the blizzard and was desperately trying to drive home on his motorcycle when he was hit in the face by a 20-pound owl that swooped out of the night and almost took his head off—which caused him to lose control and run his bike off the road and through the wall of a nearby barn that was full of roosters and hay and plastic drums full of gasoline.

The explosion was triggered by the sparks of a red-hot cigar butt that he was smoking at the time, and the flimsy tin barn was now a fiery tomb full of shrieking animals. The blast sent 10 or 12 burning guinea hens up in the air like rockets. One was still clinging to Cromwell's back as he fell. Another one dropped with a thud on the hood of my red convertible, where it sizzled and steamed until dawn.

Cromwell staggered and babbled as we helped him into the house. He was still in deep shock and seemed to think he was somewhere in Egypt with some good-humored strangers or ski bums, but he was cheerful about it, and he thanked us for giving him gin. We humored him carefully for a while, until he came back to life and seemed almost normal.

He relaxed with a bottle of Tanqueray and talked casually about the tragedy, as if it had happened a long time ago and was a matter of small importance. "I never liked that bike anyway," he said with a smile. "I've taken worse falls than that on Aspen Mountain. And I've hated that owl for 10 years."

The XFL game was long over and nobody cared who won, so we turned our attention to the heavyweight championship fight that was about to start on TV from South Africa.

Lennox Lewis wasn't the only one to be dazed and confused that Saturday night. On most Saturday nights I would have passed on it—Lennox Lewis was a 15-to-1 favorite to quickly demolish some obscure challenger from Baltimore. The fight had been widely ignored by the ranking elite of the boxing press—but I was, after all, a professional, and I had a column to write. And besides, the 15-to-1 odds were impossible to resist. I didn't even know who the challenger was. . . .

But it didn't matter. I have never forgotten that other widely ignored fight about 10 years ago, in Tokyo, when another heavyweight champion got ambushed and whipped like a chow by some no-name bum who was such a ridiculous underdog that the fight was actually taken off the Board in Las

Vegas. . . . Right. That would be the famous Mike Tyson vs. Buster Douglas upset, which remains near the top of my list of the most incredible heavyweight fights. I still have it on video-tape.

Larry Merchant was there, as I recall, so when I saw him at ringside from Johannesburg—along with George Foreman and Jim Lampley—I felt a tingle of rising excitement in my spine. I quickly picked up the phone and called people with professional access. . . . Why not? I thought. On a night like this I could use a cheap thrill or two. This yokel Hasim Rahman suddenly looked like a wise investment.

It was right about then that we began having trouble with Cromwell. His mood had deteriorated and he was losing his sense of humor. The Sheriff had just made an idle joke about his sworn duty to arrest Cromwell and jail him for killing the owl. "You murdered that beast," he laughed. "That's a felony crime in this state. You'll have to stand trial for it." But the joke didn't work.

"You bastards," Cromwell yelled. "Stop laughing at me! I can't stand it. It's driving me crazy. I'm getting the fear. . . . I feel weak," he said hoarsely. "I feel like I'm dying."

He fell back on the couch, and his eyes rolled back in his head. "Oh, God!" he screamed. "I'm afraid. Something is rolling all over me! It's the Fear! I have the *fear!*" His body went tense, then suddenly jerked up in a spasm, twisting wildly back and forth, as if struggling desperately in the grip of some assassin when nobody else could see.

It was Terrifying. We watched helplessly as he grasped and clawed at the top of his head, which was beginning to blister and bleed. The room was heavy with a stench of burning hair. . . . The situation was getting out of control.

Cromwell was a huge and dangerous man, even when he was happy—but with him in a frenzy of Fear and Rage, we knew it was out of the question to try to deal with him physically.

I saw my friend Curtis trying to wrestle a giant Red fire Extinguisher off a hook on the wall. "No!" I yelled. "Not that!" I knew it was a high-powered A, B, C, & D–type FX that would fill the whole room with a cloud of white glue. So I quickly reached over and gave Cromwell a sharp jolt between the shoulder blades with my 200,000-volt PowerMax cattle prod. And that was that.

He collapsed in a coma and said nothing for 20 minutes. It might have seemed cruel and unusual, but we knew at the time that it had to be done, and he would thank us for it later.

The fight came to an abrupt end with an amazing knockout in round ten. We had a new heavywight champion and my bet would pay off handsomely. . . . The rest of the night was quiet. Cromwell went home with the Sheriff, and I was soon back to work on my typewriter.

—April 23, 2001

Can the Three Stooges Save the NBA?

There is too much ignorant squawking these days about the Decline and Fall of the NBA Empire. Nielsen ratings are down, the fan base is shrinking, and even the Commissioner's office says radical changes are needed to keep the game healthy.

Many alarming statistics are cited to show that the NBA, as we know it, is withering away right in front of our eyes.

But none of it is true. It is a landslide of gibberish dutifully parroted by sportswriters.

What the hell? Somebody has to fill all those holes in the

widely cursed 24-hour news cycle. We live in faster and faster Times. Big news that only 200 years ago took nine weeks just to cross the Atlantic Ocean now travels everywhere in the world at the speed of light, and gossip travels faster.

Any geek with a cheap computer can log on to the World Wide Web and spread terrifying rumors about Anthrax bombs exploding in Dallas or half the population of San Francisco being killed in three days by a brown fog of Ague Fever that blew in on a vagrant wind from Mongolia. . . . And never doubt for an instant that these things might be true. That is the wonderful perversity of gossip in the 21st Century. Nothing is impossible.

Some things are more impossible than others, however, and the collapse of the NBA is one of these. The only thing wrong with the NBA—or any other professional sport, for that matter—is a wild epidemic of Dumbness and overweening Greed. There is no Mystery about it, and no need to change any rules. The NBA's problem is so clear that even children can see it—especially high school basketball stars, half-bright manchild phenomena who don't need college Professors to teach them the difference between Money and Fun.

There is a famous Three Stooges film clip that says all we need to know about the NBA. Here is how I remember it:

On a warm afternoon in the summer, the Three Stooges decided to cool off by going out on a nearby Lake in a small rented rowboat and feeling the breeze in their hair. Why not? they thought. Floating around in the middle of a nice cool Lake was the smartest thing they could do on a sizzling summer day.

So they dressed up in their normal black business suits and set off across town to the Lake—where, after long haggling about money with the boat rental man, they took possession of a 6-foot dinghy with two oars and a small tin bucket for bailing out the odd leak or two of stray lake water. . . . There were other boats on the Lake, and young couples were drifting around happily in the shade of wide sun umbrellas. It was just another idyllic day in the American Century.

The trouble started when the boat sprung a leak, as rented rowboats will, and one of the Stooges noticed that water was rising around his ankles. He pointed this out to his companions and they began bailing water out of the boat with their handy tin bucket. . . . But they couldn't stay ahead, even by using their black bowler hats as bailing buckets. The leak was worse than they'd thought. The boat was filling up.

It was then that they put their heads together and came up with a brilliant solution—they would use the oars to punch a hole in the bottom of the rowboat, so the water could more easily flow out. . . . And when that didn't work, they punched another hole in the bottom of the boat. And then another. They were getting desperate, and the boat was in danger of sinking.

Still they bailed crazily with the bucket and three hats. They were far out in the middle of the Lake and none of them knew how to swim. Other boaters ignored them, or laughed when they screamed for help. . . . What a fine Hoot it was to see these three stupid, fat men flapping around like wild rats in the middle of a calm little lake. . . . Yes sir, that was the Three Stooges for you, Real Jokers.

The moral of this story is as clear as a new pane of glass to everyone in the world—except the greed-crazed owners of the NBA franchises. They are dumber than the Three Stooges, and so is that babbling jackass of a Commissioner. Stern should have been put out to pasture a long time ago. But don't worry. Quick exit, Soon come. And it won't even be noticed.

The Game will go on.

—*April 30, 2001*

Kentucky Derby and Other Gambling Disasters

Betting against the Lakers in the NBA playoffs has never been a sound investment for gamblers—especially not in a lazy year like this one, with the Lakers being the defending NBA champions & favored to win again, despite a lackluster season & more internal bitching & squabbling and crazed jealous treachery than in a tribe of Hyenas in heat. . . .

It may be worth noting here that Hyenas are the only beasts in nature that are born physically bisexual & remain that way all their lives. They are also cannibals that routinely eat their young & everything else that looks helpless. People who know Hyenas describe them as "the filthiest animal in nature—with the possible exception of English cows & corrupt big-city police officers in 21st-century America."

Indeed. But that invidious comparison to Hyenas and crooked Cops was not my real reason for betting against the Lakers on Sunday night. My real reason had to do with The Spread—which had the Lakers giving 6½ or seven against Sacramento, a fast and flaky team that appeared to have everything necessary to beat LA, except a cure for Shaquille O'Neal Disease. . . . Which appearance turned out to be true: Shaq ran totally wild, dominating the game so completely that the whole Kings' front line came away looking like they'd been Beaten & battered all night by a 300-pound Meat Hammer.

O'Neal totaled 44 points, 21 rebounds, & seven crushing blocks at crucial moments in the game. Poor, rich little Kobe added 29, and the rest of the Lakers scored only 35 among them. That was all LA needed to win—but not enough, ho ho, to beat The Spread. The final score, 108–105, was deceptively close for a game the Lakers should have won by 19 or 20. They played at the top of their form, against a Sacramento team that couldn't do anything right & played their worst game of the season, and still lost by only three. . . .

If the line doesn't change for the next game, take the Kings & the points. They have a knack for figuring things out in a hurry, and Shaq won't score 40 points again this season. The Lakers are so bitchy that it would be shameful for the whole NBA if they won another championship.

That game was not my only gambling experience of the weekend. I also bet heavily on the Kentucky Derby & suffered huge losses.

The Derby is not my favorite sporting event of the year, despite my deep Kentucky roots & my natural lust for gambling. I have had more truly heinous experiences linked to Churchill Downs than any other venue. And I can tell you, for sure, that Derby week in Louisville is a white-knuckle orgy of Booze & Sex & Violence that, 99 times out of 100, swamps anybody who goes near it in a hurricane of Fear, Pain, & Stupefying Disasters that will haunt them for the rest of their lives.

The behavior of the crowd at Churchill Downs is like 100,000 vicious Hyenas going berserk all at once in a space about the size of a 777 jet or the White House lawn. Going to the Derby in person is worse than volunteering to join General Pickett's famous Charge at Gettysburg, and just about as much Fun. . . . Take my word for it, folks: I have done it nine or 10 times in a row, and I still have recurring nightmares about it that cause me to wake up sweating & screaming like some kind of pig being eaten alive by meat bats.

My memories of the Derby are extremely clear & far too obscene to describe here in any detail. Some involve jails, insane asylums, Rape trials, wife beatings, police brutality, and private graveyards filled with victims of tragic medical experiments worse than anything the Marquis de Sade was ever accused of.

I went to one Derby party where two teenage girls were deliberately set on fire & tortured by drunken rich people, who then hurled their bodies off a cliff above the Ohio River & laughed about it later. The girls' families were told by local authorities that their daughters had "run away with a gang of horse gamblers from Turkey who loaded them up with gin and told them they were going to Hollywood to get famous."

Things like that happen every year when the Derby comes to town. People "go out to the track," as they like to say in Louisville, and simply disappear into thin air. Some return a few years later with horrible disfigurements & no memory at all of what happened. Others end up in "hospitals down South" and are never mentioned again by people who knew them.

Omerta is the code of the South, especially after weird crimes are committed by rich people. The usual explanation is a brief mention on the Obituary page of another head-on collision with some unidentified truck far out on the River Road & a "private cremation ceremony attended only by close family members, who wish to remain anonymous." Horse people have very short attention spans for anything involving humans.

The best thing about the Kentucky Derby is that it is only two minutes long. It is the quickest event in sports, except for Sumo wrestling & Mike Tyson fights. Maybe Drag racing is quicker, but I have never been attracted to it. You can find more gambling action at any weekend cockfight in rural Arkansas. ... An NBA play-off game lasts for two & a half hours on live television, but it is a hell of a lot quicker if you watch it on tape without the commercials.

That is the only way you can avoid seeing that sleazy little monster, David Stern—who gets paid millions of dollars a year for doing nothing at all except jabber & giggle every two or three minutes about drafting ugly old women into the NBA as potential replacements for overpaid teenage mutants who might develop shin splints or go lame overnight if they can't take 50 shots a game & get more public love than anybody since Bill Clinton's years in the White House.

Okay. I see that I am feeling a bit nasty myself this week—

so maybe I should go back to bed & have a few more sick dreams about the Kentucky Derby & David Stern creeping in through my bedroom window with a dead animal in his mouth.

That is what happens to people who watch too much TV & make long-distance hunch bets on horses named Dollar Bill. Maybe it's true that habitual gambling really is a fatal disease worse than brain cancer. I will do some more research and report back next week on my Findings.

—*May 7, 2001*

Quitting the Gambling Business While I'm Ahead

Betting against the Lakers was Right for 2 games—but now is the time to Quit/Retire because the Auman public Rally is Monday in Denver and the DA has for some reason blamed all his "PROBLEMS" on me and I don't want to RISK getting arrested because of my "gambling background" or some other Trumped-up charge.

My speech is still secret—but I will print it next week. Beware of the CJS. It will grind you up by accident. Yes, just like Gambling and Lawyers.

That is not a healthy mix. I know this—but I am doing it anyway. But only this *once*.

That's why lawyers get Paid—to do savage work that nobody else will or Can do, except for money.

I usually have No Choice—I am usually the One on Trial

and needing help at high Risk. It is not cheap to fight back and survive against any system that you Cross or even seem to Cross: $200,000 for being Innocent. Two years to win a Corrupt DWAI case.

Stay out of Courtrooms—but if you must go in, be Well Armed and Don't compromise. You are Innocent. Remember That. They are Guilty.

—*May 12, 2001*

The Most Dangerous Sport of All

ESPN Editor's Note: Sports are about passion—but all passion is not about sports. On a weekend when most of our readers were consumed with Shaq and Kobe and Super Mario and A. J. Burnett, Page 2 columnist Hunter S. Thompson could not get Lisl Auman out of his mind. In fact, the good doctor is so outraged by Auman's case—she's a 24-year-old Denver resident whom some observers believe was wrongfully convicted of felony murder—that he helped organize a rally Monday in Denver on Auman's behalf.

Auman was convicted in 1998 of felony murder, which means in this case that she was a participant in a robbery and attempted flight that resulted in murder. In this case, the murder was of a pursuing Denver policeman by another robbery suspect, who then committed suicide. The crux of her guilt or innocence is the debate over whether the items were stolen or were in fact hers, whether she was a participant in the flight or a hostage, and whether she handed the rifle to the shooter or was a victim of fabricated evidence.

Though Page 2's editors aren't making a judgment about the case one way or the other, we believe strongly in indulging passion—especially a passion for justice. And so, though this is a sports site—first, foremost, and almost always—today we are sharing our columnist's political passion with our readers.

I am a rabid basketball fan and a veteran sportswriter, but on Monday I had serious business to do. I am a Warrior, and the time had come to Rumble. Many things have happened since last week—many weird things, radical things, Savage 180-degree swings between totally opposite poles like Joy and Fear, Wild passions and violent rages, sudden Love and sudden hate. . . . I have known them all, and I fear I have come to like them too much. I am an Addictive Personality, they say, a natural slave to passion—and many Doctors have warned me against it. I am a High-risk Patient.

But not all of those doctors are still alive today. Two committed suicide, and two others had their Medical licenses lifted for abusing Hospital drugs. Another misdiagnosed his own wife's Cancer and was forced to retire from Medicine. After that, he went into the psychiatric business and destroyed the mental health of a whole family by convincing all of them, one at a time, that they were fatally Dysfunctional and probably Insane. Their only hope, he said, was to have each other committed to long-term, fearfully Harsh, and impossibly Expensive private Insane Asylums. . . . The children got the most painful sentences. One spent two years in the lockdown ward of the Menninger Clinic in Kansas; another was put in a straitjacket and turned over to the notoriously cruel Cocaine Addict Wing at Jackson Memorial Hospital in Miami, where "Isolation Therapy" is mandatory for the first nine months.

Quacks are a part of our culture, and we all fall prey to them. Who among us can say, for sure, that even our own personal physicians are honest and competent? Ho ho. Don't bet on it, Bubba. Remember Dr. Nork.

But not today. No. On Monday I was a main speaker at the "Free Lisl Auman" rally in Denver, which drew thousands of people and attracted widespread Media attention. Pictures of me, Warren Zevon, and Benicio Del Toro have been all over the Denver TV news in recent days. The National Committee to Free Lisl Auman has been joined by hundreds, even thousands, of very high-end professionals and volunteers. A Defense Fund has been legally established. Hollywood people have joined up.

A famous microbrewery has offered its hospitality to speakers and guests of the Lisl rally. Whoops. I almost wrote "Riot" there, instead of "Rally." But I caught myself just in time. No doubt it was a Freudian slip of some kind, or maybe just an old habit. No! We were not going to have a riot in Denver. It was out of the question. We hired uniformed State Troopers to drop a wire net on any freaks or booze-addled Crazies who got out of control. We are a finely organized Team now—and we were, after all, standing on the white-marble steps of the Colorado State Capitol, with its gold-plated Dome looming just above us. It was a majestic scene, and it was decidedly Not dull. I Guaranteed that.

Warren Zevon opened the hour-long rally with a few inflammatory words about the Free Lisl Auman crusade and why he is part of it—and then he turned up the amplifiers and burst into his famous song, "Lawyers, Guns, and Money."

Five thousand Criminal lawyers were also in town for the Rally. Monday was the day when the two (2) formal Defense Appeal Briefs were formally Filed with the Colorado Supreme Court: one by Lisl's public defender and the other by an elite Team of Appeals Attorneys from the National Association of Criminal Defense Lawyers, which decided in March to join our team, pro bono, and file a solemn, intimidating Amicus Brief in Lisl Auman's defense. . . .

A finely honed speech was uttered by Dr. Douglas Brinkley, Presidential Historian from the University of New Orleans and author of many distinguished books—most recently, *Rosa Parks*, about the legendary black woman who touched off the whole Civil Rights Movement of the Sixties when she refused to move to the back of a city bus in Montgomery, Alabama.

I was a part of that, incidentally, and I have been proud of it all my life. Many of those who stood on the Capitol steps Monday were veteran warriors from the Civil Rights Movement. It was good training for the even More brutal confrontations we would face later. . . . It is very important to learn, early in life, that you can beat City Hall and that You can change the System. You might be beaten and gassed by Police a few times before you succeed—but that stuff goes with the territory. And you will be proud of it later, just as you will make many smart friends who will stand with you all your life.

Lisl Auman, a 20-year-old girl with no criminal record, was convicted of Felony Murder in Denver for a crime that occurred while she was handcuffed and chained in a Police car. She is the only person ever Convicted in the history of Colorado for a murder committed while the defendant was in official police Custody—and then she was sentenced to spend the rest of her Life in state prison, without any possibility of Parole.

That is what this case is about, and why we had this major Protest Rally at the State Capitol on Monday. We are making the people of Denver (and the Colorado Supreme Court Justices) aware that the original Auman trial was a shameful farce and a disgraceful mockery of the whole "Criminal Justice System."

The Lisl Auman drama has been played out on a painfully unequal surface, so far. Victory—getting her out of Prison immediately and overturning the savage and unnatural Felony Murder statute—seemed 95 percent impossible at first, even to me. . . . But no longer. Now I believe we will win.

The playing field got leveled out in a hurry when the NACDL came in. That was back on Super Bowl Sunday, when the Lawyers gathered here for the game. Of course. Remember that story—when my house was hit by Lightning? Yes sir. That was when the worm turned.

The first signal of change was the massive response to my

Hey Rube column by 100,000 loyal ESPN.com readers in ten (10) days. . . . Hot damn! I want to Thank all of you very sincerely. You made a huge Difference. Abe Lincoln would be proud of us today and so would Bobby Kennedy. If it is true, as Edmund Burke said, that "the only thing necessary for the triumph of Evil is for good men to do Nothing" (and I have always believed that is true), then we are sure as hell not doing Nothing. I salute You.

Justice is expensive in America. There are no Free Passes. . . . You might want to remember this, the next time you get care-less and blow off a few Parking Tickets. They will come back to haunt you the next time you see a Cop car in your rearview mir-ror. Or if you notice your teenage daughter hanging out with a rotten-looking Skinhead. . . . There is no such thing as Para-noia. Your worst fears can come true at any moment. . . . What happened to Lisl Auman can happen to Anybody in America, and when it does, you will sure as hell need Friends. . . . Take my word for it, folks. I have Been There, and it ain't Fun.

Thanks again for your help on this. It is good Karma and also very wise.

—*May 14, 2001*

Patrick Roy and Warren Zevon— Two Champions at the Top of Their Game

Warren Zevon arrived at my house on Saturday and said he was in the mood to write a few songs about Hockey. "Thank God you're home," he said. "I had to drive all night to get out of Utah without being locked up. What's wrong with those people?"

"What people?" I asked him.

"The ones over in Utah," he said nervously. "They've been following me ever since Salt Lake City. They pulled me over at some kind of police checkpoint and accused me of being a Sex Offender—I was terrified. They even had a picture of me."

"Nonsense," I said. "They're doing that to a lot of people these days. They're rounding up the Bigamists before the Olympics start. They don't want to be embarrassed in the eyes of the world again."

Warren seemed far too frantic to do any serious songwriting, so I tried to calm him down with some of the fresh Jimson tea I'd brewed up for the Holiday. I knew he was a rabid hockey fan, so I told him we could watch the Stanley Cup game on TV pretty soon.

"Excellent," he said. "I have come to Love professional hockey. I watch it all the time on TV—especially the Stanley Cup play-offs."

"Well," I replied with a smile, "tonight is our lucky night. Game 1 is coming up on ESPN very soon. We will drink some more of this Tea and get ourselves Prepared for it."

"Bless you, Doc," he said. "We can Watch the game together and then write a song about it." He paused momentarily and reached again for the teapot. . . . "This is very exciting," he said eagerly. "I can hardly wait to see Patrick Roy in action. He is one of my personal heroes. Roy is the finest athlete in Sports now. I worship him."

I nodded but said nothing. There was a faraway look in his eyes now, and he spoke in an oddly Dreamy voice. I could see that he had forgotten all about his troubles in Utah, and now he was jabbering happily. . . .

When the phone rang, he ignored me and picked it up before I could get to it. "Patrick Roy fan club," he said. "Zevon speaking. We are ready for the game here—are you ready?" He laughed. "Are you a Bigamist? What? Don't lie to me, you yellow-bellied pervert!" Then he laughed again and hung up.

"That will teach those Bigamists a lesson," he chuckled. "That fool will never call back!"

I jerked the phone away from him and told him to calm down. "You're starting to act weird," I told him. "Get a grip on yourself."

The game was the most dominating display of big-time hockey either of us had ever seen. The Avalanche humiliated the favored defending champion NJ Devils.

Patrick Roy got his shutout and "could have beaten NJ all by himself," Zevon boasted. "He made midgets of us all. I will never forget this game. Our song will be called 'You're a Whole Different Person When You're Scared.' "

Which proved to be true, when we played it back on his new age Hugo machine 40 hours later.

Zevon is famous for his ability to stay awake for as long as it takes—often for 85 or 90 straight hours. "I wrote 'Hit Somebody' in 75 hours," he said, "and look what happened to that one."

Indeed. It rocketed to the top of the charts and was hailed as "the finest song ever written about hockey" by *Rolling Stone* and *Songs of the Rich and Famous.*

Warren Zevon is as adept at songwriting as he is with a .44 magnum. Warren Zevon is a poet. He has written more classics than any other musician of our time, with the possible exception of Bob Dylan. . . . He is also an expert at lacrosse—which we also watched while we worked. He went wild when Princeton beat Syracuse for the NCAA Championship on Sunday.

He disappeared in the middle of the night, still without sleep—saying he was headed to Indianapolis to write a song with Colts owner James Irsay, who had just returned from buying Kerouac's original manuscript of *On the Road* for $2.43 million at Christie's Auction House in New York. Irsay is another one of Warren's heroes.

Warren is a profoundly mysterious man, and I have learned not to argue with him, about hockey or anything else. He is a dangerous drinker, and a whole different person when he's scared.

—*May 28, 2001*

Wild Days at the Sports Desk

It will come as no surprise to anybody who has ever had to work for a living when I say that there are Fast days and slow days in Every business. It is a Universal Truth that no one but a certified Moron would deny—not even the Filthy Rich who have never worked a day in their lives and still believe in Santa Claus, if only because they can afford to think that way.

Not even professional Journalists can deny a thing like that with a straight face. It is an open secret on any newspaper that the Sports Desk will see more Action, on any given day, than any other Desk will see in a month. . . . That is why Sportswriters are almost always the lowest-paid people on Newspaper staffs: They are charter members of the Too Much Fun Club, and they like it that way.

"Why should I work for a living," they say, "if I can get paid doing something I love?"

And who will argue with them? Not me. I am a Natural-born Sportswriter. I have a knack for it, a God-given talent. After I first learned that it was possible to sleep late and go to work at Two in the afternoon, and still get Paid for it, I never did anything else.

You bet. Some people call me lazy, but they are Wrong. If I am lazy, then so is Chris Berman of ESPN and Bob Costas of NBC. Both are members of the Too Much Fun Club, and they both learned their trade from former New York Yankees Hall of Fame shortstop Phil Rizzuto—who went from Playing baseball for a living to talking about baseball for an even better living. Rizzuto was my hero as a youth, and I wanted to be just like him when I grew up. I too played shortstop for many years (in Louisville's version of what is now the Little League), until I was struck down by Acne and Baby Fat.

It was Beer that finally ended my career as a full-time Athlete—first Beer, then Girls, and finally a brief fling with Crime. That is a fatal mix for any star athlete, and for a while I thought I was Finished. I went into shock when I no longer heard cheers. My life turned weird overnight, and people snickered when I lumbered out on the Diving Board. It was horrible.

But not for long. The shock quickly wore off, and I soon found a home at the sports desk—any sports desk, from the *Louisville Courier-Journal* to the *Tallahassee Democrat* to *Time* magazine and the *Brazil Herald* to the *New York Herald-Tribune*. They all have a sports desk.

—June 11, 2001

Eerie Lull
Rattles the
Sports World

Some weeks are ugly in the world of Sports, and last week was definitely one of them. Millions of serious basketball fans—80 percent of them rooting feverishly for the Philadelphia 76ers (according to *USA Today*)—watched in painful disbelief as the preternaturally arrogant Los Angeles Lakers stomped the helpless 76ers into quivering Blood sausage (on their Home court in front of 19,000 Philly supporters). The Philly fans had been conned into betting huge chunks of their own money on their Homeboys to somehow prevail and bring home the Bacon—and toward the end they got Bitter about it. The whole vast city of Philadelphia was humiliated, once again, and even the Mayor freaked out when he had to pay off his bets.

He was far from alone in his grief. The whole nation was plunged into mourning for one reason or another (from floods in Philadelphia to suicidal despair in the White House) when they heard the news of the U.S. Navy running amok with bombs and heavy Artillery on the war-torn beaches of Vieques, where local Protesters were stripped naked and brutally beaten by wild-eyed U.S. Marines.

The White House was blindsided and fatally paralyzed by the horrible news from Vieques, which broke on Page One of the *New York Times* and was reported in such bloodcurdling detail that not even the hapless child-president dared to deny it. . . . "He has his own problems right now," said one high-ranking White House official who refused to be named or even quoted except on conditions of total anonymity. "As far as I know, the President knows absolutely nothing about the island of Vieques. As far as I know, he doesn't even know where it is."

Whoops! Enough of that. Back to sports.

We were all taught in school that right-thinking people go to Work on weekdays and relax on Saturday and Sunday, and that Bad things happen to people who don't. That is why high school football games are scheduled on Friday night and College teams play on Saturday. It is the American Way, and I learned it like everybody else did.

But things changed when I grew up and went into the Sportswriting business. All of a sudden I found myself going to Work on weekends, which caused my life to change radically. . . . I still went to Football games on Fridays and Saturdays, and I still drank beer on those nights, but I no longer sat with my friends in the carefree Student section, and I no longer took my girlfriends along with me to the games—no more than normal people take their girlfriends with them to the Office. It was out of the question.

So I was forced to change my ways. It was awkward at first, but not for long. The first time I got a real-money Paycheck for watching a football game from the Press box or covering a Muhammad Ali fight from ringside, I quickly saw the Light.

The sporting world is faced with an eerie lull this week, and many people are nervous. The winter is over, the harvest is in, and the Revenue Stream from Hockey and Basketball profits has dwindled down to a trickle. The next few months will not be a happy time for winter sports executives who failed to meet Expectations, as they say in the Bean Counters' cubicles. Dr. Chop is coming to town.

It happens every year in every sport, like a game of Musical Chairs in a grade school classroom. There are only 32 professional basketball teams in the NBA and only 16 slots in the Play-offs, so the math is not difficult. At least 16 well-paid professional Coaches will be Terminated With Prejudice before Labor Day, and not one of them will be surprised. They learned the difference between Winning and Losing a long time ago.

—June 18, 2001

Olympic Disaster
in Utah

The barren state of Utah took another cruel beating in the public prints last week, and the 2002 Winter Olympic Games slipped another foul notch toward the Abyss.... First it was felony bribery, then a rash of scandalous Sex crimes, and finally a plague of meat-eating crickets.... It is an open secret now that Salt Lake City's giddy ambition to host the first Winter Olympics on U.S. soil since 1980 is doomed to Shame & Failure.

Third-term GOP Governor Michael O. Leavitt, who is now the chairman of the EPA, appointed by Bush, has been fatally smeared, and three officials of the all-powerful Church of Latter-Day Saints are accused of covering up Bribery, Fraud, & shameless Prostitution. Even the mayor of Salt Lake City was staggered by the overweening Lewdness of the charges—which ranged from Pimping and Gross Sexual Imposition to Perjury and Wife Beating. Two prominent members of the original Salt Lake Organizing Committee were indicted by the U.S. Justice Department and will go on trial in July on a grab bag of State and Federal antibribery charges that could put them in prison for the rest of their lives.

Hosting the Winter Olympics is always a high-risk venture. The last winter festival in Nagano was a financial disaster for the Japanese Government and a monumental failure for the U.S. winter sports establishment.... And next year's train wreck in Utah will be no different.

Everybody who goes there will be walking in the queasy shadow of punishment. Salt Lake City has developed such hideous worldwide Karma that success is out of the question. The SLOC has put Utah so deep in Debt for the next 30 years that No money will be available for anything except bribes, whiskey, and the mandatory 10 percent membership fee to the

Church of Latter-Day Saints—the same corrupt greedheads who ran up the debt in the first place.

Corruption is a Way of Life in Utah, and they seem to like it that way. Mormons have been beating and cheating each other since the arrival of Brigham Young in 1847. . . . He was a stern and gentle man, they say, and nobody argued when he made Utah the permanent Kingdom of the Mormon Church and everything it stood for.

"So what?" my friend Cromwell snarled when I showed him the latest list of bizarre crimes allegedly committed by state of-ficials and Church leaders in the ongoing Utah Olympics nightmare. "Nobody cares what happens in Utah anyway. It has always been a sinkhole of Vice and Corruption. The last time I went to Utah, I got busted for Soliciting a Prostitute in the Salt Lake Airport. It cost me $2,000 just to leave the State."

"Yeah," I nodded. "It's the Mormon way of life—a handful of Gimme and a mouthful of Much Obliged. I know it well."

Which was true. I am all too familiar with Utah.

—*June 26, 2001*

The Wisdom of Nashville and the Violence of Jack Nicholson— A Football Story

It was raining in the "City of 10,000 Whores" on Sunday night—a heavy, drenching rain that only added to the pain of the 69,000 Tennessee Titans fans who packed themselves into the immense new Adelphia Coliseum to watch the hometown Titans be embarrassed by Miami in a game that was deeply scarred by human dumbness. It was also deeply painful to local gamblers, who were forced to give Miami six (6) points, which added insult to injury. By halftime many of them had the look of people who had just been hit in the kidneys by Lightning.

Nashville is a river town with a long and sleazy history. It was a capital of commerce before the Civil War, when it became a vicious war zone and a swollen mecca for gamblers and prostitutes. The population doubled during the War, and most of the newcomers had Syphilis. . . . But that was before Football was invented, and Nashville today is a thriving city of 520,000 relatively healthy sports fans who don't mind admitting that they gamble a lot of money on many football games.

That is what happens in sweltering cities with no team in the NFL—like Los Angeles, where high-dollar gambling is by far the most popular sport in town. Millions of dollars go up for grabs every weekend. "Real football fans were happy when the Rams and the Raiders left town," Jack Nicholson told me. "Now we can watch the goddamn games on TV, instead of driving all the way out to Anaheim, or down to that monstrous Coliseum. Nobody wants an NFL team in LA, except maybe the TV networks."

That is because of the "mandatory TV blackouts" that the league imposes on any Market where the local team fails to sell *all* the seats in its "home stadium." The LA Coliseum, for instance, seats slightly more than 100,000, and neither the Raiders nor the Rams ever had a sellout crowd. "It was a hateful situation to put yourself in," said Jack, "sitting out there in the smog with a mob of criminal swine full of warm beer. At a Raiders game you could get beaten and robbed without ever leaving your seat. It was like an outdoor jail."

Jack is famous for spending most of his winter nights in the glitzy *Indoor* jail where the Lakers play, but I didn't want to complicate our conversation by introducing perverse elements, so I didn't bring it up. He is a serious basketball fan and he gets a whole different perspective by sitting in his profoundly expensive courtside seat, which he's maintained for almost 30 years in three different venues. The difference between sitting on the court for a game and sitting in row 99 is the difference between living in the Hollywood hills and renting on the outskirts of Nashville.

"You should move to Tennessee for football season," I told him. "You'd like the games a lot better if you knew you were surrounded on all sides by thousands of whores and gamblers."

He smiled wanly and scratched at his groin. "Who the hell do you think I sit with now?" he muttered. "A crowd of innocent children?"

Indeed. I have attended football games in both towns, and I have to admit that I do prefer Nashville. You can get a lot closer to the action there, and on most days you will lose a lot less money. The whores and gamblers will rub up against you, down south, and they have a nicer way of speaking. The closest seats in the LA Coliseum are about 40 yards from the field, far across an Olympic-sized track and field pavilion, and you can't even see the players' numbers without powerful binoculars. Even the occasional roar of the crowd seems distant and vaguely impersonal. It is like sitting in a traffic jam on the San Diego Freeway with your windows rolled up and Portuguese music booming out of the surround-sound speakers while animals gnaw on your neck and diseased bill collectors hammer on your doors with golf clubs.

O. J. Simpson doesn't live in LA anymore, but that doesn't mean the city is not full of extremely dangerous freaks. You are far more likely to be randomly killed on your way to a football game in Los Angeles than you are in Nashville—but there are potential killers in Any crowd larger than two these days, and even Two can be dangerous after midnight.

In any case, I have watched football games from every angle from the sideline in Oakland and the huddle in Frankfort, Kentucky, to the top row of the Superdome in New Orleans and the press box in Washington—I have watched them in Kezar Stadium and from the deck of a big sailing yacht 500 miles south of Bermuda with naked women lolling around—and I can tell you for sure that the best seat in any house is right in front of a high-end TV set with a few good friends who know football and like to see green money moving around the room. That is how it should be done. *Selah.*

And thank you. It feels good to be back in the Fast lane, for good or ill—and I did, incidentally, Lose big on the Miami-Tennessee game, along with Carolina-Minnesota and Cincinnati–New England. I won with the Raiders, San Francisco, and the Colts. . . . But what the hell? It is a far far better thing to lose Now than in December, when the humor goes out of the gambling business. That is when I plan to spring the final ambush on gloating screwheads like John Walsh. He thinks he's Ahead now, but in truth I am just baiting him into the trap. He will learn soon enough. Don't worry. I know exactly what I'm doing.

—*September 10, 2001*

PART TWO

WHERE WERE YOU WHEN THE FUN STOPPED? FEAR AND LOATHING IN AMERICA: BEGINNING OF THE END.... EVEN ESPN WAS BROADCASTING WAR NEWS.... GUERRILLA WARFARE ON A GLOBAL SCALE.... WELCOME TO THE STADIUM LIFE.... ALL WAR AND NO FOOTBALL MAKES JACK A DULL BOY.... I AM SEAN PENN, SHOULD I ENTER THE HONOLULU MARATHON? ... WHY DIDN'T YOU TELL ME YOU HAD SUCH A BEAUTIFUL SISTER, OMAR? ... FAILURE,

FOOTBALL, AND VIOLENCE ON THE STRIP. . . . GETTING BRACED FOR THE LAST FOOTBALL GAME. . . . ARE TERRORISTS SEIZING CONTROL OF THE NFL? AND WHO LET IT HAPPEN? . . . HAD I FINALLY LOVED SPORT TOO MUCH?

Fear and Loathing in America: Beginning of the End

It was just after dawn in Woody Creek when the first bomb hit New York City this morning, and as usual I was writing about sports. But not for long. Football suddenly seemed irrelevant, compared to the scenes of destruction and utter devastation coming out of New York on TV.

Even ESPN was broadcasting war news. It was the worst disaster in the history of the United States, including Pearl Harbor, the San Francisco earthquake, and probably the battle of Antietam in 1862, when 23,000 American soldiers were slaughtered in one day.

The battle of the World Trade Center lasted about 99 minutes and cost 20,000 lives in two hours (according to unofficial estimates as of midnight on Tuesday). The final numbers, including those from the supposedly impregnable Pentagon, across the Potomac River from Washington, will likely be higher. Anything that kills 300 trained firefighters in two hours is a world-class disaster.

And it was not even Bombs that caused this massive damage. No nuclear missiles were launched from any foreign soil, no enemy bombers flew over New York and Washington to rain death on innocent Americans. No. It was four (4) commercial jetliners.

They were the first flights of the day from American and United Airlines, "piloted" by skilled and loyal U.S. citizens, and there was nothing suspicious about them when they took off from Newark, Logan, and Dulles on routine cross-country flights to the West Coast with fully loaded fuel tanks—which would soon explode on impact and utterly destroy the world-famous Twin Towers of downtown Manhattan's World Trade Center. Boom! Boom! Just like that.

The towers are gone now, reduced to bloody rubble, along with all hopes for Peace in Our Time, in the U.S. or any other country. Make no mistake about it: we are At War now—with somebody—and we will stay At War with that strange and mysterious Enemy for the rest of our lives.

It will be a Religious War, a sort of Christian Jihad, fueled by religious hatred and led by merciless fanatics on both sides. It will be guerrilla warfare on a global scale, with no front lines and no identifiable enemy. Osama bin Laden will be a primitive "figurehead"—or even dead, for all we know—but whoever put those all-American jet planes loaded with all-American fuel into the 110-story-high Twin Towers and the Pentagon did it with chilling precision and accuracy. The second one was a dead-on bull's-eye. Straight into the middle of the skyscraper.

Nothing ever Claimed by George W. Bush's $350 billion "Star Wars" missile defense system could have prevented Tuesday's attack, and it cost next to nothing to pull off. The efficiency of it was terrifying. Fewer than 20 unarmed Suicide soldiers from some apparently primitive country somewhere on the other side of the world took out the World Trade Center and half the Pentagon with three quick and costless strikes on one day. That is terrifying.

We are going to punish somebody for this attack, but just who or where will be blown to smithereens for it is hard to say. Maybe Afghanistan, maybe Pakistan or Iraq, or possibly all three at once. Who knows? Not even the Generals in what remains of the Pentagon or the New York papers calling for *war* seem to know who did it or where to look for them.

This is going to be a very expensive war, and Victory is not guaranteed—for anyone, and certainly not for a baffled little creep like George W. Bush. All he knows is that his father started the war a long time ago, and that he, the goofy child-

President, has been chosen by Fate and the global Oil industry to finish it off. He can declare a National Security Emergency and clamp down Hard on Everybody, no matter where they live or why. If the guilty won't hold up their hands and confess, he and the Generals will ferret them out by force.

Good luck. He is in for a profoundly difficult job—armed as he is with no credible Military Intelligence, no witnesses, and only the ghost of Bin Laden to blame for the tragedy.

Okay. It is 24 hours later now, and we are not getting much information about the Five Ws of this thing. Not even the numbers of dead and wounded can be established. CNN reports "more than 800 people standing in line to donate blood at St. Vincent's Hospital in Greenwich Village, but only fewer than 500 victims brought to the Emergency Room." The numbers don't add up. I am confused.

The numbers out of the Pentagon are baffling, as if Military Censorship had already been imposed on the media. It is ominous. The only news on TV comes from weeping victims and ignorant speculators.

The lid is on, Loose Lips Sink Ships. Don't say anything that might give aid to The Enemy.

—*September 12, 2001*

When War Drums Roll

Johnny Depp called me from France last night and asked what I knew about Osama bin Laden.

"Nothing," I said. "Nothing at all. He is a ghost, for all I know. Why do you ask?"

"Because I'm terrified of him," he said. "All of France is terri-fied. I was in the American Embassy today when they caught some terrorists trying to blow it up. I freaked out and rushed to the airport, but when I got there my flight was canceled. All flights to the U.S. were canceled. People went crazy with fear."

"Join the club," I told him. "Almost everybody went crazy over here."

"Never mind that," he said. "Who won the Jets-Colts game?"

"There was no game," I said. "All sport was canceled in this country—even *Monday Night Football.*"

"No!" he said. "That's impossible! I've never known a Mon-day night without a game on TV. What is the stock market doing?"

"Nothing yet," I said, "It's been closed for six days."

"Ye gods," he muttered. "No stock market, no football—this is Serious."

Just then I heard the lock on my gas tank rattling, so I rushed outside with a shotgun and fired both barrels into the darkness. Poachers! I thought. Blow their heads off! This is War! I fired another blast in the general direction of the gas pump, then I went inside to reload.

"Why are you shooting?" Anita screamed at me. "What are you shooting at?"

"The enemy," I said gruffly. "He is down there stealing our gasoline."

"Nonsense," she said. "That tank has been empty since June. You probably killed a peacock. . . ."

At dawn I went down to the tank and found the gas hose shredded by birdshot and two peacocks dead.

So what? I thought. What is more important right now—my precious gasoline or the lives of some silly birds?

Indeed, but the New York Stock Exchange opens in thir-teen minutes, so I have to get a grip on something solid. The Other Shoe is about to drop, and it may be extremely heavy. The time has come to be strong. The fat is in the fire. Who knows what will happen now?

Not me, buster. That's why I live out here in the mountains with a flag on my porch and loud Wagner music blaring out of my speakers. I feel lucky and I have plenty of ammunition. That is God's will, they say, and that is also why I shoot into the darkness at anything that moves. Sooner or later I will hit something Evil, and feel no Guilt. It might be Osama bin Laden. Who knows? And where is Adolf Hitler, now that we finally need him? It is bad business to go into War without a target.

In times like these, when the War drums and the bugles howl for blood, I think of Vince Lombardi and I wonder how he would handle it. . . . Good old Vince. He was a zealot for Victory at all costs, and his hunger for it was pure—or that's what he said and what his legend tells us, but it is worth noting that his career won-lost record in the NFL is not even in the top ten.

No, that honor goes to George Seifert, who inherited a 49er dynasty at the top of its form and won a Super Bowl in his first year. His winning percentage in three downhill years was .75. Then he retired and went fishing. It was a good career move.

The San Francisco empire crumbled after that. It was a horrible process to watch. Bill Walsh went to Stanford, Joe Montana to Kansas City, and the owner was busted for trying to bribe the monumentally sleazy Governor of Louisiana—who argued successfully that while it may have been a crime to offer a bribe to him, it was not a crime for him to accept a bribe.

It was profoundly twisted legal reasoning, but it worked in Louisiana. Gov. Edwin Edwards walked on that one, saying cheerfully that the Law would never get him unless he were "caught in bed with a live boy or a dead girl."

Good old Edwin. He was a barrel of laughs in his day, but he is in Federal prison now, for fraud—or at least that's what they say, but who knows where he really is. The slippery little bugger might be hunkered down in a salt cave near Kabul—probably with Osama bin Laden, disguised as a teenage whore.

Whoops. This may not be the time for eerie humor. We are At War now, according to President Bush, and I take him at his word. He also says this War may last for "a very long time."

Generals and military scholars will tell you that eight or ten years is actually not such a long time in the span of human history—which is no doubt true—but history also tells us that ten years of martial law and a wartime economy are going to feel like a Lifetime to people who are 20 years old today. The poor bastards of what will forever be known as Generation Z are doomed to be the first generation of Americans who will grow up with a lower standard of living than their parents enjoyed.

That is extremely heavy news and it will take a while for it to sink in. The 22 babies born in New York City while the World Trade Center burned will never know what they missed. The last half of the 20th Century will seem like a wild party for rich kids, compared to what's coming now. The party's over, folks. The time has come for loyal Americans to Sacrifice. . . . Sacrifice. . . . Sacrifice. That is the new buzzword in Washington. But what it means is not entirely clear.

Winston Churchill said, "The first casualty of War is always the Truth." Churchill also said, "In wartime, the Truth is so precious that it should always be surrounded by a bodyguard of Lies."

That wisdom will not be much comfort to babies born last week. The first news they get in this world will be News subjected to Military Censorship. That is a given, in wartime, along with massive campaigns of deliberately planted Disinformation, and it makes life difficult for people who value real news. Count on it. That is what Churchill meant when he talked about Truth being the first casualty of War.

In this case, however, a next casualty was Football. All games were canceled last week. And that has Never happened to the NFL. Never. That gives us a hint about the Magnitude of this War. Terrorists don't wear uniforms, and they play by inscrutable rules—the Rules of World War III, which has already begun.

So get ready for it, folks. Buckle up and watch your backs at all times. That is why they call it "Terrorism."

—*September 17, 2001*

Will Sports
Survive
Bin Laden?

There was strangeness in the NFL on Sunday, weird upsets that baffled fans and rattled the teeth of gamblers from Boston to Morro Bay.

The Vikings got waxed by the supposedly Lame Chicago Bears, Miami punctured Oakland, and the mighty Baltimore Ravens were blown off their pedestal by the wretched Cincinnati Bengals. Thus, there were three sure-thing play-off teams beaten like curs in the second week of the season. I was stunned, frankly, and I wept for my long-term bets.

A few things were normal in the NFL last week: St. Louis beat the 49ers, Denver trashed Arizona, and the Colts flogged Buffalo. Miami's last-second victory over Oakland was an exceptional piece of football, and Tennessee's second loss in a row was not a real shock—not like seeing the Ravens get whipped by Cincinnati. Even bookies cried about that one. It was horrible. In the old days I would have bet both my thumbs against it, but I didn't. No. I am older and wiser now—and I have a powerful need for my thumbs, if only to write about football.

I broke more or less even on Sunday, but it was not an easy trick. In any case, 50-50 is unacceptable in this business, unless you're skimming 10 percent off the top—in which case you're just another bookie with rotten self-esteem.

That is tempting, on some days. Ten percent of everything looks pretty comfortable in the ominous new economy—compared to being a ticket agent at Dulles International Airport, anyway, or working as a skycap in Boston. I have done both of these things in my time, and all things considered, I think I'd prefer to be a bookie.

I have never done that, but I have some friends who still do it vigorously, regardless of the risks. Most bookies bear the scars of workplace disasters that go with the territory, such as pain, cruelty, and violence in all its forms. It can be a brutal business for losers. A plunge into debt can be a life-altering experience, even terminal. Death and disfigurement are routine punishments in the trade, and fear is a constant companion. A long losing streak can mean the end of the world as you know it.

Ah, but never mind those things. I must be watching too much bad news on TV. Let us turn away from ugliness and embrace our Happy thoughts.

Breaking even on our football bets is extremely good luck, compared to being on trial in Afghanistan for trying to subvert the Taliban religion. That is where the rubber meets the road.

Osama bin Laden is like a vampire that casts no shadow, yet his shadow is over us all. People call me on the phone and jabber like fruit bats in heat.

These are not triumphant times for people with bullish hopes for the future—unless you are part of the Military-Industrial complex, and then your future is bright, very bright. If you own stock in military/munitions suppliers like Raytheon, Lockheed, Northrop Grumman, L-3 Comm, or General Dynamics, your profit picture is golden. Your ship has come in. The power balance has shifted drastically in this country since the World Trade towers were destroyed September 11, and your people are in charge now. We are at War, and I'm glad to be your friend. We are all in this thing together.

What business are you in, brother? Your face is familiar. Do we know each other? Where have I seen you before? Was it Hong Kong? Beirut? Johannesburg? Where do you live?

Where indeed. The universal soldier has no home. He is always on the move. He has many names, and he pays his rent with cash. Yes sir, cash and carry. I know him well, I think, and I know his habits better than I like to admit. Beware, he comes quietly, but with terrifying force. Raw gold is his only currency, and Death is what he sells. We all know him, but describing him is difficult. He is a "Master of War," in Bob Dylan's words, and Warren Zevon has called him "Roland, the Headless Thompson Gunner."

Now is a good time to buy Disney stock, they say, because sport and entertainment are undervalued now, and they might be all we have left. "War is hell," say the Generals. "Prepare to make many sacrifices, especially in your Standards of Living." Our Enemy is cruel and evil and strong, but our Faith will be victorious, sooner or later.

The big thing now is to make sure the football season continues without interruption, which I think it will. Football is necessary now. Until recently, it was only a brutal diversion, but now it is a key to the national sanity. We are still deep in shock from the attacks on New York and Washington. We still can't figure out what it all means, or how to keep it from happening again—and who is this horrible bastard bin Laden, anyway?

That is a serious question for a country on the brink of a $400-Billion-a-year war against an unseen enemy. That is almost half a Trillion dollars, which is sure to make a dent, if not a bottomless pit, in many budgets. It is a staggering number to behold, and the President says this War will continue for many years, against many enemies in many countries all over the world, until America feels safe again.

Wow! Stand back! That is likely to be quite a while, eh? The NFL could play for 600 years at that price. We could have football every Day, with money left over for beer and Polish sausage. Rabid football fans—and even nonfans, for that matter—would happily queue up to buy time-shares in high-end luxury boxes in gigantic new stadiums, which would also serve as their Homes for as many days of the week as they could afford to pay. Stadium living would become a whole new Way of Life. Hell, most of those boxes already have full-service kitchens and 36-inch TV sets with close-up seating and personal parking spaces. It would be like a dream come true—the new American Dream, I suspect, with 21st-Century features and supermodern gimmicks in every drawer. I have already drawn up the plans, and my patent is pending.

—*September 24, 2001*

Stadium Living in the New Age

If Washington Redskins owner Daniel Snyder thinks his life has gone south on him now, he is in for a series of frightening shocks when he gets a dose of the rage and despair building up in the hearts of his once-loyal football fans in the terrorized metro Washington area. It is a huge and far-flung fan base of millions of rabid supporters in the wealthiest per capita metropolitan area in the U.S.—and these people are extremely stirred up by the disastrous fate they feel Snyder has brought down on their once-beloved Redskins. Which is true. The Redskins are doomed, lost like pigs in the wilderness—a gang of squabbling losers with no pride and no shame and no hope at all of anything but failure for the next 20 years. In 3 games this season they have been outscored by 112–16.

I was a Redskins fan, in the pre-Snyder days. It was impossible not to like a winning team led by rogues like Sonny Jurgensen and Billy Kilmer. They were wild boys, anarchists, boozers, and freaks who could win or lose on a whim and torture the hopes of their fans. Betting the Redskins to cover the spread on any given Sunday was like throwing your money to the winds of fickle chance, something only a common junkie would do—but there were many junkies, and not all were "common," by any standard. They were big-time people—U.S. Senators, Presidents, evil pimps, and gold-plated whores from mysterious harems in Hong Kong, Turkey, and Liechtenstein. The power they wielded in the years after World War II was enormous. They traded in diamonds and rubies and atom bombs. They rarely slept, and their blood was always boiling. Those were wild and lawless years in the Capital District.

Which brings us back to the much-despised Daniel Snyder.

The Washington Redskins were whipped again like rabid skunks on Sunday, but only a few people cared. Brooding on the fate of the Redskins is no longer considered cool, in Washington or anywhere else in the English-speaking world. Not even the President of the United States gives a hoot in hell about the pitiful fate of the Redskins. They are the worst team in the NFL, and their owner is widely vilified.

But that doesn't bother Daniel Snyder. He is a rich and busy man. Public scorn and ridicule Don't faze him.—Mr. Snyder is not a frequent flier to Afghanistan, these days. He is too busy owning the Redskins and the brand-new, state-of-the-art Federal Express stadium, where his team plays nine games each year.

Snyder bought these properties in 1999 for eight hundred Million dollars, which some people said was too much. But Dan ignored their warnings and spent $100 Million more for "stadium improvements," like creating new Luxury Suites and replacing new steel girders with newer glass ones, so that people in $100 seats could better see the field. The average price of a seat at FedEx Field is $92, the most expensive seat in the NFL, and that doesn't include $12 hot dogs and $8 cups of beer.

That is a very pricey ticket for a sports event—though not up there with bizarre things like Jack Nicholson's seats for Lakers games and folding metal chairs in the Governor's Box on Kentucky Derby Day. But those are the best seats in the house, and cheap at any price—particularly for real estate developers and shrewd Hollywood stars who need massive publicity for their movies but would rather not be seen on the Letterman show.

Tell me, Britney, why did the chicken cross the road?

Because he wanted to be seen. The chicken is smart, he is cool. He is making a sound investment in himself—unless he is drunk, and then he has no future. But he wins either way. If the chicken is Flamboyant as he crosses the road, he will soon be rich and famous. If he is bitchy and neurotic, he will be eliminated. This is the Law of the Road.

But what is Daniel Snyder really up to? Is he as stupid as a chicken on a freeway? Is he a natural fool?

No. The Redskins' owner has been called many things—from a treacherous greedhead and a savage jackass to a leech and a whore-beast—but he is rarely called a fool. Snyder is a high-rolling businessman in Washington, DC, the crossroads of power and politics in a nation of dangerously frustrated warriors who love football and hunger for personal Security. It is a nervous climate for businessmen: they crave a solution—and Daniel M. Snyder thinks he has one. All he needs now is a proper market for it.

That is where the Redskins come in. The team itself is a loss leader, a pawn in Snyder's larger scheme—which is to lure confused rubes into his futuristic football stadium and sell them highly secure space, where they can relax and be entertained in peace and personal comfort for as long as they feel afraid.

It is a pretty good scheme, on its face—a walled city with a high-tech security system and rigidly controlled access, like a perfect Super Bowl experience with all-American people and all-American fun that never ends.

Yes sir, young Daniel is definitely on to something. There is method to his free-spending madness. He is crazy like a fox. Ho ho. I have already signed up as a charter member of the first true Redskins Club, in Landover, MD, which Michael Jordan and his supercool Washington Wizards also call home. Snyder doesn't own the Wizards yet, but a deal is said to be pending. Michael will play for another 20 years, and Dan will call him a Partner.

As for the Redskins, they will dump the whole roster, including Coach Schottenheimer and all his failed relatives, then slowly rebuild through the draft. It will be a long and painful process for fans, but in the end they will know Victory and Joy for the rest of their jittery lives. Snyder guarantees it. He already owns the most expensive football franchise in the history of the game, along with FedEx Field with its 88,000 new seats and the indoor shopping mall and 20 acres of parking space, with armed guards to punish evil strangers. They will be flayed and turned into germ-free hamburgers, with just enough purified animal fat to make them sizzle.

We are talking about a new kind of City, folks, a danger-free mecca of sport without fear and without bogeymen to make innocent football fans nervous. Daniel is ambitious. He loves music and friendly people with green money. That is his dream and his passion. He has plenty of Luxury Suites, and plenty of beer for club members. Welcome to the Stadium Life.

—*October 1, 2001*

Football in the Kingdom of Fear

The Washington Redskins lost again on Sunday, but they were not the worst team in the NFL. The Detroit Lions earned that label when they went belly up against St. Louis on Monday night, losing 0–35 in a monumental display of failure in all its forms that made the Lions' new General Manager visibly ill. Matt Millen tried to hide from the ABC cameras. Toward the end of the nightmare they showed Millen sitting alone in a desolate box as the dazzling St. Louis offense sprinted up and down the field like water running downhill. I gave 31 points and still won my bets. On some days even victory can be too bleak to celebrate.

When the game was over, I drank some Persimmon juice and called John Wilbur in Hawaii. "Cheer up," I said. "Think about the war news. We are winning handily, and the British are still with us." Wilbur was a famous pulling guard for both the Redskins and the Lions, in better days. And I feared he was wallowing in suicidal gloom out there on the western edge of America.

But I was wrong. "Never mind the war," he chirped when he picked up the phone. "The worm has finally turned! Washington covered! They finally beat the spread. I won big!"

It was true: Washington had been a 14½ point underdog, and they had only lost by 14. It was one of those technical victories that only gamblers can enjoy. Just ten days ago Wilbur had been selling Honolulu real estate at a frightening discount—but now he was giggling like a fat young boy and talking about his new Mercedes convertible. "It's beautiful," he babbled, "maroon and gold with Spanish leather seats."

"Good for you," I said. "You are a hero of consumer confidence. When will you take delivery?"

"Who knows?" he said. "I got it for eight thousand dollars—maybe it's a stolen car."

"Don't worry," I said. "We will all be driving stolen cars before this thing is over. Think of it this way: a stolen Mercedes is a hell of a lot better than no car at all—especially in Hawaii."

"That's what the salesman said. He said I should shrug it off and feel proud to be a patriot. Hell, I already feel a lot more optimistic about everything—the war, the market, even the filthy Redskins."

"You bet," I said. "Washington is a powerhouse, compared to the Detroit Lions. Things are definitely looking up. I can hardly wait to get out there for the Marathon."

"Have you gone into training yet?" he asked. "Are you ready to race 26 miles?"

"Don't worry," I told him. "The war news freaked me out for a while, but I'm back in training now. Do you have my official number yet?"

"No," he replied. "They won't give out the numbers until Pearl Harbor Day. You're sure to get a low one. Just keep on training and don't worry about things you can't control."

"Thank you for saying that," I said. "All I want is for things to get back to normal. The war will be over soon."

"Sure it will," he said. "How about some action on the Dallas game next week? It should be a hell of a game! I'll take Washington even. How's that? I feel confident about this one."

"Nonsense," I said. "I want Dallas and ten."

I could hear him thinking, but I knew he had a weakness when it came to Dallas. He hated the whole franchise. The Dallas Cowboys had given him a lot of pain when he went against them in the glory days. Wilbur originated the famous Redskins death dance. "Rot, Rot, Rot in Hell," he would screech from the sidelines—and then his teammates would join him, screaming "Die! You yellow dogs, Die!" He was a Redskin to his core.

But that was in the old days. Things are different now: both teams are winless this year. But not for long. One of them will almost certainly win this game on Monday. A scoreless tie is possible, but the odds against it are 500 or 600 to one. This is a good game to bet Dallas and the low side of the over/under. Dallas almost beat the Raiders last week, while Washington hasn't scored a touchdown in the last 10 quarters. They are both extremely bad teams, but Dallas can at least penetrate the end zone now and then—and they will also be playing in front of a pumped-up home crowd.

The biggest game this week is the Colts-Raiders clash in Indianapolis. I am a serious Colts fan, but I have a queasy feeling about this one and I don't see them winning against the Raiders—not after taking that horrible beating by New England. Oakland will double up on whatever the Patriots did, and they have enough ex-49ers to win by 10.

I will not bet that way, however, if only because I won't have to. The Colts are favored at home, but Peyton Manning will have to stop throwing interceptions if he wants to stay even with Miami in the AFC East.

St. Louis looks like the class of the league right now—almost too good to be true, in fact—but that's what they looked like last year after four games, and in the end they couldn't even beat New Orleans. The NY Giants are not like the Detroit Lions, and their hot rod defense will give St. Louis the fear. This game will be decided by turnovers and Jason Sehorn—so why not have some fun and go with the Giants? We could use a little fun right now, with all these unverified rumors of war and anthrax going around. All war and no football makes Jack a dull boy.

—*October 10, 2001*

Foul Balls and Rash Predictions

Two teams that will not play in the Super Bowl for another eight years are the Denver Broncos and the screwy Indianapolis Colts. That much is clear beyond doubt. They are Losers, doomed like blind pigs in a jungle of snakes and hyenas. The Colts are chickenshit, and the Broncos won't even make the play-offs. They have humiliated me for the last time.

Aside from that, I feel juiced up and ready to make a few rash statements and irresponsible predictions about this week's games. So stand back and prepare to be enlightened. The fat is in the fire.

San Francisco and Cleveland will meet in the Super Bowl, and the Browns will be stomped like cheap grapes. The Yankees will lose the World Series and R. J. will throw two no-hitters, then overdose on tobacco and announce his retirement from the game.

Are we cooking yet? If not, let's blurt out some more. I see the Rams losing to New Orleans by one point, Oakland whipping the Eagles by 10, and the 49ers beating the snot out of the phony Chicago Bears in a blinding fog-storm. Dallas will win big over Arizona, New England will beat Denver by 15, and UCLA will embarrass Stanford.

These are only a few of the many far-reaching visions I've endured in the past two days. I have been working around the clock to finish the first 88 pages of my long-awaited Memoir, titled "Sex and Justice in the Kingdom of Fear," which will be in bookstores next year.

Last week was extremely busy. I spent most of it doing top secret surveillance work on some of my neighbors who are obviously up to no good and need to be watched closely. I have always hated Evildoers, and now that the President has given us a green light to crush them by any means necessary, I see my duty clearly. Dangerous creeps are everywhere, and our only hope is to neutralize them with extreme prejudice. These freaks have taken their shot(s), and now it is our turn.

The first thing I did was beef up my guest list for the weekend football games. Running full-time surveillance on unsuspecting people is extremely taxing work for quasi-professional operatives with no funding, but I am blessed with deep background experience in the spook business, and I know a few top secret shortcuts that simplify the process enormously.

One of them is to always act normal and calm in situations of extreme danger. If your job is to surveil and record every moment in the life of a Foul Ball who might be growing Anthrax spores in his basement, for instance, you will learn far more about his brain patterns by inviting him into your home for a nine-hour marathon of disturbing football games on TV than you will ever learn by surveiling him through a telescope from a frozen creek bed in a pasture near his hideout. With luck, you might catch him in the act of fondling a foreign flag or prancing around his parlor wearing nothing but a turban and a black jockstrap—but that will not be enough, in the way of hard evidence, to justify terminating him with extreme prejudice. There is a big difference between croaking a harmless pervert and callously murdering a close relative of the Saudi Ambassador.

Any Evildoer with the brains to plot lethal damage against our national infrastructure will also be degenerate enough to protect his Evil cover by faking great enthusiasm for watching and gambling on American football games.

He will not want to talk about his job, but ask him anyway. "How is it going at work, Omar? Are you cool with it? Are you meeting enough girls? Are you a gambling man? Do you have any extra hashish? Why are you looking at me that way? What's eating you?" It is better to load him up with booze and goofy chatter than to make him suspicious by staring at his hands and constantly taking notes.

Whoops! I think I see him jogging out there on the road, right in front of my gate. Why not go out and offer him some hot water? Yes, of course, do it now. Remember to watch your back. I'm out of here.

—October 23, 2001

Getting Weird
for Devil's Day

Hot damn, it is Halloween again, and I am ready to get weird in public. Never mind Anthrax for today. The Yankees won, but so what? That's what I said to that fruitbag who claimed to be Sean Penn when he called earlier. "Screw you," I said. He was drunk, so I knew right away that it wasn't Sean Penn. "Get out of my face!" I screamed at him. "You are the same squalid freak who called here a few days ago and said he was Muhammad Ali. What's wrong with you?"

"I need advice," said the voice. "Should I jump into the Honolulu Marathon this year? I desperately need a Personal Challenge to conquer. My blood is filling up with some kind of poison."

"Nonsense," I said. "You are just another jackass looking for attention. I'll give your lame ass a beating if I ever catch you sneaking around My house, you sleazy little Freak!"

I didn't care who he was, by then. He was just another geek in a Halloween parade, to my way of thinking. And for all I knew he was dangerous—maybe some kind of murderous off-duty cop with two guns and a bottle of whiskey in his pocket. I wanted no part of him, especially not on a day like Halloween.

But why not humor him, I thought. Nobody needs this kind of Foul Ball drunk coming into his yard at night. So I lowered my voice and gave him a break. "Okay," I said. "I will help you, just don't come anywhere near me."

"I am Sean Penn," the voice said calmly. "Should I or should I not enter the Honolulu Marathon in December? That's all I need to know."

"Yes," I said. "You should definitely enter it. I will go with you if necessary. But don't call them today. Do it tomorrow, not today. Nobody will believe a thing you say on a horrible day like Halloween. . . . And don't use the goddamn telephone anymore! They'll hunt you down and dice you up like a squid—just go to bed and stay out of sight until noon. That is when the bogeyman sleeps, and so do I. So get out of my face and never call me again!" Then I howled in a low animal voice and hung up the phone.

"These freaks should all be put to sleep," I said to Anita. "Let's go out on the town and get weird."

"Wonderful," she chirped. "We will put on our costumes and throw eggs at foreigners. What are you going to wear?"

"Only this turban and a jockstrap," I said. "And some lipstick. They love lipstick."

Anita was dressed up as the coach of the New York Giants. "They are Losers," she said. "It is okay to mock Losers, right?"

"Yes," I said. "It is righteous to mock Losers in this country. We are Number One."

"Thank you," she said. "You must be a sportswriter."

"You bet," I replied. "We are going to fly to Hawaii with Sean Penn next month. You will probably need a new Rolex."

"Yes." She nodded. "We will have to be inconspicuous for that kind of travel. Is he still Drinking?"

"No," I replied. "He is going into training for the Honolulu Marathon. Perhaps we should stop drinking too."

"Not today," she said with a wink. "Today is the Devil's day."

She was right, of course—although some people will tell you that the Devil has had a lot of Days recently. They see him behind every bush. He lurks like an Evil spirit. He is terrifying.

And who is to say they are wrong? Which of us will hurl the first stone at these chickenheads? Not me, buster. I know these people. They are Devils. . . . Which may be true, but so what? Even a blind pig finds an acorn now and then.

Just then my phone rang. "Not that Freak again," I muttered—but I was wrong: it was my old friend John Wilbur, calling from Hawaii, and his voice was very excited.

"You'll never believe this," he said. "Sean Penn wants to run in the Marathon. He just called Doc Barahal and confirmed it."

"No!" I shouted. "That's impossible. He's asleep downstairs in my basement, and there is no phone in that room. Don't you know what day this is? It's Halloween, you jackass!" And then I quickly hung up on him.

"I can't stand this crap anymore," I said to Anita. "Let's get out of here. We can watch the game at the Jerome. What do these swine think I am—a fool?"

"Who cares?" she said with a shrug. "Can I drive?"

"No," I said. "I'll do the driving tonight. We might run into the Saudi Ambassador along the way—and you know how he flies off the handle if he thinks he sees a woman driving a car."

She agreed, and we drove into town without incident and

got to the Jerome Bar just as the Knicks-Wizards game was getting under way. . . . But no. I was wrong again. All five TV sets, including the 50-incher in the back room, were tuned to the World Series. And the bartender laughed when I asked him to switch at least one of them over to the basketball game. "Are you nuts?" he jeered. "This is a men's bar! We don't watch no stinking basketball here."

"You brainless animal!" I snarled at him. "You just lost the whole ESPN account. You'll be fired for this!"

"Get out of here!" he yelled. "Or I'll set fire to that rotten-looking turban you're wearing!" He lit a book of matches and waved it at me.

So we left and went down to the county jail, where I knew the prisoners would be watching the NBA game, because I knew the jailer hated baseball. He was a Michael Jordan fan— so I gave him the Wizards and five points, and I was wrong again. They lost by only two, which completely ruined my night. I had to pay off all the prisoners too. I can still hear them laughing at us on our way out.

—*October 31, 2001*

The Yankees Are Dead: Long Live the Yankees

That evil warpo from up the road appeared at my door on Sunday night and asked if he could watch game Seven of the World Series with us. He said he wanted to bet big money on the New York Yankees because he felt so sorry for them. "They are incredibly brave men," he said. "But there is no dishonor in losing to better and braver men."

Whoops, I thought, Welcome to the night train. This is the same suspicious pervert I've been watching 24 hours a day for the past month with nothing to show for it—why is he suddenly knocking on my door and begging to gamble on baseball? "What do you want?" I asked him. "Why are you hanging around my house at night? Are you Omar?"

"Exactly," he responded. "I am Omar and I want to watch the Yankees with my neighbors."

I went into a knife-fighting crouch, although I had no knife—and just then a sultry-looking woman about 25 years old appeared beside Omar, and he introduced her as "Princess Omin, my little sister. She also loves the Yankees."

Ye gods, I thought. This creep is more evil than I thought, and now he brings this Woman! I was confused. Princess Omin was extending a delicate little hand to me now, so I took it and kissed it nervously. She was wearing a light blue shawl that kept her face in shadow, but I sensed she was smiling at me, and I felt my fear disappearing.

"Wonderful," I heard myself saying, "Come right in. Why didn't you tell me you had such a beautiful sister, Omar? This changes everything. How much do you want to bet? Come inside and meet my other guests. Does Princess Omin also want to gamble?"

An odd mix of people had gathered in my lounge that day for the games. The County Coroner was there, along with the Sheriff, an extremely bigoted astrophysicist, and four elegant blond women looking to work out on somebody—but not necessarily Omar, who was viewed in the neighborhood as an extremely dark influence and they were not entirely ready to have him sitting behind them on a stool for the next four hours. All they knew about him was that he hung around the Post Office every afternoon, whistling at women and muttering to himself in a language that none of us knew. The Coroner said he was a dangerous creep who was pushing his luck and should probably be put to sleep.

"Stop talking like that," I told him when we went out on the porch to speak privately. "That sister of his isn't going to hurt anybody, as long as we give her a seat. Why don't you ask her if she wants to sit on your lap."

"Screw off," he replied. "I'll fry in hell before I let that woman sit on my lap! She is a lot crazier than Omar."

"Nonsense," I said. "They want to bet a Thousand dollars ($1000) on the Yankees and give three to one."

"Well, that's different," he said quickly. "We know the Yankees are going to lose, don't we?"

"You bet," I said. "I guarantee it."

"Oh?" he said with a slow nod, as if he were lost in thought. "Will you give 3–1?"

Just then Princess Omin came out on the porch and clapped her hands over the Coroner's eyes, from behind. He screamed something incoherent and dropped to his knees, then he fell against the woodpile and passed out.

The girl rushed to help him, but I waved her off. "Never mind that fool," I said with a cruel chuckle. "He is history."

It was true. The Coroner had given up his chair, and he would never get it back. Princess Omin accepted it gracefully and quickly became the center of attention. Omar took a stance behind her, massaging her shoulders and looking more like a dangerous pervert than I felt I could tolerate.

"Get away from that girl," I barked at him. "I thought you came here to gamble, not to fondle your sister in public!"

"Exactly," Omar replied suavely. "We will bet ten thousand dollars on the Yankees. They are very brave men."

"They are Losers," I said. "You are nutty as a fruitcake, Omar, but I can't resist gambling with you."

"We will see," he hissed. "I have plenty of money—and if I lose, I will leave my sister with you until I pay."

Anita came into the room and slapped him sharply on the side of his head. He staggered momentarily but said nothing. The sight of it filled me with dread, so I quickly fell asleep and left the others to deal with him.

When I woke up four hours later, the Yankees were leading

2–1 in the bottom of the ninth. My friends were laughing greed-
ily and Omar was gone. I felt queasiness in my stomach, but I
refused to cave in to it—and just the Yankees made a horrible
error that loaded the bases with only one out. Yes, I thought,
this dynasty is ready to fall. Princess Omin was weeping softly,
but I tried to ignore her. The whole room understood that
whatever happened next was going to be awkward.

There was no time to brood on it, however, because the
next Diamondback hitter looped a single into left center and
the game was over. . . . And that's how the story ends, folks.
Omar's little sister is living with us now. She sleeps in the attic
and never talks. We are trying to take the situation one day at a
time. Anita has come to like her, and I have abandoned all hope
of Omar's ever paying off. But so what? At least he is gone from
the neighborhood, and that is what really matters. He was an
evil freak, and I hope he never comes back. Life can be strange
in the wilderness, especially when foreigners wander in and
say unfortunate things for no reason at all. The Yankees are
dead, long live the Yankees.

—*November 5, 2001*

The Man Who Loved Sport Too Much

There was not much gambling in the Rockies last week, but my
own home was swarming with it. Sean Penn arrived just as the
Sheriff was leaving for Las Vegas to endure harsh antiterrorism

training—and I had a dark feeling, even then, that these two absolutely diss-connected events would somehow combine to cause trouble. . . . Which was true, although neither one of those things were as traumatic as the bizarre arrival of Princess Omin in my home. That changed things dramatically.

Our gambling situation went all to pieces, as it usually does when you start betting with strangers who have no sense of values and don't mind losing heavily. People who don't speak English and pay their gambling debts by selling relatives into slavery are always loaded bazookas. I could have handled Penn's arrival and the Sheriff's departure with no trouble, under ordinary circumstances, but when Fate added a fine young Arabian woman to the mix, my gears began to grind. I felt my brain wandering. A little confusion can be interesting, in the Oriental sense, but too much of it with no apparent end is demoralizing.

There was a time, not long ago, when I looked forward to the Sunday NFL games with a certain giddy expectation, like a vacation coming up. But no longer—not after the 49ers failed to cover and the Raiders blew up right in front of my eyes on Sunday night like swollen sheep. They were beaten and disgraced.

Whoops. Lighten up on the bombast, Doc. Stick with the facts. . . . Okay. The once-mighty Raider defense was ripped to shreds by a rookie running back from Alabama named Shaun Alexander who sliced and stomped through the fourth-toughest defensive unit in the NFL for 266 yards and utterly intimidated the Oakland linebackers. They were shamed like animals who urinate on themselves.

The Oakland offense played like a gang of drunkards, moving well enough at times to run up 388 yards in a baffling display of classic West Coast Offense and butterfingered sleaziness that made owner Al Davis beg to be taken out of the stadium in a bag at game's end. Hall of Fame receivers Tim Brown and Jerry Rice dropped enough passes in the fourth quarter to throw the game away. It was a shoddy performance, at best, bordering on criminal fraud and cowardice. To see the proud Raiders disgraced like this caused my heart to fill with hate.

BOTCHED SURVEILLANCE

I was brooding on this and other systematic failures when Princess Omin came down from the attic and silently joined us as we bitched and whined and watched the football games on Sunday. I was not sure she even understood the game, if only because of her unrelenting silence, but I couldn't help noticing that she took a decidedly focused interest in Mr. Penn, despite his spastic drunkenness. "Maybe she speaks your language," I said to him. "Try to get her to talk to you."

"Oh no," he said quickly, "I'm not that drunk. Don't deceive yourself." He had been drinking a vile-smelling liqueur called Fernet-Branca for two days and nights, falling asleep frequently in the middle of conversations and fouling his pants when he got excited—but I sensed a sly duplicity in him, like a teenage girl acting drunker than she really is, so I gave him plenty of room.

"Princess Omin seems to like you," I said casually. "Would you like to snuggle up with her and talk openly?"

He gave me the fish-eye and took another snort of that evil booze that he carries. "Is this the girl you got from the terrorist?" he asked. "Why are you keeping her here?"

"Don't act paranoid!" I snapped at him. "I am not Keeping her. She's waiting for her brother to come back and pay his debts."

"That's obscene!" he said. "She has been here for eight days and she has no intention of leaving! Don't take me for a rubberhead. That smarmy bastard you fleeced on the World Series is never coming back!"

"Nonsense," I said. "He is Omar, a prince of the royal blood."

"You fool!" he barked. "He left her deliberately. She's a human listening device. One of these days you will wake up with a bomb in your mouth. You should call the police and have her locked up."

I stared at him, feeling a shudder in my spine. Ye gods! I thought. What if he's right? Is it possible that I am willfully harboring a Terrorist? Could this woman be making a jackass of me? ... "That's ridiculous," I said to Mr. Penn. "This is Princess Omin—little sister to Omar, who owes me $40,000."

He sneered at me. "That's rich," he chuckled. "Isn't Omar that creep you've been investigating for war crimes?"

I said nothing, struggling to digest it all. The mere possibility that Omar had run a game down on me was repulsive. "What are you saying?" I demanded. "That some foreign freak has bamboozled me?"

"Yes," he answered. "He has planted a Mole in your life. This bitch will destroy you!"

Just then the Coroner came into the room and laughed brazenly in my face. "You are too dumb to live," he cackled.

I swung a hockey stick at him, but he dodged away and slapped Princess Omin on the back of her head, which instantly changed her attitude. "Don't touch me, you swine!" she screamed. "You are a dung heap!"

"Well, well," said Penn. "She speaks pretty good English, for a deaf-mute." He reached over and tweaked her throat. "Don't worry, Princess—you're Safe here."

A wealthy man named "Cleverly," known all along the Continental Divide for his outbursts of public lewdness, burst into laughter and hooted at me. "How about that $40,000, Doc? Why don't you boys take this girl to Hollywood? That's where she belongs."

He was Right. They were all laughing at me. I grabbed some whiskey off my leather-covered icebox and went outside to be alone. My worst fears had come true. I was a public Dupe, soon to be jailed for crimes against the nation. How had it happened? Had I finally loved Sport too much?

—*November 12, 2001*

The Shame of
Indianapolis

Indianapolis Colts owner James Irsay called me last week and demanded to know what I meant by calling the Colts "chicken crap." He sounded very agitated.

"Nonsense," I told him. "I would never say that, James. The term I used was chickenshit—as in dung, cowardly dung."

"Oh God," he moaned. "I thought you were my friend. We are a lot better than chicken crap!"

"Not for me, James," I said sternly. "The Colts are a rotten team to bet on. You have fleeced me for the last time. Fortunately, I bet on New Orleans last week." Which was true. I had bet on the Saints, Green Bay, San Francisco, and even the Washington Redskins to beat Denver—which was three out of four, and I still don't understand what happened to the Packers. How can a solid team with Brett Favre at quarterback beat Chicago, Tampa Bay, and Baltimore, then lose to bums like the Vikings and the Falcons? It was embarrassing.

Those failures will hurt when January rolls around. Losing once to a Good team is not fatal in the NFL, but losing to a bad team is unacceptable. Indeed, don't let this happen to you. Avoid Bad teams when you gamble, and never mind your powerful last-minute Hunches. Lay off bad teams—like Indianapolis, for instance, or Denver. They are downhill teams, because toward the end of the season they have a tendency to Lose important games. They are Losers.

Bugwa! Any half-bright Waterhead coach can win if he inherits a team that won last year's Super Bowl. Look at George Seifert with the 49ers: they couldn't lose—at least not until Crimes against the salary cap forced them to send most of their star players across the Bay to Oakland, where they continue to tear up the NFL, despite the sleazy greed of Al Davis.

Whoops. Never mind Al Davis. He is a swinesucker, but he

does have a fine eye for bargains and overripe fruit. The Raiders' roster has been stocked from the start by veterans and malcontents from other teams on the slide. That is what makes them a winning Team—or at least a Good team as opposed to piles of puss like Carolina or Buffalo. The Raiders may be Losers, individually, but as a team they are a reliable bet, most of the time. Let's say 77.8 percent of the time, which is not a bad batting average.

Only St. Louis is better, at .889, and the Rams are clearly the class of the league. New Orleans beat them by two, San Francisco came Close, very close, losing by four. . . . The 49ers would be 88.9 percent right now, tied with the Rams for first in the NFC West—except for that horrible disaster in Chicago, when the Bears scored twice in 30 seconds and won in overtime.

Right, but that's like saying, "I would have won all the sprints at the Sydney Olympics, except for this gosh-darn wooden leg."

Ho ho. If is a big word, to sane people. Hell, the New York Giants would be Super Bowl champions today if not for the Baltimore Ravens. And Bill Clinton would be President if he could have run in 2000. If the queen had balls, she'd be King.

Yes sir, and if I hadn't flipped out over Terrorism, I wouldn't be having these hideous problems that plague me today, with this Woman stuck in my attic and Cops hammering on my door. It seems impossible, but it could happen to anybody. I was only trying to be a good citizen, to help my fellow man—or Woman, as it happened—but somehow things went sideways, and now my standing in the neighborhood is diminished. I am under suspicion of being an enemy sympathizer, a jackass, and a bigot.

That is why I don't want to talk about Princess Omin and that skunkish Omar at this time. People started snickering at me when I went out in public. Obviously they don't understand My side of the story. Every time I pick up a newspaper, I see grim headlines about Bombs, Economic disasters, and unknown foreigners being put on trial and even Executed by ad hoc Military Tribunals for secret reasons. The White House laughs it off, but we are creating what looks oddly like a police state in this country. Secret trials with secret evidence are not what George Washington had in mind at Valley Forge. He well understood the political meaning of Terrorism—and Anthrax, for that matter: it was a wool handlers' disease.

Ah, but that is a different story, and we will save it for later. Our motto now is Thank God for Football.

It was just before halftime of the Indianapolis–New Orleans game on Sunday when Police invaded my house. I paid no attention to them at first—Peyton Manning was running for a touchdown with no time left on the clock and people were getting excited—but the cops refused to stop hammering on my door. "Get away!" I shouted. "We are asleep." It was a weak thing to say, but I needed a few seconds to sweep a pile of money off the table and hide the Jimsonweed.

I heard a jiggling noise in the lock. *Whack!* The door flew open and they swarmed in. "Hello, Hunter," said Grady, who seemed to be in charge. "Don't worry, we're not after You this time—but where is that woman you're hiding?"

"What woman?" I said. "Wait a minute! I am confused. Was that a touchdown? Did Manning score?"

"Never in hell," snapped the Coroner. "He was cheating. They called it back."

Just then the Colts kicked a field goal, with no time on the clock, to tie the game 17–17. The cameras switched off to show cheerleaders and players running for the locker room. None of it made any sense.

The cop laughed. "She is on the White House list of suspected terrorists, and that makes You an official Terrorist sympathizer." He leered at me and jerked a new ESPN magazine off my leather-covered refrigerator. "What is this?" he snapped. "Is this the issue with the Olympic Venue maps?"

I grabbed it out of his hand and threw it in the fire. "Watch your mouth!" I told him. "I am on my way to Utah right now. I am a member of—"

"Freeze!" he yelled. "Put your hands on your head!"

I saw the other cop moving to get behind my back, so I fell against the icebox and cut him off. "Stand down!" I shouted. "Don't embarrass yourselves professionally." I flashed a badge at them—a Lyle Lovett security badge, as it happened—and they momentarily stood down. "I am a Sportswriter," I said calmly. "I am a member of the SLOC press security committee!"

What happened next is open to interpretation—but to make a long story short, they wound up taking Princess Omin away and telling me that I was under formal Quarantine, for Health Reasons. "And don't argue," the big one barked. "This is perfectly legal. We have a lot of New Laws these days. You Have No Rights." He handed me a small blue card with a list of numbers on it, along with some dense small print about Terrorism and National Security Emergencies and Military Tribunal Judgments.

I had read it all before, but the presence of armed policemen in my home somehow put a new and more human face on it. I saw that I was about 95 seconds away from being locked up as a hostile foreign agent, so I caved.

"Thank God you've come," I said. "She's right up there in the attic. You are saving my Life! She Threatened me! Please take her away."

I was sorry to see her go, but in truth I had no choice.

—*November 19, 2001*

Failure, Football, & Violence on the Strip

Okay, folks, we have a problem here. My new cashmere blazer is drenched with rain, and I am having a nervous breakdown. Bad vibes are all around me and I feel paralyzed by fear and desperation, my brain is out of gear, Anita is cringing outside on the balcony, our plane leaves for Honolulu in seven hours, and I can't wear short-sleeve shirts because my left forearm is disfigured by a huge spider bite that bleeds constantly.

Why even try? you might ask. What kind of jackass would be obsessing on his professional correspondence at a time like this anyway? Here's a dime, go tell it to somebody who cares.

A lot of people feel that way in this eerie hotel, but not me. I am a hopeless optimist, and I believe I have something to say. (Whoops. I am hearing the desperate screech of a large animal right outside my window, then the sound of men laughing.)

"What was that?" Anita yells, jumping in from the balcony and quickly shutting the glass doors behind her.

"Who knows?" I say, as I close my own window and drop the slatted blinds. "That was horrible," I say. "It sounded like something being killed!"

I am feeling a little desperate now. It is not just the animal screeching, but everything else that is happening: my life is falling apart. It is like an earthquake in slow motion. Howls and curses drift up from the midnight street below us and people are blowing horns and crashing into each other. I hear police sirens and the high-pitched roar of motorcycle engines in the rain.

* * *

Did I forget to tell you boys that we are smack in the middle of downtown Hollywood tonight? How careless of me. Yes. We are in a top-floor balcony suite in the venerable Chateau Marmont, my usual working headquarters when I come to LA. They know me here. My blood is on these walls, and my spirit haunts the elevators.

I have suffered grievously in this place, many times, for reasons we need not discuss now. The memories are intolerable when it rains and I come under stress—and I am very much under stress Now. Extreme stress, I think. Most people would go all to pieces from it.

I have been in the grip of Agony since last Wednesday, when I arrived. Things have gone downhill in a hurry since then. On Thursday a quack with a dentist's drill botched my wisdom teeth, and on Friday (or was it Saturday?) I tripped on a balcony ledge and sustained a nasty Subdural Hematoma that almost ended my life.

The WHACK of a fully weighted Head shot is an unforgettable sensation that will stay with you Forever.

It happens very suddenly, as high-speed collisions always do, and everything in your world disappears in a bright orange flash. There is no immediate pain, because you are knocked out cold like a dead fish. No noise, no feeling, no consciousness. That terrible THUD of impact is the last thing some people ever hear. You are "on your way out," as the Doctors like to say.

Indeed, and so much for violence, eh? Let's get back to football, which has been very good to me recently. Some people will tell you I am on a big-time winning streak, but for powerful reasons of karma I will deny it. One thing I have learned in my painful career as a gambler is that bragging when you get lucky and Win a few games will plunge you into gloom and unacceptable beatings very soon. It happens every time.

That is why I have been so quiet about the San Francisco 49ers. I don't want to hex my people while they're winning. It has happened before. The last time I shot off my mouth about San Francisco, they got stabbed from behind by the evil Chicago Bears. I was baffled and humiliated in public. People called me a Dunce and tried to crowd me into sucker bets. I felt so damaged that I started betting on Dallas.

Ho ho. And look what happened next. The Cowboys snuck up on the Washington Redskins and whacked them off their inexplicable winning binge. The Redskins are down in the ditch with all the other bums now. Ashes to ashes and dust to dust.

Meanwhile San Francisco is on a roll and tied with St. Louis for the best record in the NFL—along with Pittsburgh and Chicago.

Chicago? You bet. I owe the Bears an apology. I called them "phony," but I was wrong. They are a gang of Assassins and I fear them. They will croak St. Louis in the play-offs. The Rams have the best individual Talent in the league, but they are wiggy in the clutch and they have a terminal fumbling habit.

The 49ers only lost to the Rams by two (2) points, and that was a long time ago in Week 2. But I will go far out on a limb tonight and say that things are different now. We have a gigantic football weekend coming up in the NFL, so let's get stupid and make a few rash predictions. Why not?

So yes, the 49ers will beat the Rams by at least eight (8), and the Bears will beat the Packers by two (2). And I say that without knowing who on any of those teams might be injured or locked up. I haven't even seen the point spreads. Yes sir, make no mistake about it, Bubba. I am running on a thin mix of Hubris and whiskey luck now. Anything can happen in these games: the Rams and the Packers are serious business. They may be the best teams in football, and I will be shocked if they turn out to be underdogs. But so what? I am shocked every day by some ugly kink in the news, and I am prepared to be shocked again.

It is not particularly Fun, but I enjoy it on some days, and I feel that Sunday is going to be one of them. I will be far, far away by then anyway. On Sunday I will be running in the Honolulu Marathon with Sean Penn and former Redskins guard John Wilbur—who has never won the race in 20 years of trying but can always be depended on to knock about 2,000 other runners off their pace with his profoundly disturbing style. Wilbur is given a lot of room when he comes up to the Starting line. He is amazingly fast, and he runs in a phalanx of longtime Samoan friends who clear a lane for him and keep him highly focused.

Penn and I will be in the official Pace Car, once we've come to our senses and dropped out. And that, I suspect, is certain. Only a madman would think about running for 26 miles at top speed at my age. Wilbur tried it once, and they ran right over him when he passed out down the stretch. It was horrible.

Penn's style remains a mystery, however, and race officials are very leery of him. He is known to be capable of extreme speed for short bursts, and some of those people are right to be afraid of him. Sean is batty as a loon and is prone to taking extraordinary risks in foreign towns, often with no awareness at all of what he's doing. He is seen as a Dark horse, but I doubt it. He will croak himself before noon, and we will watch most of those crucial games from bamboo chairs in the Tiki bar at the elegant Kahala Mandarin Oriental, where Keith Richards will also be staying.

And that's It for now, folks. There is no more. *Aloha, Mahalo,* and so long for now.

—*December 6, 2001*

Madness in Honolulu

Okay, folks, let's talk about the good life in Hawaii now, about beautiful beaches and naked women and ukuleles wailing in the darkness of a football Sunday morning in Honolulu. I am familiar with these things, and I want to pass them along to you, because I am a writing fool on the run with a charming smile and a total-access Press pass. Yes sir, I am a tortured man for all seasons, as they say, and I have powerful friends in high places. Birds sing where I walk, and children smile when they see me coming.

Are you impressed yet? Are you ready to cough it up? No? Well stand back and try this: we are all Beasts, when it comes right down to it, and the only thing that really matters in the end is Who wins the Rose Bowl.

What? That is nonsense. That is Gibberish in overdrive. Nobody believes it and Nobody should. I pass it along only because it came to me in a random e-mail blurb from the Greedheads who run a College football racket known as the Bowl Championship Series, the ill-fated BCS.

Those people are dirtbags, hired swine in the pay of other swine who control the glitzy machinery of College Football.

Right, and so much for that, eh? How did I get off on that evil tack anyway? I was sitting here in this elegant beachfront Suite in the Kahala Mandarin Oriental hotel, thinking of nothing at all except the vastness of the Pacific Ocean and the incredible language skills of George Bush, when my brain locked up and I veered off on some meatball rap about the upcoming Miami-Nebraska game. Who knows why? It means nothing at all, absolutely nothing—except to both teams, who will pocket $15,000,000 each for showing up in Pasadena on January 1. Suck on that, Bubba. Ho ho.

Whoops! Have I discussed the world-famous Honolulu Marathon yet? Have I done my job as a suave professional? If not, I will do it now. When the going gets weird, the weird turn pro. That is my personal motto, and it has made me what I am today. I am a generous man, by nature, and far more trusting than I should be. Indeed. The Real world is risky territory for people with a natural generosity of spirit. Beware.

I was reminded of this when I chanced to see my notebook

from last weekend and saw what was happening back then. It seems like the good old days now, but in fact it was not so long ago at all—less than five or six days, my notes tell me, but I can only dimly remember it.

That is what notebooks are for, I think, so let's have a look at what I wrote, to wit:

It was four o'clock on a rainy Sunday morning when the long white limousine came to the hotel to take us downtown to what they called the Starting Line, where 20,000 half-naked fanatics were waiting to grease us up for the race. I was nursing a green bottle of Gin and feeling vaguely desperate, but I saw no way to escape. We had made the wretched commitment long ago, and now the time had come. The deal was about to go down.

Far across the deserted lobby, dressed in a cheap black suit and orange running shoes, Sean Penn was slumped on a leather bench and weeping dumbly and pounding his fists against a wall of orchids. I bit my tongue and tried to ignore him, but he cried out when he saw me, and I had no choice, so I paused. "I don't think I can do it, Doc," he sobbed. "I am going all to pieces. I am weak and I'm afraid. Please help me."

I had never seen him like this, and I knew I couldn't help him. Quitting now would be humiliating. We had shot off our mouths and now we were going to pay for it. "Get a grip on yourself," I said sharply, "people are watching us!" Then I handed him my green bottle of gin.

He grasped it eagerly and put it to his lips, swallowing deeply and rolling his eyes—then he dropped it on the floor, where it bounced and skittered away.

"You fool!" I shouted. "You stupid little Bastard! We can't get any more of that stuff until Noon!"

"Oh no," he mumbled. "I have money. They will give me whatever I want."

Just then I saw our limo driver. "Get away from us!" I yelled. "Can't you see that Mr. Penn is feeling poorly?"

"So am I," he replied. "It's raining Hard outside and my wife ran off with a sailor—but I have a Job to do and I am going to do it. Get that Sot in the car."

What? I thought. Are you calling Sean Penn a sot? Are you nuts? I had dealt with this driver before, and I knew him to be a thug with no morals at all. Two days earlier he had abandoned us for three hours in a dangerous downtown park where criminals lurked in the darkness. There were nine of us, including six women and children. We were utterly helpless. So we huddled behind a concert stage where sleazy old men wearing wigs were singing "God Bless America" and pretending to be the Beatles. It was disgusting. Our only weapon was a knobby-headed cane about four feet long, which I waved at the trees and occasionally pounded on the hood of a nearby Cadillac. It was a long and nasty three hours.

And now, on this horrible Sunday morning, the same irresponsible thug was spitting insults on a major Hollywood talent. It was ugly. We were the biggest celebrities in the race. I stared down at Penn for a moment, saying nothing, then I turned away and walked quickly back to the elevator, which I took upstairs to my suite and locked both doors. Anita was still asleep, so I called room service for some Crab St. Jacques and watched the War on TV until dawn. That is how we handle emergencies in the tropics.

—*December 13, 2001*

Break Up
the Ravens

Ed Podolak had just been strip-searched for the second time in 40 minutes by foreigners at the Denver airport when I met him in the Smoking Lounge, and his temper was rubbed raw. Podolak, formerly of the Kansas City Chiefs, is known all over the West as "the last great white running back"—which is not true, but that is his story and he has stuck to it for 30 years, for good or ill, and on this day he was looking sick.

"This country is turning rotten, Doc," he said as he cleared a place at the bar for me. "I don't know why they are picking on me, but they grab me every time I come near an airport. Last week in Dallas I was subjected to a cavity search."

I have known Ed for many years, and I had never seen him so helpless and demoralized. "Are they doing it to everybody? Or is it just me? Pretty soon I won't be able to travel at all."

"Get a grip on yourself, Ed," I told him. "Don't you know there's a War on?"

"So what?" he snapped. "I'm not a terrorist. I'm not carrying any bombs. I am a stand-up all-American patriot."

"That's what they all say," I said. "Let's face it, Ed. You are swarthy and you have black, bushy hair. You look guilty. Are you carrying any hashish?"

"Don't say that word!" he hissed. "You'll get us both locked up—and the answer is No, so get off my back."

"Where are you going?" I asked him.

"New Orleans," he replied. "But I don't dare go anywhere now—not if this ugliness keeps up. What the hell, I may as well just stay here and watch the games on TV."

"Good thinking," I said. "They'll never find us here in the Smoking Lounge. Let's hammer a few."

Watching the Baltimore Ravens play football is like watching scum freeze on the eyeballs of a jackass, or being stuck for 6 hours in an elevator with Dick Cheney on speed. The Ravens will pounce on you and gnaw you to death, which can take eight or nine days.

The Raven is a queer and dangerous bird, far worse than the Crow. A pack of crows can destroy an owl or an eagle, but a single boss Raven will attack a whole gang of crows and rip the lungs out of its leaders. Most crows would rather commit suicide than go head to head with a boss raven.

You bet, so what does this tell us about this week's play-off games?

Almost nothing, now that I mention it—except that Pittsburgh beat the snot out of the Ravens (at home) about a month ago. The score was 26–21, but the beating was far worse, so we can only hope that the Steelers can do it again, and knock this horrible saltwater Tar baby out of the play-offs as soon as possible, so they can't dull out the rest of the season. Betting on a Baltimore game is like betting on a three-hour sumo wrestling bout. It is wrong for the Game.

—*January 15, 2002*

Pay Up or Get Whipped

Ed Bradley stopped by my house yesterday and said he wanted to watch the Rams-Packers game in peace, far from the madding crowd he'd been hanging out with, and perhaps bet a dollar or two on the Packers. Wonderful, I thought. These suckers are everywhere. They are sentimental people, and they want to make sentimental bets. Why not indulge them—if only to restore balance to my own ledger, which was badly depleted as a result of my own stupid bets on the previous day, and also the previous week.

Indeed, I had caved in to the deadly temptation of betting like a Fan again, instead of like the cold-blooded Gambler that I like to think I am.

It was the 49ers who put the bite on me first, then the Bears, and finally the Raiders—although New England needed the game officials to get past the Raiders by three, which was exactly the spread. It was the only real contest of the weekend, played in a classic Boston blizzard and marred by wretched calls. So it was no shame to break even on that one—or the Bears-Eagles debacle either, for that matter, given that Chicago lost its quarterback in the first quarter, could not run at all, and played most of the game with no more sign of an offense than a herd of giraffes.

The worm turned on Sunday, however. After two baffling losses, I recovered nicely at the expense of Bradley, the Sheriff, and ESPN boss John Walsh, who went down with the Packers' cruel beating in St. Louis. I took my own shrewd advice and bet favorites for a change. Both Sunday games were unnaturally savage beatings, and the Rams-Eagles game this week should be a holocaust of speed and savagery. I think I will stick with St. Louis on this one, and also with the Steelers. In matters of sport, you always want to go the Southern way and "dance with the one who brung you."

It is definitely possible that we will see a Philadelphia–New England Super Bowl, but don't bet the farm on it—unless of course you get about 10 points with the Eagles and 18 with the Patriots. One of the underdogs will win or at least cover, but it will be more trouble than it's worth to decide which one has the true fire in its nuts. This is not the time of year to start Doubling up on underdogs.

Let me tell you an ugly little story that happened to me, a few years back, when I made that mistake. I was betting more money than I had, in those days, and doing it through a big-time bookie who came to me through a well-known (then and now) White House advisor. His name need not be spoken, in this evil context, but I should say that it was not Pat Buchanan or Sandy Berger or Henry Kissinger.

Names don't matter much in this business anyway. Not compared to the numbers, which matter hugely. And numbers were exactly what got me in trouble, especially those rotten zeros. I got a little desperate towards the end of that year, or maybe it was just hubris. In any case, I quickly found myself about $75,000 in debt to a gambling operation somewhere on the outskirts of Boston, which led to a series of increasingly nasty telephone conversations with ill-tempered strangers.

My White House connection was unable or maybe just unwilling to cope with my problem, although it was more and more bothering him.

Impossible as it seemed to me at the time, we both faced the possibility of a horrible beating, or worse, if I didn't pay up immediately. Suddenly all the fun had gone out of the gambling business. I was missing mortgage payments, borrowing from friends, kiting checks, and feeling far too nervous to write anything longer than a French postcard. I aged about six years in three months, and things were getting worse every day. Suicide began to look like a far, far better option than living with grief and debt forever.

Finally my friend in the White House came up with an eerie solution to our problem: I would have to go out on a relentless Speaking Tour that would continue at top speed until I made enough money to pay the bookie. He even arranged for at least two of the bookie's "agents" to be with me at all times for the duration of my Tour.

It was a horrifying notion, but I clearly had no choice. It was an offer I couldn't refuse. The bookie would even arrange when and where my lectures would occur, and how much I would be paid for each one. On top of that, they would also arrange for the limos, hotels, plane tickets, and editorial assistants on the road. Most important, they collected all my speaking fees at once, usually in an unmarked brown paper bag or a locked bank pouch. Yes sir, and I still have a drawer full of those pouches downstairs in Johnny Depp's dungeon suite, just to remind me about drifting into unacceptable gambling habits.

In truth, it was not a bad life. I made many friends in a world that I would never have known otherwise. They were good people and good company, and a wonderfully efficient collection agency for me, as well as from me, and they made sure I traveled First Class at all times, and they were a hell of a lot more fun to work with than any professional agent I have ever worked with in my own business. What the hell, they were straight shooters, and they got me out of debt almost in spite of myself. So thanks again, boys, if any of you happen to be reading this. You were good at your work and you were good for me. *Vaya con Dios.*

—*January 21, 2002*

Getting Braced for the Last Football Game

Of all the turnovers and screwups and suicidal mistakes that football is famous for, throwing a pass that gets intercepted is the most painful and crippling of all. A wobbly off-target airball that gets picked off and run down your throat is the most costly of football errors. Five (5) points, only one short of a touchdown, and two more than a fumble. The list is long, with many depressing subcategories, from "missing a tackle on punt coverage in overtime," to running the wrong way with a loose ball.

With this scoring system, Brett Favre would have contributed exactly 30 points, all by himself, to the Rams' total of 45 against the Packers last week.

That is huge. If one (1) interception can be fatal, six mean certain doom. The Eagles' Donovan McNabb gave up only one (1) against St. Louis. That is five (5) points; the final score was 29–24. You do the math.

Kordell Stewart lost three wild balls (15 points) aga

New England, baleful 10-point underdog to Pittsburgh—but incredibly, the Steelers were still in the game with two minutes left. Or at least it looked that way—but in fact the Steelers' disastrous Special Teams' blunders were impossible to overcome, especially that horrendous blocked kick: it was a 10-point turnaround, not to mention a savage morale-crusher.

Simple mistakes are the difference between winning and losing a football game, particularly a Big game—read Play-offs, read especially Super Bowl. We are talking about small failures here—basic mechanical failures, mental errors, and blind spots of memory. Foolish laziness that nobody noticed in the first three games of the year will loom gigantic in the play-offs. A simple dropped pass in the fourth quarter will haunt a football player for the rest of his life and cause him to scream in his sleep. Those things will never be forgotten.

Indeed. There are many cruel Rooms in the mansion, and many deep holes in the Road. Keep alert or be stabbed. Of all the shocks and pains that every football season brings, the worst of all is the ending of it. And that is what we face now—this coming Sunday night, in fact, before the midnight bell. There will be no appeal, no extension, no replay. That will be the end of the football season, no matter who complains.

A few geeks will, of course. A few swine always do. No barrel is utterly clean. That would be atmospherically impossible, eh? And rest assured that nothing on this earth is 100 percent clean. Nothing. . . . Are you one of these people who honestly believe that Cats are clean? I hope not, because you are riding for a serious fall. Cats are filthy, and they don't mind passing it around. The smell of a large cat (as in Lion or Tiger) at room temperature in a sea-level house is so powerful and so disorienting as to derail the human brain. The odor of a mountain lion in the wild is far more terrifying than the sight of the beast, even on a frozen night in the snow. It will literally "take your breath away" at 10 or even 20 yards. Your whole nervous system will seize up and be paralyzed, even your lungs. So stay away from all animals that are bigger than you are, especially at night when they are nervous. Even a brown bear will eat your whole body in 24 hours. Beware.

What? Why are we worrying about Bears at this time of year, right on the eve of the Super Bowl? I'll tell you why: because every time I think about New England and Football and Patriotism all at once, I think of Richard Nixon and dangerous wild animals and his lust for unspeakable violence. Nixon was a football fan—and so am I, as it happens, and I can tell you from 44 years of keen observation that us football fans have a way of getting together, no matter where we are.

There is nothing supernatural about it, but I have seen it happen over and over. Football fans share a universal language that cuts across many cultures and many personality types. A serious football fan is never alone. We are legion, and Football is often the only thing we have in common. We recognize each other instantly even if we have to speak in sign language. No doubt it has something to do with the gambling instinct, which is also universal.

The next time you find yourself in need of conversation in some backwoods foreign airport, as I have from time to time, take this tip and look around for the nearest public TV set that is tuned to a football game. That will be your oasis, no matter how long your layover may be. You will get your questions answered.

Gambling is another universal language, along with simple mathematics, cold beer, and wild sex with Jimsonweed. Any traveler who is conversant in these tongues and football too will find friends in any town. Take my word for it.

It goes without saying, of course, that extreme behavior in all these lines is not recommended. Heavy drinking and berserk gambling among strangers will usually lead to trouble on the road, and you want to keep in mind that airport bars are no longer as tolerant as they used to be. Last year's fun is today's crime. Even tying your shoes in an airport can get you locked up.

It will not be long before all major airlines will require all passengers to disrobe and change into standard Hospital gowns before they board a plane. This is already in the planning stage, according to a lawyer from Miami who also assures me that sleeping gas will also be introduced later this year on flights of 40 minutes or longer. "The gas has already been marketed," he said. "Passengers are heavily in favor of it."

"What passengers?" I asked him. "Not football fans on their way to New Orleans, I bet, or people who have to write speeches on airplanes."

"There will be no exceptions," he assured me. "Only uniformed soldiers and police officials licensed to carry concealed weapons."

"That's good," I said. "I have a machine gun license."

"Very Funny," he said. "Don't push your luck these days. That's why we have these new secret prisons."

I hung up and crossed his name off my guest list for the Super Bowl. Nazis are not welcome in this house. They can't be trusted.

So how about the Big Game, sport? Who is going to win?

Who indeed? But if I were a betting man, I would go with St. Louis by 10. I would even go double on that. Why not? It's the last game of the year. I can't lose.

—*January 29, 2002*

Sodomized at the Airport: Are Terrorists Seizing Control of the NFL? And Who Let It Happen?

Recent polls by a secret U.S. government agency indicate that 83 percent of teenage girls in America say they would rather be sodomized at airport Security checkpoints than board a commercial airliner with potential Terrorist passengers who have "not been thoroughly searched for bombs and deadly weapons." More than 90 percent said they were "very frightened by Arabic-looking strangers," and 42 percent said they had "willingly granted sexual favors to uniformed law enforcement officers since September 11, 2001."

—USDD SOURCES

The news out of Washington is getting darker and weirder by the hour. On some days it has the look of a full-bore Terrorist cell operating out of the White House basement, spewing fear and desperation on a nation of suddenly impoverished patriots. Where is Bill Clinton, now that we finally need him?

Where was Mr. Bill at the Super Bowl, now that you mention it? Was he even there? Was he whooping it up with his skull-people? Or was he wallowing lewdly in one of those chic and famous orgies on South Canal Street?

Not on your life, Bubba. Bill Clinton was long gone from

New Orleans by the time the Troops arrived, and the angel of Fun was not with him. He was hunkered down in Beverly Hills with two fat young whores from Oxnard and a heart full of hate for those Texas freaks who scuttled him.

Now, only one year later, the whole country is broke and bogged down in some bogus foreign war that our children will be paying off for another 99 years. Our national economy is in ruins, Harvard-trained crooks have destroyed the roots of investor confidence, public school systems from Maine to California are downsized to death by greedheads, and our baseball-loving President comes back to work after a weekend of unspeakable football adventures with a nasty-looking puncture wound on his face.

Who needs that kind of berserk chickenshit, in this hour of national crisis? It is exactly the kind of sleazy, Third World behavior that we have always denounced as "unacceptably corrupt" when it happens in primitive banana republics like Haiti or South Texas.

Bill Clinton is looking pretty good these days, compared to the criminal craziness of Enron and Wall Street. Good old sex-crazy Bill never asked for any more job-related booty than a high-style Hollywood blow job. You bet—if Clinton could run for President in 2004, he would win handily. We will see. . . .

Meanwhile this blizzard of mind-warping war propaganda out of Washington is building up steam. Monday is Anthrax, Tuesday is Bankruptcy, Friday is Child Rape, Thursday is Bomb scares, etc., etc., etc. . . . If we believed all the brutal, frat-boy threats coming out of the White House, we would be dead before Sunday.

It is pure and savage terrorism in the classic Nazi tradition. Joseph Goebbels would be proud of our bullyboy PsyOps capability today. Goebbels hated Jews, along with everything else he could get his murderous hands on. Down here in the PSYCHOLOGICAL WARFARE COMMAND, we know him as "Dark Joey," the beast who ran Hitler's brutal GESTAPO Secret Über-Police, who feverishly terrorized everybody in Europe back there in the salad days of the Thousand-Year Reich, when uniformed Cops were also public heroes and blond people worshipped Public Sex.

Adolf Hitler was a sports fan. He would have been right at home at the Big Game in New Orleans. It was his kind of Show—Beautiful athletes, savage gladiators, and a monumental display of Military Firepower. That is why our creepy child-president is crying poor-mouth on TV again today, at a National Prayer Breakfast somewhere in the mountains near Pittsburgh. He smiled warmly and spoke in a powerful voice, announcing drastic cuts in every new U.S. category except Military spending and overweening top secret War Emergencies.

Yes sir: it was all guns and no butter when our superfriendly young warrior-president went to market. It was a public feeding frenzy for the global Military-Industrial Complex.

Whoops! That's it for now, folks. The bell has finally rung for this ill-tempered rant. I have to get a grip on myself now—but I will not forget the ugliness of having crazed religious messages from the White House and the FBI jammed into my face when I'm trying to watch a football game. Help. Has the NFL been drafted into the "war effort" now? What kind of horrible experiment are we being subjected to, in the name of Football? Have the whore-hoppers at Fox TV finally run amok like fiendish zombies?

Who is responsible for this Rudeness? What kind of bigoted freak came up with the idea that Terrorizing 200 million football lovers on Super Bowl weekend is "Good for national Security interests"?

That is something that Adolf Hitler might have said in the summer of 1942. . . . And the "Thousand-Year Reich" lasted 12 years and 3 months. *Caveat Emptor.*

terrorism n. *the act of terrorizing; use of force or threats to demoralize, intimidate, and subjugate, esp. such use as a political weapon or policy.*

—WEBSTER'S NEW WORLD DICTIONARY

—*February 11, 2*

Slow Dance in Rap Town

I have abandoned all hope of winning at this amateur farce of a game by now. How low the mighty have fallen. This is like watching a pickup game between convicts in a federal prison: shoot & miss, shoot & miss, shoot & miss—even the CBS gents are sneering as these bums ignominiously kill the clock. These are clearly not championship teams that we are watching.

It has been this way from the start. Where was the confident precision of Duke last year and the year before? Where is the fabled speed of UCLA, or the kinky muscle of Stanford? We miss these things. Nobody is going to get excited about Kansas-Maryland or Indiana-Oklahoma—especially when they are playing lame basketball. These are routine neo-annual clashes between high-profile, big-budget basketball programs, like Ford vs. General Motors. They are embarrassing.

Ed Bradley called on Friday and tried to bully me into another one of my famous doomed bets on Kentucky, but he failed. "Never in hell," I told him. "Not unless I get 11 points." That is precisely the spread that I predicted last week in this column, and I refused to take anything less.

Indeed. This is what my new maturity has done for me. I have learned to never make hysterical last-minute bets on big-time sporting events—unless it is necessary rather than lose the action.

That is exactly the kind of rat-brained, junkie thinking that makes gambling dangerous. You bet. There is a gigantic, life-and-death difference between betting the underdog plus nine points, and the underdog plus 10 or 11. It is the difference between winning and losing, between victory and defeat—between fun and pain, on rainy nights in some cowboy towns—so you want to be thinking clearly when you start dealing in numbers like One or Two.

The final spread in the Kentucky-Maryland game, for instance, was an evil, humiliating 10—which would have been perfect, if I had stuck with my original eleven. But I didn't. I allowed giddiness to take over my brain, just before tip-off, which caused me to get mushy and settle for nine.

How long, O lord, how long?

Surely I was not the only rabid basketball fan to feel joyous at the sight of a taxpayer-funded Marijuana message on all of our TV sets last week, in conjunction with the CBS broadcast of the annual NCAA championship tournament. It was relentless—popping up, as it did, at what seemed like every other time-out or crowded commercial break.

The message itself was terrifying: Marijuana means Death, for You and many others, including the judge and who knows how many U.S. Marines. It is a truly frightening thing to see on your TV basketball screen. One toke over the line is no longer a harmless joke. No sir, it is Felony Terrorism, under this brand-new American Patriot "law" that came in with the new century, the new president, the new morality, etc., etc. . . .

College basketball is riddled with harmless dope-smokers, of course—no worse or better than any other segment of American society. Wow! Maybe that explains the diminishing quality of play in the Big Dance every year. Hell, yes. These freakish young brutes are too stoned to compete in anything more serious than a public sex contest. They are addicts. Their brains have been fried. They are doomed. We have spawned a whole generation of lazy, brain-damaged show-offs.

That is the view from the White House and most of the U.S. Congress these days. It is World War III forever, by the look and the language of it, and the Meanness quotient of the U.S. image in the world is growing logarithmically with every passing day.

Whoops! No more of that stressful gibberish, eh? Exactly. We don't need it. Our world is full of exciting options—the Oscars, spring training, the NBA play-offs, heavy golf, the Gonzo beauty pageant, the War, the Stock market. . . . We are blessed.

The NCAA Tourney is always a time of visions and confusing hallucinations. It is spring and the sap is rising. Every dawn is another righteous challenge, another test of faith, another fateful notch in the national TV ratings.

There is a lot of happy talk on the great American street these days about the "amazing jump" in ratings for the NCAA games this year, but none of it is true. The TV numbers are the same as last year and the year before, which were mediocre.

So rest easy, folks. We have nothing to fear but Fear itself. The Kentucky-Maryland game is cheap history now, and good riddance. Maybe you remember this: 11:43 p.m. Friday. We are nearing the end of the game now, the Terps are up four, Kentucky has croaked, and this may be the sloppiest college basketball game of the year. The shooting is miserable, the passing is rotten, and so far we have seen 28 turnovers. This is embarrassing. "Very uncharacteristic of teams of this caliber," says Jim Nance as Kentucky throws the ball away twice in 30 seconds. I will not watch it on tape or anywhere else. It sucked.

But today is a new world. We are coming up on another Final Four, and I feel the urge to gamble. My pre-Dance bracket sheet shows me with two out of four teams still alive—which is nothing to brag about, but it beats the dim performance of one longtime gambling antagonist (whose name I dare not speak aloud), and I feel vaguely happy about it.

I see Kansas über alles, with Oklahoma as runner-up. Maryland is eminently beatable, and Indiana can't possibly continue to hit all those 3-pointers like they did against Duke and Kent State. The joke is over for those people.

That is how it looks from out here in the Rockies, sports fans. A pretty slow weekend, all in all.

—*March 28, 2002*

Dr. Thompson
in Beirut

ESPN Editor's Note: Dr. Thompson has gone to Beirut for a few weeks, and we will not be able to reach him from time to time, except by personal courier. We still respect him and await his safe return. *Vaya con Dios,* Doc. May the wind always be at your back.

Meanwhile, in the space below, the man utters some random warnings and predictions for those among you who don't mind going out on a limb.

For openers, the Fix is in at Churchill Downs, so adjust your bets accordingly. The Derby itself is always a little suspicious. What would you do, for instance, if you thought you knew that Saturday's KY Derby was going to be won by a colt named "Patriot"?

> A) Buy U.S. War Bonds immediately?
> B) Smell a Rat and call the FBI?
> C) Move to Beirut and grow a beard?
> D) Bet heavily on "Patriot"?—AKA Johannesburg

The answer is D, of course. The Fixed beast will always win, if word comes down from the top. It is a natural law, and in this case it translates to bet Johannesburg Now, while you can still get 50–1 odds. And if you can't find a reliable bookie, find a friend who believes you are honest and thinks he is pretty smart about horses—then fleece the poor bastard just for the fun of it. . . . Hell, bet with two or three good friends who trust you. Why not? They would to the same thing to you, if they knew who was going to win the Derby. Yes sir, this is horse-racing season, and a lot of people are going to get fleeced before it's over. That is what the Sport of Kings is all about.

And now that you mention it, how about this ugly flock of

nags that we have in the Derby this year? What happened to the 2002 crop of thoroughbreds? And why is *Sports Illustrated* saying all those horrible things about Johannesburg? Are they in on the Fix?

My hunch is Yes. They Know something that we don't, and some of their top secret information has leaked out. It says that a cabal of playboy speculators in the racing business have conspired to destroy the Irish colt's reputation (see *S.I.*, April 29, 2002) in public while privately betting him at 50–1, then pump him full of Mandrax on Derby Day and watch him win like the freak he is. The payoff will be $50,000,000,000 cash.

On other fronts—Dallas will whack the Lakers and win the NBA title, the Red Sox will fail spectacularly to win the AL pennant again this year, San Jose will seize the Stanley Cup, and *Sports Illustrated* editor Terry McDonnell will be present in the winner's Circle at Churchill Downs when Johannesburg, the much-maligned beast, gets his collar of roses. . . . And guess who we will see on the cover of *S.I.* next week—yes, it will be good old reliable Johannesburg, the amazing streaker from Ireland. Take my word for it, folks. I know what's happening.

Indeed. I just spoke with McDonnell, and he brazenly confirmed that it's all true. He and 35 staffers will be in the clubhouse at the Derby, and they are all "betting heavily" on Jo-burg.

And that's about it for now, friends. What the hell? I am going to Beirut anyway, so why not kick out the jams. Truth is beauty, beauty truth—that is all ye need to know.

—April 29, 2002

Dr. Thompson Is Back from Beirut

Hi, folks. My name is still Hunter and I am still a fool for football—or maybe just a fool, because last night I had a strange vision that featured Miami and New Orleans playing in Super Bowl XXXVII when (and if) it finally rolls around in February, and I think I saw the Dolphins winning it by a score of 31–17.

How's that for jumping the gun, eh? Some people will call it premature, but not me. A vision is a vision, whether it reveals itself 24 hours ahead of the actual game or 24 months, and I never ignore these creepy little flashes—but I RARELY BET real money on them unless I can get 22–1 odds. . . . That way I can honor just about every vision that comes to me in the course of a season, and still break even.

Ho ho. Don't try this at home, folks—at least not until you have checked your visions against the record for at least 22 years, like I have. The downside in this kind of gambling is that it can mean Grief, humiliation and, in some cases, an agonizing reappraisal of your whole life.

So why am I saying these things? You might ask. If pain has made me so wise, why am I trying to hurt myself again by betting on long shots? Am I a fool?

No. I am a sportswriter and a lifelong football addict—so why not?

That is what I said to my odd neighbor, Omar, last night when we were discussing pro football in my secluded attic office. . . . Omar has been in the neighborhood for a while now, along with his star-crossed little sister, Omin, and they have both become High-end football fanatics who love to gamble (Omar more than Omin, who rarely appears in public and has another home in Big Sur, where she lives in the winter with her family), and Omar has learned enough about the game to gamble shrewdly on most days.

"I will give you 22–1," he said, "but only if you give me the same bet with New England and San Francisco."

"Never in hell," I said.

We finally settled on 15–1, which seemed about right.

"Why Not?" I said. "We have 22 more weeks of football to get through. Hell, we might both be dead from Anthrax by then."

"Nonsense," he said quickly. "But what about the Broncos? Why won't you bet on your homeboys?"

"I will," I replied. "I will bet against them, at 20–1."

Omar's grasp of American football was improving. Two years ago he thought a football was round.

"How did you get so smart so fast?" I asked.

"Well," he said after giving my question some thought. "Maybe it is because I studied American football very intensively for 10 years before I even met you."

I laughed at him. "We will see," I smirked. "I will bet you $100,000 dollars that I will pick more winners than you do this season."

He reached into the pocket of his long black jacket and pulled out a fistful of money. "Yes," he muttered, "I think I have it right here." He smiled faintly and dropped 100 big ones down on the bar.

I was stunned but not entirely surprised by his bold maneuver. "Fair enough," I said. "I will go along with just about anything, in September. Can I give you a cheque?"

"Of course," he chirped. "Money means nothing to me, nothing at all." He paused. "Why are you staring at me like that?"

"Because I hate people like you," I said sharply. "Your instincts are Evil and you are overcharging me for petroleum products." I flashed a grotesque-looking grin at him, a face he had never seen before. "You might get away with that oil rip-off," I told him. "But you will never get away with pretending to know Football. I will beat you like a gong."

Just then a loud knocking came on the front door, and

Omar disappeared out the back. Moments later I heard his gray, high-powered Land Rover disappearing up the road with a dull atavistic roar.

And that was that for last Sunday. Other people came by to try their luck, but they all looked like amateurs compared to Omar.

"Well," I thought, "Buy the Ticket, Take the Ride."

—September 23, 2002

The NFL: We Will March on a Road of Bones

Gambling on the National Football League got off to a slow start out here in the Rockies this season, and nobody blamed it on Baseball—or NASCAR racing either, for that matter, or even the annual Texas-Oklahoma showdown. . . . Not even the LA Lakers opening in Oklahoma City could compete with War, Fear, and Terrorism on the national stage. The Great American appetite for total War seems to have finally triumphed over its love of Sport and Gambling.

I deplore this, but so what? How many Oil Wells do the Denver Broncos own? Or the New York Yankees?

It is nothing, compared to the long-suffering nation of Iraq. That is elementary, Mr. Blue. The USA has dominated Baseball and (U.S.-style) Football from time immemorial, but nobody east of the Hudson seems to care.

*   *   *

Last weekend was a Monster for the NFL and everything it wants to stand for. There were awesome displays of Speed and Violence, on a scale that made baseball look like slow motion. . . . The contrast was day and night. . . . One so-called evening baseball game took four and a half hours, and that was just a run-up to the horrible tedium of the World Series. Which once again is overstaying its welcome. The season should be trimmed back to about 110 games, which would give it a whole new back-to-school DEMOGRAPHIC that would have the baseball season officially over with by Labor Day.

Why not? Baseball is a summertime game, in most all-American towns, and Football is not. The seasonal confusion is only a factor of human Greed. It has that good old familiar odor, the stench of Mendacity, More games = more money. More money = more teams. More teams mean more NFL T-shirts sold and a dark new wave of public lewdness and promiscuity among innocent teenage girls.

There is a rumor around sporting circles in Denver that the Broncos plan to market T-shirts with nipple holes cut in the chest next year, or even this one. . . . But it gets cold out here in the wilderness as autumn wears on. Last night it was 22 degrees F and sinking steadily. Any scheme to sell topless football shirts would meet with public ridicule and rejection, if only because of the Colorado weather. That fine new stadium they have over there may be huge and modern and finely manicured—but it ain't weatherproof; there is no escape from the vicious blizzards and ice storms.

And so much for that, eh? Who needs public lewdness in a time of fear and depression like this? Not me, Bubba. Watching Denver lose to Miami with six seconds to go on Sunday night was hard enough on TV—and hell, we had a big stack of apple-wood burning in the fireplace. . . . I won heavily for the second week in a row, leaving me nicely ahead in the W-L column, but way behind on the total money earnings.

The reason for this, of course, is that people are betting less money on football games this season, because they have less. A broke person doesn't mind making a small bet or two here or there, but a poor person won't, because he can no longer afford to spend cash on anything. He (or she) is far beyond being temporarily "short of cash" in this brutal winter of 2002. . . .

No. That is what "broke" used to mean. But "poor" means permanent.

I have lived through almost 50 pro football seasons, thus far—along with five or six major economic depressions and constant wars all over the world—but I'll be dipped in shit if I can remember a year in the life of this nation that was played out against a bleaker and more ominous historical backdrop than the one we have today.

The quality of the football we see today is no doubt better than ever. The players are bigger, faster, and enormously richer. There are three or four current teams in the NFL that would have visibly intimidated the best teams of yesteryear, including the '85 49ers and the '68 Packers.

Either one of the teams in that bloodcurdling Sunday night game would run away from those sluggards who ruled their roost in the old days. The Dolphins and the Broncos played a genuinely brutal football game that both teams lost. Denver lost on the scoreboard and Miami lost its quarterback, all for a silly little "W" on their record. Both were once-beaten coming in, and now—after inflicting many crippling wounds on each other in public for three ball-busting hours—both Miami and Denver are structurally weaker than they were on Sunday morning. . . . What is a bloody two-point victory worth, if it costs you your starting quarterback and your strong safety for the rest of the season? The Broncos are better off in defeat than the Dolphins are in victory—which is a dismal thing to say about the two best teams in the league at this stage of the season, but it's true. That Sunday night game was qualitatively hurtful on both sides and opened the Super Bowl up, once again, to some squirrelly team like New England or New Orleans. Even the winless St. Louis Rams came out of their injury-plagued funk long enough, last week, to torpedo the unbeaten

Raiders. Both the NFC and the AFC look oddly scrambled this year. We are entering a time of Extreme Parity.

At least the Super Bowl will be better, bigger, and faster than the World Series. Not even George Steinbrenner's deeply tainted millions will keep baseball alive forever. The Yankees' payroll would cover three or four teams in the NFL, maybe 16 or 17, and they are no more dependable than goats when the weather turns cold anyway. Baseballs freeze in the winter, so they can't bounce normally. . . . I know this from horrible experience: I once walked 22 consecutive batters on a chilly night in Taylorsville, Kentucky.

But that is another story, and we will save it for later— maybe for some warm summer night when bands are playing and children shout and perverts work the bathrooms under the bleachers. You bet. That is where baseball belongs.

—*October 14, 2002*

PART THREE

LOVE AND WAR

A Wild & Woolly Tale of Sporting Excess

Okay, boys, this one is going to be short and hopefully quick, because of my wound and the terrible excitement it has generated—along with the grief and the pain and public humiliation. . . . Yes, we are living from one moment to the next tonight in the Chateau Marmont, never knowing if the next word on this page will be the last—for now, at least. . . . Who knows what will happen by midnight?

After my unfortunate encounter with an oddly configured hotel window (now shattered), I lost enough blood yesterday—or was it Friday?—to keep two or three people alive for 22 hours. Or at least it looked that way to the manager and the frightened workers dressed in biohazard suits who were ordered to mop up my blood. The manager wrung his hands and tore his hair when he saw the damage and tried to call an ambulance for me.

Harsh words were spoken, as I recall, and several suites had to be closed off, on a max-capacity weekend. . . . There was a flashy convention of Gucci executives, a movie crew busily filming the last days of Warren Zevon, and a profoundly violent gathering of famous actors and huge dogs who were here to launch the production of a gamey film called *The Rum Diary* in 2003.

This was the reason for my own participation, if only because I wrote the book. Johnny Depp was here, along with Benicio Del Toro, Nick Nolte, and the goofy child prodigy Josh Hartnett of *Black Hawk Down* fame. . . . The idea was to meet and quarrel calmly for two or three days during the final weekend of the World Series.

Events went wildly astray on us—like they did for those

people who went to that theater in Moscow last week expecting to take in a stirring performance of *Nord-Ost*.

Indeed. We are living in unnaturally savage times, folks.

My own individual record for spontaneous blood contribution in public will hopefully stand forever. . . . It was something like 2.4 pints, liberally distributed on the walls of a top-floor suite that need not be identified at this time. . . . It is enough to say that the spectacle was far beyond the visual horrors of anything ever involving my old friend John Belushi or even the Manson family. . . .

Whoops. Strike that. Nobody was killed because of my episode, and the only obvious casualty was me. I was sliced up so grossly that I almost. . . .

What? Get a grip on yourself, Doc! Remember your manners. We are, after all, dealing with longtime friends. . . . Calm down and tell us about Sunday night and the great victory.

But first, let me tell you about this vision I had. Maybe it was all the blood. Who can know for sure about these things.

USC doesn't have the horses, but Carson Palmer deserves the Heisman Trophy. In my vision, Beano Cook is saying he "has no idea who will win the Heisman Trophy this year."

But I do.

Try Carson Palmer from USC, who has a bitching arm and a nice habit of lulling a defense to sleep with normal stuff, and then breaking their backs with long weird strikes to the heart. . . . Sudden death: WHACK! Right down the middle—so fast that it catches you flat-footed, two steps behind and stupid.

Indeed. We have all known that feeling from time to time— even Deion Sanders and Jerry Rice. There will always be somebody faster. But not many. . . . And just about everybody will be significantly slower. Always. Speed is a precious commodity in America.

Carson Palmer, however, is not faster, and USC is nowhere

near unbeaten—which is fatal for the Heisman, I suspect, so he is a very unlikely long shot in December. . . . Miami's hot rod QB, Ken Dorsey, is truly impressive, and no doubt the favorite, but only as long as Miami keeps winning. Dorsey is fast, strong, and scary confident. He is a winner—just like I would be if I played QB behind that offensive line. That is what makes Miami so daunting. They have the horses.

It would be nice to believe in a Miami–Notre Dame finale, but that is probably too much to ask for in these bleak and deadly times.

There are too many bleeding X-factors running around, too many holes in the boat. . . . It makes me oddly nervous today about feeling happy in public. And I don't feel any urge to be 22 years old again.

By Sunday my nerves had gone all to pieces, along with my attitude, and I was sorely in need of a football orgy. The time had come to laugh out loud at something, anything, even a frenzy of subhuman violence like pro football. It was also time to gamble heavily and take long risks for no good reason at all. That is the nature of unacceptably rotten losing streaks.

The first disaster was my own near-death experience with the bloodbath after my hand went through the window and the walls began turning red—a rich crimson as in arterial spurting from what appeared to be my palm. . . . It was more human blood than I had ever seen in my life.

That includes more experience with public bleeding than your average bloodthirsty sports fan will ever conceive of, much less than I would admit—not because I feel guilty about anything, but because I have learned over time that most people simply don't like blood. It is as simple as that.

There may be a nice way to deal with too much blood all at once, but I'm damned if I know what it is. . . . There is vampirism, of course, but I don't recommend it—or anything else that involves uncontrolled bleeding. It is one of those specialties that is best left to the handful of queasy specialists who do it professionally, like combat medics and blood bankers.

Right. And so much for that ghoulish raving, eh? Many worse things happened last week. Washington, DC, was paralyzed by killer snipers who murdered nine or 10 innocent bystanders, Moscow was stunned by another mass slaying of hostages by Russian soldiers, and Sen. Paul Wellstone of Minnesota was killed in a disturbingly familiar plane crash that very nearly included Sen. Ted Kennedy of Massachusetts.

But that is another story, eh? For another time, another place, like they say. . . . Yes, but you don't always get that choice, in the real world. And Sen. Wellstone's death hit the *Rum Diary* Crew especially hard. It would have ruined my weekend, even without the bloodbath. . . . And it utterly destroyed Josh Hartnett, age 21, who was on his way back to Minneapolis to personally campaign for Paul Wellstone when he heard the news of his death. It will be a nasty scar on his brain for the rest of his life.

I know these things. My brain is covered with scar tissue. I was 22 when JFK was murdered, and I will never recover from it. . . . Never. And neither will Josh recover. Take my word for it. Those things are forever.

—*October 29, 2002*

My 49er Habit

Some people called me a fool for betting the 49ers to beat Oakland last week, but they were wrong. It is true that I bleed 49er scarlet and gold on some days, but I am no longer ashamed of it like I was in the good old days when I was trapped in the nasty habit of betting on San Francisco every week like some kind of helpless junkie.

That addiction is still with me to some extent, but it is no longer quite as painful as it was back then when I lived three blocks up the hill from Kezar Stadium.

Freelance writers almost never make enough money to live on, much less ride exotic motorcycles and buy season tickets to 49er games. But I am here to tell you that it can be done—and done without ever resorting to shadowy gigs like pimping or selling drugs. There were times when I was sorely tempted, due to overweening poverty, but I have always believed that any-body with a personal lifestyle as flagrant as mine should have a spotless criminal record, if only for reasons of karma.

I still believe that, and it has served me well and honorably over the years. Knock knock. And I still try to live by it.

But it was not just karma that quasi-justified my spending habits in those wild and elegant years of the middle Sixties. No, there were good reasons. . . . My brand-new silver and red 650 BSA Lightning (the "fastest motorcycle ever tested by *Hot Rod* magazine") was absolutely necessary to my work. Nobody will argue with that. It was the best investment I ever made.

The 49er tickets, however, were a touch more difficult to explain. I was a professional sportswriter, even then, and I have been hopelessly addicted to NFL football ever since I watched the legendary Giants-Colts championship game in 1958—but that was not enough, at the time, to justify spend-ing our rent money on my football habit.

Perhaps there was no justification, but I did it anyway, be-cause I had to. It was necessary to my mental health. . . . My comfortable apartment on Parnassus Hill looked out on the Bay and the Park and the Golden Gate Bridge—and, thusly, straight down on the wretched hulk of Kezar.

Indeed, who could ask for anything more? . . . Ho ho. But we could only see half of the playing field. John Brodie would fade back and throw long to Dave Parks or Gene Washing-ton—and the goddamn ball would disappear in midflight behind the roof of a building. We could hear the roar of the crowd and the howls of despair that usually followed, but we never saw the end of the west-bound play. Never. And that was too painful to live with, too hard on my nerves. So I borrowed enough money from my lawyer to pay for a season ticket. (And thank you again, John Clancy, for the loan.) It was another good investment.

But it took about 20 years to "mature," as they say. It was not until Bill Walsh and Joe Montana came along that the worm turned, and after that came Steve Young and Jerry Rice, along with five Super Bowls, many victory celebrations, and the delicious habit of winning, which I highly recommend.

And that—to make a long story short—is why I bet heavily on San Francisco to beat Oakland last week. The 3 points helped, but in truth I honestly believed, in the pit of my gambler's heart, that the 49ers would Win, and that is why I bet on them.

It was a vicious game, and by the time it was over I was ready to sic the Hell's Angels on that flaky punk of an EP kicker. That swine. If the Raiders had won in OT, Al Davis would be ordering a new Mercedes 500SL to send Jose Cortez for Christmas. . . . The game was that important for Oakland, especially with the hated Denver Broncos coming up next.

The spread should be about six for that one. And the Broncos are riding high. . . . But what the hell? I'll take Oakland and six anyway. It will be life or death for the Raiders—and if it's not snowing in Denver on Monday night, I suspect they will win.

Probably not, but those six points are what this business is all about. . . . And so long for now, folks. I have to get to bed so I can go into town tomorrow and vote. That is another habit I recommend. It ain't much, but it's the only weapon we have against the Greedheads. *Mahalo.*

—*November 4, 2002*

Don't Let This
Happen to You

There were some very weird football games on Sunday—amazing comebacks, stunning failures, and one stupefying tie in Atlanta that turned out to be my only win of the day. It was the ugliest thing I ever saw. . . . And ye gods, I have another game coming up within hours, and I fear it. Perhaps the time has come to give up gambling.

What? No. That would be impossible. It would be like donating all my blood to a charity event. Without gambling, I would not exist.

Right. And so much for psychomedical gibberish, eh? Let's get back to the real reason for my degrading streak of dumbness that has brought me so low. . . . It was hashish, a vile and dangerous resin that can be ruinous or even fatal if it ever gets mixed up with significant gambling decisions.

Indeed. I know this from profoundly negative experience. Even secondhand hashish smoke can tip your mental balance in painful ways. . . . This is what happened to me when I placed my Bets on Saturday. I was ripped to the teats on secondhand hashish smoke, and I made a fool of myself. I also lost so many greenback dollars that I was reduced to paying off with cardboard IOUs before the game even started.

So what? you might say. It can happen to anybody, and it does. Disaster goes with the territory in this business. You just don't want to make a habit of it.

I have nobody to blame but myself, of course, and I have long preached that Dumbness deserves no sympathy—but in my heart I believe that what happened to me could happen to any one of us, at any time, so I guess the moral of this story is Don't let this happen to you.

Not *all* of my choices on that day were the direct result of my drug experience. A few were based on entirely logical assessments of the teams and the point spreads. . . . What kind of squandering jackass, for instance, would have risked real money on the giddy idea that the flaky Indianapolis Colts would beat the living snot out of the Philadelphia Eagles? It was so unlikely and so shocking that I would have been embarrassed to be seen betting on it in public.

The final score was 35–13 for Peyton Manning and my man, Marvin Harrison, who ran wild on the vaunted Eagles' defense. At the end of three quarters, the score was 28–6 and Donovan McNabb had piled up 199 yards of total offense. It was pitiful.

Just then the phone rang: it was Warren Zevon, calling for advice on how to deal with Donald Rumsfeld, our Secretary of Defense. "He keeps calling me," he said. "But he never says why. It's giving me the creeps. I'm afraid to answer the phone."

"Don't worry," I told him. "I know Don. We were in the Nixon Wars together. I recognize his footprints. This is just another publicity stunt for his new image, as a closet rock & roll guy."

"That is bullshit," he said. "He's a cold-blooded monster. I used to date his daughter." He chuckled. "That's why he's calling me. He wants revenge."

"You are right," I said. "He heard you were dying, and he wants a piece of your ass before you go. He Wants to be known as your buddy."

"That swine!" Warren snapped. "I don't have time for him now. I'm in the studio with Bob Dylan every day. Tell him I'll see him in hell."

"Don't get sentimental on me," I said. "I just got wiped out on my football bets. I was humiliated. I lost everything!"

"Yeah," he replied. "How about them Rams? Was that a beautiful game, or not?"

"Not." I said. "I had the Chargers and three. Yes. I also had Miami plus two and a half. My own editor beat me like a gong. He keeps betting the Jets and the Giants, and they both keep covering."

"Why don't you quit gambling?" he said. "You are turning into a loser."

I hung up on him and went back to analyzing the scores and the numbers, trying not to sink into a coma of grief and loss. . . . Why had Warren refused to let me tell my story about Princess Omin and my accidental dose of secondhand hashish smoke? And about why I lost all my bets? What was wrong with him? Nobody wanted to hear it. All they wanted to do was laugh at me. Hell, I never dated Donny Rumsfeld's daughter. All I did was follow those tire tracks in the snow until they went straight off the cliff—so I stopped my Jeep to investigate. . . . Ah, but that is another story and we don't have time for it now.

—November 11, 2002

Grantland Rice Haunts the Honolulu Marathon

I was deeply engrossed in the Tampa–New Orleans game on Sunday night. They were locked in one of those "classic defensive struggles" that Grantland Rice used to write about—in the good old days, before he turned queer.

That's what the sportswriters said, anyway, but who knows? I knew Grant, from a chance meeting in my childhood, and he never seemed weird to me . . . but rather like some old and mysterious uncle who took his work so seriously that we rarely saw him, except for times like the Derby or the frantic week of the SEC basketball tournament, when Kentucky was riding high and I would see him out playing golf in Cherokee Park.

We knew him as "Mr. Rice" in those days, and we knew that he did some kind of extremely important work that may or may not have had something to do with sports, but we never quite knew what it was—and because of that, we were vaguely afraid of him. Mr. Rice told good sports stories, and he had a friendly way of putting his hand on your shoulder or your arm when he talked to you—and he would stare right at you when he talked, so you had to pay close attention to everything he said.

Indeed. There was something distinctly sinister about "Uncle Grant," as he liked to be called, and I kind of liked him for it. He was suave, in a sentimental way that seemed to reek of heavy drama and dangerous, romantic adventures involving secret murder and violence and desperate foreign intrigues that would forever be unspoken, at least by him. He was far too professional to go around babbling and bragging about this se-cret life or what he really did for a living. We had no need to know, anyway. Hell, we were just a bunch of curious neighbor-hood kids who called themselves the dreaded Hawks A.C.

We were powerful, back then. We controlled a vast terri-tory that stretched from Cherokee Park all the way down to the Municipal Armory in downtown Louisville, only a few blocks from the river, and I think this is why Mr. Rice seemed to like us, and even respect us on some days. . . .

He was extremely helpful, for instance, in getting some kind of official sanction that allowed us to do our own little shootaround drills at halftime and between games at the SEC tournament—on the court and using official game balls from the teams who were playing that day, or night: maybe Georgia vs. Alabama, maybe LSU vs. the mighty Kentucky Wildcats, who were riding very high in those days. We mingled with the players and retrieved loose balls that went into the crowd, we hung around the Press table with Uncle Grant and his friends,

or sometimes we would climb the long narrow ladder up to the
TV booth, far above and behind the feverish fans in the wooden
seats below. We more or less had the run of the place, as they
say, and we tried hard not to abuse our inexplicably privileged
situation.

Wow! Those really were the good old days, eh? That kind of behavior today, in 2002 America, would get you locked up by
some quasi-legal Military Tribunal in a cage at Guantánamo
Bay . . . and it was not that long ago, either: barely 20 years
since the days when people could speak openly to each other
without fear of the police and wander around freely, wherever
they wanted to, as long as they weren't hurting anyone else,
when a nationwide panic like the one we have today was inconceivable, when some hideous bogeyman like "War on Terrorism" would have seemed more like a vengeful Communist
Plot than like something that could ever happen in the good
old USA.

Whoops. I seem to be wandering here, so let us drag ourselves from those innocent days of yesteryear and confront the
terrifying reality of NOW, today, in these grim years of the
post-American century, to wit: I lost all my bets on the once-
proud Tampa Bay Buccaneers, along with five or six other
games, and these dumbfounding losses plunged me into such a
fit of melancholy that I almost canceled my trip to Hawaii this
week for the 30th annual running of the weird and dangerous
Honolulu Marathon, which will happen on this coming Sunday, December 8—exactly the same day as the final deadline
for declaring War on Iraq and also the last day of existence for
the debt-ridden hulk that was once United Airlines. . . . And all
of these ominous developments, taken together, mean certain
disaster for millions of people all over the world.

That is when being stranded in Hawaii, with no money and
no way to get off the islands for what may be the rest of your
life, will look like paradise on earth, compared to what the rest

of the world will be enduring. It will be like a series of horrible earthquakes with an epidemic of Dengue Fever occurring in slow motion all over the world in the same week. Not unlike the Book of Revelation, now that you mention it. When Hell erupts out of the earth and the four Horsemen of the Apocalypse ride everywhere, everywhere, with permanent flood tides of blood and filth and murder that will destroy our lives forever—

Right, and so much for that, eh? You bet, so lighten up with your preaching, Doc. Just why have you decided to fly to a profoundly remote island in the central Pacific Ocean that is probably closer to North Korea than it is to Beverly Hills and which is guaranteed to be one of the most unhappy places in the world to be when the sun comes up over Waikiki Beach on Sunday morning? If you don't get your legs blown off by an airport bomb, you will be taken into custody by military police and held for further questioning as a suspected terrorist sympathizer with no local address and no apparent reason or purpose or even a good excuse for being there at all.

That is where the fun starts, but not for you. No. You will be treated like a spy from somewhere on the Axis of Evil, until you can prove otherwise. . . . That is when you will find out how many friends you have left.

So that's about it, folks, for the reasoning behind my tortured decision to fly with Anita to Honolulu tomorrow to participate, with many of our friends, in the oppressively lewd spectacle that is called the infamous Honolulu Marathon, which I have "covered" in my fashion for something like 21 years and never been disappointed by.

"Why are we doing this again?" I asked Anita as we packed for the trip. "Are we stupid? Don't you remember what happened last year?"

"Of course I do," she replied. "But I want to go anyway. We must go. I crave it. I want to lounge on the balcony, and swim with the dolphins, and drive naked across the mountains in a silver convertible with Don Ho crooning on the radio. . . ."

"Hot damn," I said quickly. "I must have flipped out from massive stress for a minute when I was even thinking about canceling this assignment. I too crave the wonderful excitement of the race, and the rain beating down, and running along Kahala Avenue in the tightly packed mob of naked strangers who are all whacked on Ephedrine and crazed by too many pheromones in the air above the mob and the race and the mainly fanatical spectators who line all 26 miles of the race. And we will be there at the finish line, me and Mr. Rice."

—December 4, 2002

Honolulu Marathon Is Decadent and Depraved

Trouble can come at you from any direction these days, like being chased through a crowded parking lot by a pack of vicious stray dogs, knowing they want to kill you, but not knowing why—or being hit by a wing that has just fallen off a military jet plane that ran out of gas and exploded. . . . The world situation has become so nervous and wrong that disasters that would have been inconceivable two years ago are almost commonplace today. They are not our fault, to be sure, but still we live in fear of them—and so do professional athletes.

I learned these things and many others on my recent assignment to Hawaii, where I did some special coverage of the

Marathon and evaluated some of the newest Nike equipment, along with my usual public muttering, intense listening, and distended body shots in the evening, when the sun sank toward Japan. . . . On these nights I spoke extensively with players, coaches, and one University president who must confront and cope with the fears of modern athletes on an almost daily basis.

My old friend June Jones, head football coach at the state university, told me more and more of his younger players are plagued with a genuine fear of dogs.

"Dogs?" I said. "That's weird—these islands are full of dogs, thousands and thousands of them."

Hawaii's football team isn't a dog anymore, thanks to June Jones. "I know," he replied. "They are like cockroaches, I hate the bastards."

I laughed. "Don't be silly, June," I warned him. "Are you trying to tell me that the University of Hawaii football program has languished for all these years because the players are afraid of dogs?"

"Oh, no," he said quickly. "Not just dogs—about half my freshmen believe they'll be killed if they ever fly on an airplane."

"What's so weird about that?" I snapped.

He stared at me for a few seconds, saying nothing, and then he turned away.

I wanted to tell him that I was just kidding about the UH football program languishing (the exact opposite is happening, in fact: Hawaii has the look of a school on a fast track to becoming a major football power—but more on that later), but just then I was seized by two very small women from Russia who laughed and said they had something to show me.

Which was true. They had a gold Russian coin with my face on it. I was stunned and even shocked, but not for long. Of course, these were Marathon winners, wild girls from St. Petersburg who won here last year, extremely impressive little beauties who had made such a fool of me then. I knew their names, but this incredible gold coin had momentarily scrambled my brain.

"Don't worry," the more aggressive one told me gently. "We forgive you. Meet me at the finish line tomorrow and I will give you a big Russian kiss."

"Where is Sean Penn?" asked the other. "I want to kiss him too."

"Forget it," I told her. "Sean has gone to Iraq, maybe forever."

"So what?" said the first girl. "Who needs a screwhead like Sean Penn? I would rather kiss a dog."

I smiled and wished them good night, so we could all get a few hours' sleep before the big race. It was getting late in balmy Honolulu.

We arrived at the starting line sometime around 4 in the morning—one hour before starting time—but the place was already a madhouse. Half the runners had apparently been up all night, unable to sleep and too cranked to talk. The air was foul with the stench of human feces and Vaseline. By 5 o'clock huge lines had formed in front of the bank of chemical privies set up by Marathon President Doc Barahal and his people. Prerace diarrhea is a standard nightmare at all marathons, and Honolulu is no different. There are a lot of good reasons for dropping out of a race, but bad bowels is not one of them. Will they finish? That is the question. They all want that "finishers" T-shirt. Winning is out of the question for all but a handful: Mbarak Hussein, Jimmy Muindi . . . Ondoro Osoro maybe. These are the racers. For them, this is a race.

The others, the runners, were lined up in ranks behind the racers and it would take them a while to get started. The top Kenyans were halfway finished, running four abreast, before the back of the pack of 30,000 tossed their Vaseline bottles to the side and passed the starting line and they knew, even then, that not one of them would catch a glimpse of the winner until long after the race was over. Maybe get his autograph at the banquet.

We are talking about two distinct groups here, two entirely

different marathons. The Racers would all be finished and half drunk by 8 in the morning, or just about the time that the pack was pouring through the halfway point. The pros run smoothly, almost silently, with a fine-tuned stride. No wasted energy, no fighting the street or bouncing along like a jogger. These people flow, and they flow very fast. Watching the Racers race is like watching Kobe Bryant in the open court or Michael Vick turning the corner. Each one of them is literally one in a billion. A Racer in full stride is an elegant thing to see.

The marathon has become too big for the original group to handle; it is now the fourth largest in the world. When I first came to cover the spectacle in December of 1980, there were 8,000 runners. Today there are more than 30,000—10,000 more than last year alone. The small group of individuals who have run this race for years are overwhelmed, and the strain is obvious. This year the race brought in more than $62.5 million to the local economy, the bulk of which is spent on painkillers and bottled water.

Marathon running, like golf, is a game for players, not winners. That is why Callaway sells golf clubs and Nike sells running shoes. But running is unique in that the world's best racers are on the same course, at the same time, as amateurs, who have as much chance of winning as your average weekend warrior would of scoring a touchdown in the NFL.

There are 30,000 of them now and they are all running for their own reasons. And this is the angle—this is the story: Why do these buggers run? What kind of sick instinct, stroked by countless hours of brutal training, would cause intelligent people to get up at 4 in the morning and stagger through the streets of Honolulu for 26 ball-busting miles in a race that less than a dozen of them have any chance of winning? This is the question we have come to Hawaii to answer—again. They do not enter to win. They enter to survive, and go home with a T-shirt. That was the test and the only ones who failed were those who dropped out.

There is no special T-shirt for the winner, but there is a

$40,000 check. In the end the Kenyan men swept the first four spots and it was all East Africans until the Japanese placed eight through 15. Hussein held off Jimmy Muindi to win by four seconds at 2:12:29—a pace of 5:03.2 per mile. Muindi ran at a pace of 5:03.4 per mile. To lose a 26-mile race by 4 seconds would be more than most of us could bear, but these men simply pack up and get ready for the next race. On the women's side, the top three places were taken by Russians. The winner was Svetlana Zakharova, who surged past Albina Ivanova, the Russian national record holder, in the 25th mile to win in 2:29:08. I do not know the connection between Kenyan men and Russian women.

At the postrace awards dinner at the Outrigger Canoe Club, one of the Ethiopian women was offering around a blue plastic gasoline jug of special homemade Ethiopian liquor. It was an iffy proposition. It tasted recently distilled. I recognized the taste as being very close to white lightning, Kentucky mountain moonshine, what we used to call thunder road whiskey.

It is not really the most logical thing to do—akin to accepting cocaine in an airport bathroom from a stranger—but in the scale of things, drinking it seemed like the most normal thing to do.

—*December 16, 2002*

Public Shame and Private Victory

I would like to take as much personal credit as possible for the San Francisco 49ers' mind-shattering victory over those poor bastards from New York last Sunday, but alas, I cannot. It would be like Jack Nicholson beating his chest and bragging/ boasting that he alone was responsible for the Lakers' last three NBA titles.

Jack would never do that, of course. He is an honorable man and a totally loyal Lakers fan. He would never think of betraying them and calling them "doomed" just prior to another doomsday play-off with the Sacramento Kings—never bet against them in public or scorn their genetic makeup, never curse them on the Internet or announce on TV that he was switching his love to the Clippers from now on. No. Jack is a decent person.

Indeed. And I, apparently, am not. Because I did all those hateful, treacherous things to the 49ers last week, and I did them as publicly as possible. . . . I raved, I babbled, I even threatened to piss down their spines to consummate our divorce.

It was horrible, frankly, and I was deeply embarrassed by it on Sunday when San Francisco erupted from out of the bowels of footballs' foulest graveyard to play 20 minutes of the finest and bravest and most beautiful come-from-behind football in 49er history, to beat the crazed and bewildered Giants by one truly desperate point, 39–38.

It was incredible, incredible. I came very close to going crazy toward the end. All around me, people were screeching and weeping and hammering on the bar like victims about to be executed. They were Giants backers, not just fans or fun bettors. No. They were Players, high rollers, serious, hard-bitten people who had come from both coasts of America, England, Poland, and even Switzerland for this annual orgy of gambling on the NFL play-offs. . . . These people have been here before, they know the rules: Unlimited betting, no violence, with no mercy expected and none given. *Caveat Emptor.*

It would not be fair, at this point, to continue this thorny saga without confessing that I had, in fact, bet heavily on the Giants to Lose by no more than three points. Ho ho. That's one way of putting it, anyway. Yes sir, I was wise, I was suave and shrewd to figure out some way to win my bet and remain faithful to the 49ers at the same time.

But that would be a lie, eh? Right. So let's have a look at what I was saying about the 49ers this time last week. To wit:

In a column titled "Death of the 49ers," I said, "They will go nowhere in the play-offs. . . . They are a puffball team with no soul and the Giants will beat them like sick rats. . . . I piss down the spines of the craven 49ers."

Wow. That is horrible, eh? That is really stupid, vengeful stuff. That is ugly and wrong. It sounds like something you'd hear out of some sleazy drunken sot. It is embarrassing.

I will not comment on that—but I will say that I owe the San Francisco 49ers a profoundly sincere Apology for that berserk outburst. It was rude, and cruel, and degrading—and most of all, it was Wrong, disgracefully wrong, dismally Wrong, painfully Wrong. . . . I fouled myself by saying it, I humiliated my family. They shunned me like some kind of filthy stinking animal with evil in its heart, and I suffered.

Hot damn! I feel wonderful now. I feel beautiful and pure, now that I finally got that dumb bitch of a Shame off my chest. I feel like my old self again, only better—and I did, of course, Win so many, many complex Bets that day that I felt like a combination of Bill Walsh and Genghis Khan. It was like winning some kind of brutal lottery, where the winner gets obscenely rich and all the losers get castrated. I felt almost Holy.

Ah, but those suckers are gone now (except for one or two that I look forward to fleecing again, this week) and things have calmed down around here, if only for a few nervous days, and then it will start building again. . . . This is a hard life, out here in the wilderness, but it is all we really know, so we do the best we can, and we cope with it pretty well.

Which reminds me that I also won heavily with the Jets and the Falcons on Saturday. Heavily. You bet. Those foreigners got what was coming to them, this time around. Their luck ran out. They lost everything, and we had no pity on them. It was fun.

In one high-visibility situation, Anita flogged the arrogant Ewing brothers from Charleston so smoothly and so cruelly that they lost control of themselves. They had given NY plus 3, and by halftime they were gloating and flouncing around the room like rich peacocks. It was disgusting. I was tempted to give both of them a taste of my 225,000-volt safety stick that I use against intruders—right then these two pompous bastards were looking very much like nasty intruders to me. . . . But cooler heads prevailed, and the second half got under way without incident.

The score went from bad to worse almost instantly. The Giants scored easily, making a mockery of the SF pass defense. The score was 38–14, and the Giants were just getting warmed up. I could see 55 or even 66 lurking just around the corner. The 49ers seemed beaten, and bored. I gritted my teeth and began chain-smoking cigars, good cigars, just to keep my nerves calm and my temper deeply concealed.

The game was interrupted now and then by White House–inspired commercials showing half-naked children smoking dope and killing each other with guns, or murdering a judge in Turkey, because stupid little Henry over here got weak and smoked a joint. . . . that Fool! He was just another useless victim of the War on Terrorism.

But so what? Wild things were happening on the TV screen. Suddenly the crowd was screaming and whipping on each other as the hapless 49er offense suddenly came alive like rock lizards. The lifeless worm of yesteryear was turning into an invincible golden snake with countless arms and legs. They were terrifying.

And the rest is History, folks—it was like seeing the Frankenstein monster come alive with a brain full of lightning. The Giants were ripped to shreds. They were utterly demoralized. It was pitiful. They were like helpless bums being chewed up and spit out, right in front of our eyes. They withered and turned to jelly. I felt sorry for the poor fools.

Okay. In closing, I'll take Atlanta and Tennessee on Saturday—San Francisco and Oakland on Sunday. That's it for now.
Mahalo.

—*January 7, 2003*

Shooting the Moon with the Raiders

I was just settling down to watch the horrible 49er game on
Sunday when a meteor crashed into a deserted pasture somewhere above my house and all the lights went out. My first
thought was that somebody in the neighborhood had touched
off an underground nuclear device, or maybe it was another
earthquake, like the one that hit San Francisco during the 1989
World Series.

I felt the house shudder for a few seconds, but there was not
much real noise—just a big Thump, then nothing. . . .

"What the hell was that?" said the Sheriff, coming up from
an underground sheep laboratory. "Are you people doing some
shooting up here?" he asked. "I just felt some kind of tremen-
dous impact shock. It felt like a plane crashing."

"So what?" I giggled. "The game is starting. Nothing else
matters now. The joke is over."

Indeed. The mob in the not-quite-sold-out coliseum was
whipping itself into a frenzy as the Raiders took the field
and began strutting and strolling around on the sideline and
snapping footballs back and forth to each other, not talking
much, just looking cool and acting sinister like any other gang
of extremely high-priced, fine-tuned assassins on a big day at

work. . . . Near one end of the Raiders bench, Jerry Rice prac-
ticed sprinter starts and quick bursts of speed, then flapped
his hands crazily to loosen them up. It is a trick I use frequently, for the same reason, and I recommend it highly.

We had just suffered through another shameful, weak-
minded performance by the chicken-crap 49ers. Their season
came to a dismal end at the hands of the hard-rocking Tampa
Bay Buccaneers, 31–6. It was horrible. I took one long, last look
at that crowd of pampered, neurotic little bastards who have
meant so much to my professional fortunes for so many years—
and I regretfully said, "So long, you swine. I'm moving my act
across the Bay to Oakland, where we still know how to win."

You bet, buster. That Tampa game was so disgusting that I
turned in my badge. It was humiliating. I wanted to hurt somebody. "Where is Al Davis tonight?" I said to Anita. "I want to be
with him."

"No, you don't," she said firmly. "You'd better start concen-
trating on this game, or these gamblers are going to make a
whimpering fool out of you. They still hold a grudge from what
happened last year, when they pushed themselves to the brink
of their own possibilities, only to be chopped off at their knees
at the last moment, and they are still bitter about it."

"Are those creepy bastards finally out of the valley?" asked
the Sheriff. "I can never relax until they leave town."

"Then stay on your toes," I warned him. "Only one of them
left. The other one will be here any minute, and he's all cranked
up about being fleeced."

Just then the creepy Ewing brother walked briskly into the
room, wearing his usual polo outfit and smacking his boot
with a stiff leather crop. "Are you boys ready to kick ass today?"
he snapped. "Are you ready to take a Beating?"

"You bet," I said calmly. "I, for one, am resigned to a terrible
beating today. I crave it."

He nodded happily. "We will bet heavily on every play, for
this game—every pass, every kick, every fumble. I want to see
money moving around this room like a high-speed cockfight."

"Don't worry," I said. "Some people are going to be hurt badly today, and I may be one of them. Did you hear what happened to the Raiders' quarterback?"

"No," he said eagerly. "What happened to him?"

"He broke his thumb in a car accident," the Sheriff said mournfully. "He is out for the year."

"Wonderful," he chuckled. "Then so are the Raiders. They don't have a chance."

"Yeah," I agreed. "Too bad I am already stuck with them. I guess I'll need some points, now that Gannon is out."

There was a moment of tense silence in the room, then he screeched at me & shook his fist. "Points?" he yelled. "Points? Are you crazy? Only a jackass would give you Oakland with points!"

I shrugged and laughed it off. "Okay," I said finally. "What the hell? Why not? Forget the points—I'll take it even."

Just then the Raiders kicked off & the game was under way. No more haggling. He nodded quickly at me but said nothing. It was a deal.

Indeed. And the rest is history, folks. It turned out that I didn't need those points, after all. . . . The halftime score was 10–10, and the Jets were looking good—so we doubled up/down and prepared for a long afternoon of raw, teeth-gritting suspense.

"Hot damn!" said the Sheriff. "We have a real humdinger on our hands, don't we? This thing will almost certainly go into Overtime, maybe two overtimes. We might be here far into the night—and never mind those rumors about a meteorite. We don't need it now."

The polo prince was deeply committed to the Jets now and he was feeling pretty uppity about it. "How are you feeling now, tough guy?" he sneered at me. "Are you ready to be wiped out? Are you ready to suffer?" He smiled smugly and raised a bottle of sweet gin to his lips, smacking his boot again. . . . He had weathered the shock of Rich Gannon starting the game at quarterback, and now he was riding high, preparing to seize what would soon be his. "I've been waiting a long time for this," he muttered. "The Raiders are doomed."

I nodded sadly but said nothing. Anita laughed at me for being such a loser—but she had also bet on Oakland. Ho ho.

Well—what else can I say about it, without totally shedding my modesty and appearing to be unacceptably greedy and cruel? Why discuss it? Nobody needs that kind of rudeness.

Of course Oakland won handily. The final score was 30–10. The Jets got run out of town. They couldn't handle the pressure and went all to pieces in the fourth quarter. Their boy-wonder quarterback got swatted around like a Ping-Pong ball and the crowd began to hoot at them, causing their nerves to crack, and the Raiders ran wild toward the end. It was a massacre.

This Raiders team is the real thing. I have been saying that ever since they beat San Francisco and Denver, back to back, to end their demoralizing streak of losses about halfway through the season. . . . Gannon will slice up the slower Tennessee secondary this week and Oakland will go into the Super Bowl as a 5-point underdog to the Eagles, and after that it is out of my hands. Who knows? That is what gambling is all about. Ho ho ho. So let us rumble, young man, rumble. Good luck.

—January 13, 2003

The Last Super Bowl

Wartime Super Bowls are always dismal and lame—if they happen at all, in fact—because of "tragic National Security disasters that we cannot, of course, disclose to you at this time, because of etc., etc., etc." Alas, I know that story well. It happens every time you find a huge police agency seizing control of all sporting events, in this country or any other.

Indeed. But that is what happens in Wartime, eh? Yes sir, the War Machine comes in and takes whatever measures are Necessary to make sure our boys have plenty of bombs, wherever they happen to be. Sacrifice, sacrifice, sacrifice. . . . Hot damn, there's a war on, Bubba. That's for sure—but at least it won't happen until the day after the Super Bowl—and that is when the shades will come down. Beyond that, Nobody knows. It will all be up in the air.

So we should all take a nice long look at the *big game* on Sunday in San Diego—because it may be the last one we'll see for a while, at least until the War ends. . . . Ho ho. That is a nasty thought, as thoughts go, but it is the melancholy truth. Certainly it will be the last peacetime Super Bowl for another five years, maybe more. . . . But by then we will all be wearing uniforms, of one kind or another, and only the "Trusted Travelers" among us will be allowed to come and go as we please—within reasonable military limits, of course, as long as we don't make waves and never gather in groups of more than three, and don't spit.

Whoops! Why are we drifting into negativity here at this hour, with the final game of the season about to happen and the war about to start? Never mind that morbid gibberish about—

"You know what?" the Sheriff interrupted. "The last place in the world I'd want to be this weekend is San Diego. It will be like hell on earth."

"Not for the Oakland Raiders," I said. "They will be on top of the world, such as it is."

"That's what I mean," he said. "The Raiders will have fun. All the others will suffer. They will all be detained, or locked up for military crimes. Military crimes. Military police, military tribunals. Military justice—Get used to it. That is the Military way."

I agreed and quickly changed the subject. "How many draft picks did the Raiders get for Jon Gruden?" I wondered aloud.

"Many," said a voice from behind me. "They also got enough money to pay off many signing bonuses. Al Davis will rule forever."

Which may be true. The Raiders dynasty is already a fact, whether they win or lose on Sunday, and the dynasty is moving in full harvest mode. Stand back. Prepare to salute and pay tribute. . . . That is how Davis and his people are seeing it, anyway, and I think I agree with them. This is a serious football team, folks.

Which is not to say that Tampa Bay is not. No sir. But the Oakland Raiders are serious in a different way. They're deadly serious, and you can take that for whatever it seems to mean. They are assassins, in a word, and they have everything they need in their arsenal: extreme speed, beautiful talent, smart coaching, preternaturally fine chemistry, and a rare level of individual intelligence among players. . . . This is a high-class unit, exactly the kind of team you would buy for yourself if you wanted to win a Super Bowl. Tampa Bay's chances of winning the game on Sunday are about one in five hundred. You're welcome.

I might be wrong, of course. I might be wrong. Hell, that's always possible. Nobody can win all the time. That would be fishy. It would mean that something is wrong with the system. Why bet on a fixed game? That is nonsense, of course. The Super Bowl can never be fixed—not in Peacetime, anyway, and even if it was, I would never offer to bet on the Raiders and give 500–1 odds. Not on the Internet. That would be illegal and probably insane. Think of the trouble I would have in collecting on my bets, eh? Or paying off. Wow. That would be horrible, truly horrible, like a plague of lizards and leeches fighting all around you on the ground. These rodents are always in heat.

Whoops. Strike that. Leeches are not rodents. They are bloodsucking members of the Hirudinea class, a subspecies of the hermaphroditic sucker worm that is frequently applied to headache victims and other human sufferers. Leeches used in human treatment range in size from three inches to thirteen inches when fully bloated. They have two ugly mouths, one on each end, filled with tiny, razor-sharp teeth by which they attach themselves firmly to the flesh, prior to sucking. The leech has many eyes.

The Oakland Raiders are the only team in football that still routinely uses leeches for treatment of serious injuries. It is an old-timey medicine, deriving no doubt from the team's Bay Area roots, with its powerful Italian community and its many neighborhood grocery stores and exotic foreign delicacies, along with sausage, fresh fish, and leeches. . . . I have many fond memories of hanging out in North Beach at elegant Italian restaurants with Raiders players in the good old days of yesteryear, when the silver and black dynasty was just getting started, long before they turned into the gigantic, high-powered winning machine that they are today.

Things were different in those years, but they were never dull. Every game was a terrifying adventure, win or lose, and the Raiders of the seventies usually won—except in Pittsburgh, where cruel things happened and many dreams died horribly. You could see the early beginnings of what would evolve into the massive Raider Nation, which is beyond doubt the sleaziest and rudest and most sinister mob of thugs and wackos ever assembled in such numbers under a single "roof," so to speak, anywhere in the English-speaking world. No doubt there are other profoundly disagreeable cults that meet from time to time in most of the 50 states. . . .

But so what? There is nothing more to say. I have obviously made my decision about the Raiders. They are simply a better football team than the Buccaneers, and they will win. A realistic line for this game would be 10 or 11, but right now it is hovering around 5 or 6.

In the end it won't matter. It will be like a track meet for tall people. Good luck, and remember this: if the Raiders lose, I will appear on national TV with big leeches all over my head and a formal confession to read. I will be ashamed of myself for being such an ass.

Indeed. But that is the nature of gambling, eh? That is why we do it. Ho ho. That is why we call it fun.

—*January 20, 2003*

Extreme Behavior in Aspen

Last week was a monster for the snowbound city of Aspen, which definitely needed the action. The merchants were crazy for it. . . . Hot damn! Yes sir! The X Games were coming to TOWN!—and a huge crowd of genuinely Wild boys was coming with them. Ho ho. Early estimates said there would be about 40,000 of them, all ripped to the tits on their *own* adrenaline and craving an orgy of speed. The weekend was going to be *crazy*, they said. The whole town was braced for it.

Why not? I thought, let's have a look at these games, this terrifying spectacle of risk and extreme danger that ESPN brings to town every year, along with TV crews and reporters and grifters and work crews and Security specialists who had been here all week. The whole valley was seething with excitement, as if the Olympics were coming to town.

"Let's get weird today," I said to Anita somewhere around dawn on Saturday. "I feel like whooping it up today—and besides, we have a professional duty to cover these games." I smiled lazily and tried to cheer her up. "I am a sportswriter, remember? Yes, and these X Games are definitely Sports. It will be a madhouse, a huge and feverish mob. I can hardly wait."

She stared at me for a long moment and then screamed, "You fool! Are you crazy? You have to speak at the Antiwar rally today. You are the main speaker. Get a grip on yourself," she said. "The Sheriff will be here to pick us up at three o'clock. What shirt will you wear?"

"What?" I screeched. "What are you talking about? I was thinking about wearing my police uniform and a wig, in order to mingle in peace with the cranked-up crowd and have a few speedy conversations with strangers."

And then I remembered. "Of course! The Rally, the marchers! . . . I must have been drinking last night," I muttered.

"Why is this happening?" I felt my confidence oozing away as I looked at the situation. In a matter of hours, just as the X Games were peaking, I was scheduled to make a speech to thousands of whooped-up antiwar protesters who had swarmed into Aspen from all over the state of Colorado to protest the looming war in Iraq and march through the center of town.

Indeed, it had the look of an action-packed day coming up, and some people even feared violence.

"Nonsense," I told the Sheriff. "There will be no violence, not as long as we are there. So you can tell those worrywarts to calm down and enjoy the energy of it, which is wonderful."

He nodded his head slowly, seeming to agree, yet apparently lost for a moment in his own thoughts. "We have nothing to fear," he said finally, "except fear itself." Then he laughed and whacked me sharply on the back. "That is what's wrong with this entire country, isn't it?"

"Exactly," I said. "We are turning into a nation of whimpering slaves to Fear—fear of war, fear of poverty, fear of random terrorism, fear of getting downsized or fired because of the plunging economy, fear of getting evicted for bad debts or suddenly getting locked up in a military detention camp on vague charges of being a Terrorist sympathizer. . . ."

These things have already happened to millions of patriotic, law-abiding American citizens, and it will happen to many more, even in the glitzy, high-rolling world of professional sports, where superstar athletes have uncommonly high pro-files and large influence in public opinion polls. . . . What would happen, for instance, if Michael Jordan made a glitzy antiwar commercial for Nike that appeared on nationwide TV about nine times a day? Think about it.

Whoops. Ye gods. My plane is leaving for New York in two hours, and I am gripped with a helpless panic. It seems impos-sible. A giant blizzard hit the valley yesterday, just after I fin-ished my impassioned speech to the cheering crowd at a park in the center of town, which included hundreds of X Gamers as well as antiwar marchers. There was not a hint of violence or even conflict. All in all, it was a good crowd to be a part of. The day was a success on all fronts.

Ah, but we are running out of time, folks. I *must* get to New York to celebrate the publishing of my new book. It is guaran-teed to be a volatile visit, for sure. Ho ho. That's it for now. *Mahalo* and remember to watch your back.

—*February 3, 2003*

Billionaire Swine and Kiwi Catastrophe

The Super Bowl happened less than three weeks ago, but to football junkies like me, it feels like 22 years. I have blocked it out of my memory now, although on some nights I have agoniz-ing flashbacks that cause me to sweat and babble in my sleep, as if a roach had crawled into my spleen to die.

These moments of total recall always leave me weak. I see Rich Gannon hurling air balls up for grabs, staggering backwards in the grip of huge, speedy brutes—rangy 300-pound sprinters who run 40 yards in 4.0 seconds and love to hurt people, especially MVP quarterbacks.

The vaunted Tampa Bay pass rush shredded the massive Raider offensive line, leaving Gannon helpless to throw or even think. It was pitiful.

The whole Raider Nation was flogged and humiliated on worldwide TV like a gang of sissies. By halftime I felt stupid and wrong in every way. It was like dying and going to hell.

Ah, but never mind that wretched game. It is a thing of the past now, for most people. We will banish it from our brains forever, along with the myth of the mighty Oakland Raiders, who lived and died on their once-proud passing game. The Raiders are dead—long live the Raiders.

Right. And so much for that, eh? For at least two weeks I thought the lopsided whipping in San Diego was the most painful moment I have ever witnessed in the pain-riddled world of sports. . . . But last Friday a new champion emerged, and you didn't even have to be a sports fan to appreciate it.

Oakland is, after all, only one city in one country.

The nightmare happened 10,000 miles away in New Zealand, the sailing capital of the world, where a whole nation got their heads handed to them in the feverishly awaited America's Cup Race in the treacherous waters of the Southern Pacific Ocean. It was a hideous thing to watch, even as an ignorant, quasi-curious foreigner.

I am not a yachting person, by nature, but I have just enough experience on the sea under sail to feel a certain nostalgia for it when I see a big white racing yacht heeled over at cruising speed on the ocean, and I still tie a mean bowline knot on just about anything in less than 20 seconds.

That is only one of the lifelong benefits of putting in some time on the sea, jerking big ropes and lines and sheets and extremely heavy sails around for 18 hours a day with your hands bleeding and all your toes ruptured from sliding around on the deck. Even in retrospect it is a harsh and painful life, punctuated every once in a while with moments of staggering beauty and wild adventure.

There is magic, for instance, in sailing out of a foreign harbor at dawn, gliding in utter silence across the water and heading out to sea for eight long days and nights on the ocean with no engine and no radio. It is madness, by any nautical wisdom. Only a fool or a desperate man would even think about it. The risks were too high and our chances of reaching the next island by dead reckoning and celestial navigation with no engine and no radio were about one in 44.

There were, of course, at least three compelling reasons for getting out of that country immediately, but there is no need to discuss them right now. So let's get back to the tragedy that happened last week in New Zealand when the defending world champion Kiwi boat blew up on the first leg of the first race, for no explainable reason. . . . It was inconceivable. Utterly out of the question. Watching it happen in real time was like seeing the Yankees lose 65–3 in the opening game of the World Series.

The next race on the following day was even worse, ripping the heart out of the entire Kiwi nation and leaving its team 0–2 in the best-of-nine series. It was a truly heartbreaking defeat, coming as it did in the final 30 seconds of a 3-hour race when the Kiwis blew a comfortable lead and stupidly allowed themselves to be caught from behind by a slower boat and beaten by a boat length by the billion-dollar Swiss yacht crew, made up mainly of the same gang of Kiwis who brought the Cup to New Zealand for the first time in 144 years and made themselves national heroes and undisputed world champions. . . . They jumped ship about three years ago, when they decided to "test the market" for their special skills and found it so rewarding that they turned pro for real and hired themselves out to the highest bidder—which turned out to be a Swiss billionaire named Berteralli, who craved the Cup so desperately that he decided to spend whatever it might cost him to hire the finest sailors in the world and seize the prize for Europe from its temporary home in Auckland. Nothing would stand in his way.

So he went out and hired the best crew in the world, which happened, back then, to be from New Zealand. Now they sail for Switzerland, a landlocked nation. That is only one of the distinct advantages of being a billionaire in this world. A billionaire can indulge any billionaire whim that pops into his mind, regardless of cost—and that is what happened in Auckland: a crew of hired mercenaries returned to New Zealand and wiped out the home team on their own turf without even breaking a sweat.

Whoops. I see I'm wandering off track here and becoming exhausted and unable to focus—probably because the Cup Races will almost certainly be over this weekend; no team has ever won the Cup after losing the first three races. The Kiwis are finished. They will lose five straight.

And so what, eh? I am into basketball now, keeping a keen eye on Louisville and Kentucky, both locks for the NCAA tourney in March. Hot damn. Yes Sir. That should be enough action to cure any junkie, and I already crave it. Football is dead, long live basketball.

—February 17, 2003

Fleeced by
Ed Bradley

March is a dangerous month for basketball people, and this year will be no different—unless you happen to be one of the many, many thousands of American unfortunates who will be forced to watch the wild and woolly NCAA championship tournament on TV in some wind-whipped U.S. Army tent somewhere in the bleak Iraqi desert. That will be an awkward situation at best, and the only real winners will be a large handful of terminal gambling addicts and committed basketball junkies who have hovered and lurked and functioned in the ranks of every military unit attached to every U.S. Army since Washington crossed the Delaware.

Sports gambling is huge in the Army, and most people will tell you (in private) that it's a good and even healthy distraction for thousands of otherwise stress-crazed soldiers forever teetering on the brink of some hideous outburst of preternatural violence that could leave them all dying painfully.

That is an adult dose of *stress*, folks, and I salute the poor bastards who are out there right now. I wish you people the very best of good luck, because you are going to need it.

Right. And so much for war, eh—or at least *this* one. I hate it and I *know* it will bring disastrous consequences. . . . But hey, what the hell? We are all basketball fans, not bone pickers, and March is our time of year. So let's get into it. Having the Big Dance on worldwide TV for the next three weeks may be the best thing that could happen to this country right now. It might save us from ourselves for a moment, and maybe longer. . . . We are basketball people, and we are legion.

And now, back to the cruel realities. Indeed, I am stuck with Kentucky again, and this time around I feel pretty good about it. You bet, let us rumble. I have already bet heavily on Kentucky against the field—at odds I see no need to disclose, at this moment, except to say that if my Bluegrass people *do* win the national title this year, I will be flying into Las Vegas on my own jet plane for the next heavyweight fight, or maybe just for a spectacular orgy at the Palms. We will see.

Let me assure you, once again, that I am not a bookie, a cop, or a shill for anything except my own whims, wisdom, and sometimes even *visions* that I have never denied or repudiated. So it's *caveat emptor*, around here, and always in flux. *Salud.*

I have not focused down on my precious Bracket selections, mainly because they are not available yet. . . . But *soon come*, eh?

Yes sir, we will all be up to our necks in it soon enough. So don't fret, there is plenty of action just around the corner.

All four No. 1 seeds for the regions—Kentucky, Texas, Kansas, and Arizona—will be around for the Final Eight, unless some eerie kink in the bracketing process somehow hurls Kentucky vs. Arizona at us in the Sweet Sixteen, or another high-stress Texas-Oklahoma clash pops up before its time.

Otherwise the early rounds look manageable for all of the seeded favorites except Arizona. I hate Arizona because they have caused me extreme grief in my gambling adventures over the years, particularly against Kentucky. Horrible, horrible. . . . I remember one monumentally rotten experience when Ed Bradley strolled into my parlor on a Saturday afternoon and beat me out of 4,000 green dollars right in front of my own eyes, in my own kitchen, with all the others watching like greedy barnyard animals. He flogged me on something like 22 straight side bets in the course of yet another painful loss to Arizona. It was one of the ugliest days of my life.

—March 11, 2003

Love Blooms
in the Rockies

The Big Dance got lost in a fiery cloud of war dust last week: almost canceled, they said, but somehow the games survived—so far, at least—despite the bitching and whining of CBS resident peacock Dan Rather, who cursed his own network for letting the annual NCAA Championship Tournament interfere with a two-day-old illegal, unsanctioned outlaw-style invasion of a defenseless country full of oil.

Why is Dan Rather complaining? Ho ho ho. Here's why:

Danny is no Walter Cronkite, for one, and Two is that Dan Rather is currently on location in Kuwait City, strutting and posing and whooping it up with all the other "embedded" journalists going to war like birds in a gilded cage.

The war was ugly enough, but that was only the start. The Horrible blizzard that shut down most of Colorado for four days and nights was far worse news for me. It destroyed our annual high-risk orgy of gambling and raving that has become a tradition out here. Ed Bradley got jerked up by the roots and sent off to war. Curtis was back in Washington to infiltrate the JDL and the billionaire degenerate Ewing brothers from North Charleston, infamous in gambling circles for their extremely aggressive gambling tactics and quasi-depraved tastes, refused to fly into the blizzard and went to Las Vegas for whatever action they could find.

The blizzard almost drove me crazy. I have nothing against snow. I am totally prepared for it, after many years of practice, and snow has never prevented me from going anywhere I really wanted to go. . . .

But *this* blizzard was different. It closed everything— schools, highways, airports, newspaper deliveries, along with food, beer, gasoline, and all human traffic across the Continental Divide for almost a week—and stranded Anita, my beautiful fiancée and soon-to-be wife, on the other side of the mountain.

I also had an elegant diamond engagement ring somewhere out there in the whiteout between me and New Orleans, where I spend a lot of time on occasional sporting business. . . . So there was no Anita and no ring, and that was heavy on my mind as the tournament got under way. No gambling, no guests, no fiancée, no ring—all this finally caused me to flip out and start trying to charter some kind of bandit jet plane to fly Anita over the hump by any means necessary. I was obsessed with it, regardless of cost. It was madness. I was in the acute stage of a total nervous breakdown.

That was when the Sheriff had to step in and strongly suggest that I get a grip on myself, which I finally did, but not until he promised me that U.S. Interstate 70 was finally cleared of the monster avalanche and Anita was safely on the road. So I hunkered down and stared at the basketball games on TV until I passed out from desperate backed-up passion and 40 frantic hours with no sleep. It was a long and restless night, full of unacceptably rotten dreams and spastic muttering about point spreads.

Anita pulled into the garage just in time for the end of the Butler-Louisville game, which I lost badly, but it didn't hurt too much, given my circumstances, because I didn't expect them to go far. There would be no heavy rematch with Kentucky this year, but it wouldn't have been worth watching anyway. The Cardinals would have been routed.

On Saturday I proposed and gave her the ring, and after that we both went a little crazy for a while, which was clearly the right thing to do.

—*March 24, 2003*

Love in a Time of War

The final mystery is oneself. . . . Who can calculate the orbit of his own soul?

—Oscar Wilde

I smiled when Marquette trounced Pittsburgh in the Sweet 16 last week, but my smile soon turned to wax. My bracket selections were murdered in the Regional finals, and I was forced to abandon all hope of victory in the office pool. It was the worst gambling disaster I'd suffered since the Super Bowl. Ho ho—but so what?

My prevailing mood has taken a drastic turn for the better since my engagement to Anita was first announced in this column only eight days ago. Saturday was our first anniversary, which enabled me to survive the rude shock of Kentucky's shameful collapse against Marquette. Jesus, 14 points. My people should have stayed in bed that day. It was humiliating.

So I will have to go with Marquette in the Final Four, which may or may not be a curse on them. This tournament has turned into a Harvest Festival for underdogs—sort of like the War in Iraq—and a long, relentless beating for the bookmaking business. There is nothing like a sudden rash of underdog victories to raise serious hell among professional gamblers. You bet. Obscure teams like Butler, Marquette, Gonzaga, and Wisconsin are not supposed to win monster games in March, not at this level—and superpowers like Kentucky and Arizona are not supposed to Lose.

Gonzaga lost, in fact, and so did Wisconsin, but they might as well have won, considering the damage they did. The Zags took mighty Arizona to two overtimes and almost to three, finally losing by a whisker and one missed final shot—but not before draining all the zing out of the top-seeded hot rods from Tucson: they shot their wad against Gonzaga, then lost to Kansas, which should be favored to seize the national championship in New Orleans this weekend. That Collison boy is a tall walking bitch of a basketball player.

But so is that human wrecking ball, Dwyane Wade from Marquette, who almost single-handedly destroyed Kentucky, which was so weakened and brutalized by its narrow escape against Wisconsin that they didn't have a chance two days later against that Jesuit gang from Milwaukee—despite being a bullish 11-point favorite, points which I nervously gave and almost immediately regretted when Kentucky's team leader and court quarterback, Keith Bogans, went down with a high ankle sprain after 15 minutes and only five points. Bogans was finished after that, and so was Kentucky. The Great Wall of bluegrass collapsed like cheap plaster. Without Bogans, needless to say, I took a nasty beating. *Mahalo.*

On any other day, a tragedy like that would have plunged me into a coma for three or four weeks, or even years, but this time I was over it in less than 20 hours, and now I can barely remember the score.

Or maybe I'm just blocking it out of my memory, for obvious reasons, but in truth, the frenzy of Love and Romance and extremely high adventure that has gripped this place since Anita finally emerged from "The Great Blizzard of '03" last week has made everything else seem small. On days like this I feel like Lord Byron and Shelley and Keats all rolled into one, as they like to say in New Orleans, and everything is possible.

Which is not true, alas. I am a Romantic by nature and a gambler by instinct—and I can tell you for sure, little Xania, that Losing goes with the territory in my business. All gamblers lose regularly, but they rarely discuss it in public. Losing is bad for the image, dude. Nobody buys Hot Tips from Losers. Remember that.

This has been a spectacular tournament, so far with a true abundance of wild and shocking games, right from the start: barn burners, many overtimes, and many desperately close games and staggering, ruinous defeats, most of them tragic in nature.

Failure in the Sweet 16 leaves a permanent scar on the hearts and minds of these innocent, once-magic athletes who suffer it this time of year. It will hurt forever. There *is* no forgiveness, never. It is a sin to lose in the Big Dance ... and remember that 64 out of the original 65 teams are doomed to failure in the NCAA Tournament and that only one can succeed. There is only one winner of the National Championship. The rest will be Losers. That is how it works in the USA—especially in times of War, and this incredibly mismanaged War on Iraq will not be going away anytime soon. This one is a Tar baby, sports fans.

It has already shot damaging holes in our national confidence and made dangerous Fools of whoever is running the Pentagon—not to mention the stunning $1,000,000,000 we are squandering every 24 hours to bomb Iraq back to the Stone Age and starve millions of helpless, unarmed, terrorized civilians to death, in the name of some hateful, ill-advised, ill-fated military Crusade on the other side of the world. How long, O lord, how long? We used to be smarter than that.

Indeed, we are truly the squanderer of what was once the American Dream, and our own dreams, for that matter. In two disastrous years, this Waterhead son of Texas has taken this country from a prosperous nation at peace to a dead-broke nation at War, and that is a very long fall.

How could it happen? you ask—and I'm damned if I can give you a sane answer in anything close to the average nine-second time of the hard-hitting, high-tech marketing message of today's average sound bite. Anything over nine seconds is wasted energy, they say in the White House these days.

That is pure chickenshit, of course. That gang of born-again geeks wouldn't know a Message from a poison meat whistle, judging by the sum of all the ignorant, wrong-headed evidence seen thus far in this dismal conflict. It is hard to ignore the prima facie dumbness that got us bogged down in this horrible mess for openers. This is not going to be like Daddy's War, old sport. He actually won, and he still got run out of the White House about nine months later.

That is the dark silver lining in this blood-spattered cloud we have brought down on ourselves, and it leaves a lot to be desired. It is almost impossibly morbid to brood on how many young Americans will have to come home in body bags before the great American voter catches on to the fact that the same greed-crazed yo-yo who slit the throat of the U.S. economy in the name of Tax Cuts and feverish warmongering gone wrong. The whole thing sucks. It was wrong from the start, and it is getting wronger by the hour. George W. Bush is doomed to the same cruel fate as his papa suffered only ten years ago.

Whoops! Dawn is up in the Rockies and I am late again for

my deadline. The bell is ringing and I must end this thing now. My beautiful fiancée is wandering around in a champagne hangover, and I have to put her to bed. I am still hypnotized by the flash and glow of her elegant diamond ring. I have never paid much attention to diamonds, until now, but this one is very different. I am utterly fascinated by it.

Right. I am wildly high on everything I see or touch. We laugh a lot, and we fondle each other constantly, even in front of the Sheriff, who recently got married himself, so he should be familiar with this kind of madness. True Romance is always exhilarating for us addicts, and I like it.

Bang! And that's it, for now. There is no more. *Aloha.*

—*April 1, 2003*

A Sad Week in America

Just about the time we were settling in for the Kansas-Syracuse game, my strange neighbor, Omar, appeared in my kitchen with a wild-looking Brazilian woman who spoke no English but seemed to understand everything we said. "Is it possible that we could watch the Big Dance with you?" he asked gently. "Today is very special for our family."

Before I could answer, he grabbed my shoulders and kissed me on both ears, then he stepped around me and came face to face with the Sheriff, who immediately lifted him off the floor and slammed him against my black leather-covered refrigerator.

"I thought I told you never to come here again!" he shouted. "I have at least five warrants for your arrest."

Omar screeched for a moment, then smiled and tried to adjust his clothes. "You know I am innocent," he said. "Don't you know who I am? I am your neighbor, Prince Omar of New York. I live just up the road. Why do you try to kill me?"

The game was about to start, so I quickly stepped between them and put my arm around the Brazilian woman, who took my arm and motioned for a cigarette.

"Of course, we have many cigarettes here," I said suavely, escorting her into the lounge and putting her on a stool between the Sheriff and Anita, my elegant fiancée, where I knew she would be safe. "There is no room up here for you at the bar," I told Omar. "You will have to find somewhere to stand."

"Yeah," the Sheriff chuckled. "You can stand over there with the losers." He pointed to a narrow spot in a nearby hallway, with no view at all of the game, which was spinning out of control for the favored Kansas Jayhawks. I was down by something like 14 points when Kansas finally made its first free throw.

The score at halftime was 53–42, and Kansas already looked beat. They were the popular choice as well as a four-and-a-half-point gambling choice over Syracuse, the Champion of the East, with its three freshman starters and its shaggy reputation for showboating. "A perennial Big East power with big potential," they said in New York. But their three (those freshman) starters were too young and too jittery to hang on for long against supercoach Roy Williams and his two big guns, Nick Collison and Kirk Hinrich, both seniors.

By halftime I was losing interest as well as money. Syracuse was simply too fast and tall and talented for the Jayhawks, who couldn't score from outside or inside and missed 60 percent of their free throws. Their defense was like a helpless punchboard and their best shots were either crushed or swatted far into the crowd, as the huge crowd jeered and my bets sank out of sight.

Anita and Princess Omin had taken my new test Jeep into town for a box of Polish sausage and some orchids to dress up the War Room. They seemed to be getting along nicely, despite the language problem that had once plagued us in the past. They were quite beautiful together.

CAN SPORT COMPETE WITH WAR?

This is a very bad week for the American nation, and next week will be even worse. The Kansas-Syracuse game was barely over when I learned to my horror that the United States Marines were randomly murdering British and American journalists in Baghdad.

Five journalists have died in Iraq so far, and not one of them was killed by Enemy Fire. They were shot down like dogs by U.S. military personnel, killed and wounded and mangled by Americans, who drive American M1 Abrahms battle tanks and eat all-American pie, just like the rest of us. American troops are killing journalists in a profoundly foreign country, for savage, greed-crazed reasons that most of them couldn't explain or even understand.

What the fuck is going on here? How could this once-proud nation have changed so much, so drastically, in only two years—almost three, to be sure. In what seems like the blink of an eye, this George Bush has brought us from a prosperous nation at peace to a broke nation at war. And why are we killing each other at point-blank range on the other side of the world—with big guns and big bombs that kill everything in reach?

Indeed, there is something going on here, Mister Jones, and you don't know what it is, do you?

Bob Dylan said that, and he is still right, now more than ever. Hell, there is nothing really new about American cops and American soldiers killing and brutalizing innocent American citizens. It happens with depressing regularity. But at least the bastards used to have the decency to deny it.

That is a big difference, sports fans, and that is why I feel so savagely depressed tonight. When the Pentagon feels free and even gleeful about killing anybody and Everybody who gets in the way of their vicious crusade for oil, the public soul of this country has changed forever, and professional sports is only a serenade for the death of the American dream. *Mahalo.*

*   *   *

Another big loser last week was the CBS-TV network, which did a credible job and put most of the games on TV—but the invasion was impossible to compete with, and ratings for the Big Dance were down almost 30 percent overall. I was not among the quitters, but I still had a hard time staying focused on basketball. The total war against Evil dominated every waking moment of our lives.

War has always been a hard act to follow, and this rotten little massacre in Iraq is no exception. It is like that permanent shit-rain that Ronald Reagan talked about in his letters to Frank Sinatra. They both believed very deeply in the book of Revelation. Reagan even went so far as to say to his buddy, "We are screwed, Frankie. We are the ones who will have to face the end of the World."

They had a good time for sure, those rogues. They were life-long sports fans, but Wars kept getting in their way.

I used to laugh when good old Dutch said ominous things like that—but it is becoming clearer and clearer that he was right, dead right, if only because he was drawing up the blueprints himself, right in front of our eyes, and we loved him for it.

I had a soft spot in my heart for Ronald Reagan, if only because he was a sportswriter in his youth, and also because his wife gave the best head in Hollywood.

The war news from almost everywhere clamped a mean lid on coverage of the NCAA tournament this year, but that didn't prevent us hoops junkies from getting an adult dose of high-speed, high-style heart-jerking college basketball last weekend. Two of the three Final Four games in New Orleans were serious ball-busters, even for those of us who had long since abandoned all hope of victory in the big-money bracket-bashing "office pools" that littered the newsrooms of the nation.

TV ratings fell 30 percent overall, and none of the favorites

survived the Final Four, which left me with no hometown favorite to focus on, once top-ranked Kentucky was scraped off
the floor after Marquette diced them up in the Midwest region
finals.

Nothing had really surprised me until then (with the glar-
ing exception of those whimpering sots from Wake Forest,
who failed so horribly against Auburn that I swore to myself,
even before that vulgar game had ended, that I was going to
drive at once to the sleepy fat village of Winston-Salem, NC,
and release a swarm of 900,000 full-grown Vulture fleas somewhere in the middle of the campus, or maybe in the basement
of the team's practice facility.

You can get anywhere from 250,000 to a million commer-
cially grown breeding fleas—or ladybugs or chiggers or moles
or even Black Widow spiders—for what might seem like a
generous price, but your purchase will definitely Not be the
end of it.

The last time I experimented with this kind of political action, the controlled release process got away from me and bad
things happened. . . . It was long after midnight when we crept
the iron cherry picker across the backyard and as close as possible to the tall brick chimney pipe that towered over the
pompous, colonial mansion on the outskirts of Aspen.

Our job, our mission, was to sneak up on the large family
home of a crooked politician, not far away, and dump a half-
million fully grown Muscatel Fleas down the huge Greek
chimney into his plush living room.

Ah, but that is another story. I was talking about Sports and
the NCAA drowned in the war news. . . . Marquette Self-
destructed. . . . Now back to the Championship. . . .

Syracuse beat Kansas last night for the U.S. college championship of the world. It was a wildly exciting game that came
down to a failed final shot, but it hardly seemed to matter,
compared to the horrible news from Iraq, and basketball faded
away. There was bigger entertainment on the screen, primarily
in the form of bombs dropping on people—mainly foreigners,

of course—and newsreaders from CNN said we were winning. Is this a great country or what?

—*April 9, 2003*

The Doomed Prefer Oakland

Good news is rare these days, and every glittering ounce of it should be cherished and hoarded and worshipped and fondled like a priceless diamond. The "war" in Iraq is all around us like one of those San Francisco death-fogs that never go away. Your immediate instinct is to flee, but to where? It is a lot easier to just go back to bed than to get in the car and look for a place where there may be no fog. The odds are stacked against you, so why even try?

That is the nervous American reality in this downhill spring of the year 2003, and I am keenly aware of it. Something is missing here, and I can't say what it is, can I?

Maybe it is spring fever, or maybe just the end of another tainted basketball season—but wait!

Ah ha! The basketball season is not over. It just seems that way, because the brittle hysteria of War has overwhelmed all sport in America, just like it did the Super Bowl and March Madness and the dismal, almost invisible beginning of another vaguely distracting baseball season. The relentless Bombing News from Iraq commanded all the front-page headlines and all the TV news shows, which drone at us 24 hours of every day. Many people don't have time to even read the sports section, much less focus on it and gamble. . . . It is impossible to truly concentrate on anything when your wallet is empty and your heart is full of fear.

But so what? Never mind the war news.

NFL Films came to my house last week, and I felt like Alice in Wonderland. It was beautiful and even historic. For a life-long, totally committed, fun-loving football addict like me, it was like being taken into the Football Hall of Fame.

A man called Tuckett led the weird expedition that resulted in my insanely ambitious attempt to explain, in vast detail, the exact Meaning and History of my intense and sometimes tangled relationship with football and gambling and Al Davis and Max McGee and Richard Nixon and Bill Walsh and, quite specifically, with the early days and legends of what is now the Raider Nation.

Indeed. I have spent far more time that I can even remember with all those violent people who surrounded and even Created the monstrous legend of the mighty Oakland Raiders in all their blighted glory.

About 40 percent of the original Raiders were criminal by nature and deliberately dangerous brutes. They were professional athletes who got paid every week to hurt people. The worse you hurt them, the more you got paid—especially if you could damage or cripple another team's Quarterback and put him on the Disabled List. That made you an automatic hero of violence, for a while, and entitled you to throw your weight around in downtown Oakland with whores and cops and animals. You were almost above the law. It was nice work, if you could get it, and winning championships made it even nicer. Being a natural-born Raider was Fun. Ho ho ho.

I fell into that groove quite naturally, back in my outlaw days. I was a fun-loving, well-paid Sportswriter. I seemed to have a bottomless expense account. Yes sir. Me and the Oakland Raiders were a match made in heaven.

But "seems" is a dangerous word, in my business, and having those brutes on my Account quickly led to trouble—not for the team or the players, but for me and my professional reputation.

Let us remember, people, that all of this happened many,

many years ago, well beyond any statute of limitations. It is ancient history now, and we can talk freely. For me, it is vaguely like watching a documentary film about a young journalist frolicking with the Hell's Angels. It was definitely weird and even perverted to some tastes, but what the hell? It is over now, lost and gone like the snows of yesteryear. *Mahalo.*

—April 17, 2003

The Tragedy of Naked Bowling

"Yo, little Suzie—how's about me and you hookin' up
for some naked bowling tonight?"
"Say what? Get out of my face!"

Naked Bowling was once a sinister sport in America, but today it is making a strong comeback, very strong. Nobody except Waterheads will deny that the recent craze for bowling naked in public makes it one of the fastest growing sports in the free world.

Wonderful. It came in the nick of time. The whole nation was getting jittery from too much war news, and the sporting public was demanding wilder and wilder government-sponsored Sport spectacles to blot out the grim horizon, and then everywhere, all at once, it happened—The Great Cheerful Naked Bowling Boom of 2003.

My friend Omar, from up the road, is opening a national chain of bowling alleys where house rules require that all human clothing be checked at the door. "It keeps them from stealing," he told me. "A naked person is an honest person.

We have very low operating costs—free labor, no taxes, new friends in strange places and extremely addictive behavior five times a week." Hundreds of thousands of otherwise decent people are already hopelessly addicted to naked bowling, which renders them all but useless for normal military work.

These Losers are like a plague of leeches on the body politic. They dim the brain as well as the body, and eventually the victim gets sucked dry and dies. That is very dead weight, which is fatal to a fast-moving army of tanks.

I have always hated bowling, and I don't mind admitting it. I can't even tolerate naked bowling, because of my tragic encounters with the "sport" and everything it stands for. The sound of a heavy black ball crashing down on anything made of wood makes me sick.

There would, of course, be no need to haggle about bowling at all—except that it *is* a recognized sport in this country, and I *am* a professional sportswriter, and I am watching a real-life naked bowling contest on my TV screen right now as I write this page. I see a team of extremely naked women with huge breast implants and fake lips going head to head with another naked team that would no doubt be wearing Hooters T-shirts if this were anything but a pure naked bowling contest—and let me tell you for sure, sports fans, that these women are really going at it. They are locked in a scoreless tie after 13 frames of pretty frantic bowling.

Sounds just about right, eh? Let's *all* get naked and go bowling. Why not?

Where can I watch this stuff? The Answer is, On the Canadian Playboy channel, which presents a few problems in itself. It is costly, for one, and Two, a subscription to Canadian Playboy almost always causes trouble in families with underage children. Any child who can multiply 5 times 6 will also understand quickly how to cut right through any of the so-called Parental Controls or sex blockers or antiporno devices. These are standard equipment and therefore penetrable by any half-bright, low-tech yo-yo in the neighborhood. Your children will soon become sex addicts.

We had a minor scandal in Woody Creek not long ago that involved a network of pampered children ranging in age from 16 down to 9. They not only copied sex films from their parents' TV, for sale at school, but made their own videotapes of each other having random public sex at home and at school and on pool tables with multiple partners, which they either sold or traded around the school like baseball cards.

Aspen High School has long been known for wildness and other quasi-criminal behavior, but even the most jaded parents in this glitzy resort town demanded police action when their 14-year-old daughters started turning up at local stag parties and Denver adult film stores.

"We haven't seen a local girl turn up on the Orgy TV channel," said the Coroner, "but it's bound to happen sooner or later. These sex channels pay good money for explicit underage sex movies."

Which somehow brings us back to bowling. All you have to do is cruise into your favorite local bowling alley and watch a while—and then smoke some fine hashish and think heavily about what kind of shuffling, screeching, hideous vision your favorite bowling alley would be if all those people were stark raving naked.

Okay, thank you for thinking. Are we clear on that?

Upon further study, I have concluded that Naked Bowling is not, in fact, a direct threat to the military security of the USA. But it should be restricted to Canada. *Mahalo.*

In other sports news last week—the Los Angeles Lakers vaporized the Minnesota Timberwolves in a terrifying warm-up for their next foe in the NBA playoffs, 117–98. . . . My man Allen Iverson went wild and scored 55 beautiful points against New Orleans and single-handedly made me a winner, 98–90, just barely covering the foolish 7-point bulge spread that I had given in a moment of weakness, while Anita and I were watching the Naked News from Canada that comes in on a different signal receiver on the same big-screen ABC broadcast of the NBA games.

Frankly, I am having a hard time staying constantly on top of the latest sporting action, mainly because ESPN has not yet delivered my upgraded HD-TV equipment for watching the basketball games. . . . I try to watch Baseball, but the hard little white ball keeps disappearing in the ever-changing maze of action between naked people dancing and small men running desperately between bases.

Weak broadband signals are to blame for my failing TV reception, and my signals are getting weaker and weaker by the day. Is it even *possible* for the Pentagon to occupy half of all available Bandwidth in the stratosphere?

You *bet* it is, Bubba. Everything in what the Brits and the Yanks call the "Free Western World" has been "freed up" for military purposes, with no explanation, due to the Military Emergency. Is this a great country, or what?

—April 17, 2003

West Coast Offense

My own Marriage was the subject of extreme excitement and big news around here last week. It dwarfed everything else, including the NBA play-offs, the Kentucky Derby, Kevin Millwood's no-hitter, Naked bowling, and the feverish search for Saddam Hussein in Iraq. A bold headline in the *Aspen Daily News* said, "Congratulations to Woody Creek's Royal Couple," flanked by photos of me and Anita smiling out at the Reader.

Surprise surprise, eh?

It was done with fine style and secrecy in order to avoid the looting and drunken violence that local lawmen feared would inevitably have followed the ceremony.

I know nothing about planning even the simplest wedding, nothing at all, and neither does sweet Anita, who is now my Wife . . . So we did it the Buddhist way. We drove straight to the County Courthouse on a stormy Thursday morning and were happily married by noon. Sheriff Bob performed the ceremony, his wife took pictures, and a black priest from Sicily handled the video camera. It was fun.

Our honeymoon was even simpler. We drank heavily for a few hours with Chris Goldstein and accepted fine gifts from strangers, then we drove erratically back out to the Owl Farm and prepared for our own, very private celebration by building a huge fire, icing down a magnum of Cristal Champagne, and turning on the Lakers-Timberwolves game until we passed out and crawled to the bedroom. *Omnia Vincit Amor.*

The Lakers made another crude mess of the Minnesota Timberwolves on Tuesday night, as most of the home crowd left early because of the hopeless beating San Antonio did to Phoenix, mauling the Suns in another one-sided game full of failures and errors and unacceptable botches.

So it is all but certain now that we will be watching some genuinely savage basketball between the Spurs and the Lakers next week—along with what will no doubt be another epic series of battles between Sacramento and Dallas, seeded number 2 and number 3 on the betting charts in the West.

San Antonio should be favored by four or five, playing the first two games at home against the number 5 Lakers. Derek Fisher and Robert Horry will have to be red hot in that first game—and the second—for LA to come out of Texas with even a 1–1 split. With Rick Fox gone for the year, Phil Jackson will need all the karma he can crank up, if his defending NBA champion Lakers hope to come out of this one alive. Beating the Spurs four times in two weeks would be impossible for the best teams in the league—especially for the shorter, slower Lakers, who played San Antonio four times this season, and lost all four. . . .

So what the hell? I'll bet on the Spurs this time, and call it four games to one. I will go far out on the limb and say No four-peat for Hollywood's team this year.

I might even go so far as to predict an all-Texas (Western) final coming up, which would make the White House very proud. We would never hear the end of it: TEXAS ÜBER ALLES.

The only way to avoid that nightmare is for the high-powered Sacramento Kings to whip Dallas—which will take seven brutal games, for sure, and leave the Kings so drained and exhausted that they will be helpless against San Antonio, losing in five games.

And so, at a glance, it looks like the Spurs whipping the shit out of some laughable underdog from the East, which has never recovered from the loss of Michael Jordan.

The whole East conference has been like a wasteland since Michael wandered away. It was the end of a glorious era. The East is a minor league now, flashy millionaire losers, roaming from coast to coast like rich gypsies fleecing the witless rubes in one town after another.

But so what? Everything I say or predict tonight could be rendered meaningless by even a single cruel injury to any star on any team. Many will be blown away and doomed, as always, when a major piece of the engine explodes. That is a natural law.

Whoever wins the championship this year will be the team that suffers the fewest injuries in the next 20 games. That is what it will take to survive these play-offs—and that team is probably San Antonio.

So good luck, Bubba. Every game from now on will have huge meaning for the Loser. Huge meaning. Thank you.

—April 30, 2003

Great Fleecing
in Woody Creek:
Lakers Staggered
in Series Opener

I am sitting here with lovely Anita at Midnight on Monday and we are whooping it up in the aftermath of what will go down in the history of rural gambling as the great Woody Creek Fleecing of the 2003 basketball season. We are slapping each other's thighs with gleeful laughter and also drinking the legendary Highland Park Scotch Whiskey (single malt, 18 years old) from a Tiffany crystal decanter and smoking Jimsonweed, for old times' sake. It is wonderful.

We all understand what a really first-class Fleecing feels like, for good or ill. And tonight I feel Good. Why not?

Tonight I lured a group of visiting priests into my gambling den and advised them to bet on the Lakers and give me the Spurs plus ten points. It was beautiful. It was a classic of big-time fleecing. And they loved me for it. Money meant nothing to them. They were messengers from the Vatican City.

A fleecee is one who has just been dramatically fleeced—as in "shearing the sheep of his woolly coat," according to the *Random House Dictionary of the English Language*. He/she has been deprived of money or belongings by Fraud, Coma, Hoax, or the like: Swindled and stripped of all human dignity, if only for one long painful moment that will never be gone from his or her memory.

Being fleeced and humiliated right in front of all your friends and peers and loved ones is every gambler's most horrible fear. It is like being stripped naked on a street not far from the ghastly hole that was once the World Trade Center—and forced to walk, or run or slither or wander, all alone to the far northern tip of Manhattan Island.

That would be somewhere close to the old Harlem River Bridge, as I recall, not far from where my friend William Burroughs was robbed and badly beaten, many years ago, by a gang of paramilitary dope addicts who had never even heard of him.

There is absolutely no end to the list of horrible things that might happen to a person who tries to walk naked from one end of Manhattan Island to the other. Nobody has ever done it. Not even George Washington, who spent a lot of time in New York and could wander around naked wherever he pleased.

But so what, eh? Nobody needs that kind of unnatural nightmare. Most of us have our own problems, and some of them are so depressing that the idea of wandering naked and alone all night to the far reaches of Central Park seem almost like a fun thing to try next weekend.

Which brings us back to the ominous fate that awaits the crippled Los Angeles Lakers tomorrow night in San Antonio. It will be the Alamo in reverse, with Shaquille O'Neal as Davy Crockett.

What? No. That is an unacceptably morbid hallucination. Shaq would never fight to the death for some cheap white man's rubble like the Alamo. And neither would I, for that matter, just for the record.

The Lakers have lost five straight games to the Spurs, and there is no smart reason to believe they won't lose three more. But probably not: the TV networks would go crazy if San Antonio swept the series 4-0. It would be a financial disaster, for them and for us. Any 4-0 sweep in any play-off series means a net loss of three spectacular professional basketball games that I will never see. And neither will you. Ho ho.

Anita is doing the math now—and ye gods, the final numbers are more disastrous than I thought. Yes. If every one of these NBA play-off series were a 4-0 sweep, we would lose a grim total of 42 major games before the summer starts.

To me, a professional Addict of the game, that would be worse than having my car stolen, or even than suddenly discovering maggots in my refrigerator. It would be a personal tragedy and very likely a Death Blow to the future of the NBA.

That means we must all pray vigorously for every series to go the full seven (7) games. That is all ye know, and all ye Need to know. *Mahalo.* Yes. Bring it on, bore it out—three games a night until the Fourth of July. I crave it, and so does Anita.

—*May 5, 2003*

The Sport of Kings

We are waiting for the Sacramento game to start now, and my phone is ringing incessantly, so I turn down its volume to zero. Fuck that telephone. I always turn it off when the game starts. That is my business.

Today has been a rough one. We had blowouts, many blowouts, one right after the other. I almost blacked out once or twice. My blood pressure ran up to about 225 and I noticed that people were giving me a wide berth.

Hot damn! The Sacramento Kings are leading the Dallas Mavericks 41–32, with four minutes and four seconds to play in the first half. . . . Mike Bibby has missed 13 out of 14 shots from the field so far, six of them wide-open layups.

Whoops. Doug Christie just stripped the ball away from flashy little Nick Van Exel and loped in for a stylish dunk, and the Kings lead 52–37 at halftime. Which is okay, but I can't help but remember that last night Dallas was down by 16 in the first quarter—and they still lucked out with a victory in two overtimes. Anita went all to pieces after that one. I had to take her into town and put her in a decompression Chamber.

She didn't take the scandal about the Kentucky Derby as hard as I did, but so what? I am a natural child of the Dark and Bloody Ground, and she is not. . . . But the horrible shock of seeing the *New York Times* go down in a blaze of fraud and treachery was too much for her, and she cracked up.

Jesus babbling Christ! The Kings have gone up 60–42—and now here comes Nick Van Exel. The crowd boos nervously, rumbling with a queer hostility. I am betting Sacramento *even*, so things are looking "good," as they used to say in Baghdad. My people are kicking ass and Anita is feeding me grapes. Ye gods, this game is a *rout!* The Mavericks are bleeding from every orifice. *Mahalo.*

Why am I still feeling queasy, with a 20-point lead at the end of three quarters? Why am I plagued by memories of false hubris and total collapse? Am I a fool?

Of course not. I am only a gambling person with a "checkered past," and I have a very keen sense of impending danger—which is what I feel now, with 6:59 left on the clock and Sacramento cruising by 19 or 20. Why am I riddled with angst?

Ah ha! The answer is not hard to see. Yes. I am faking it, trolling for last-minute sucker bets. Ho ho ho. I feel no angst at all, in truth—even though the Kings have *missed* so many wide-open shots that I fear to even count them. It is far more than 20, for sure; probably about 26. Yet they are still shooting a steady 48 percent from the field. This is not Winning basketball if only because the Mavericks are shooting 38 percent from the field. That is Losing basketball.

Strange, eh? Last night the Kings played winning basketball and lost. Tonight they are playing Losing basketball but winning. What does it all mean, Alfie?

Who cares. Dirk Nowitzki has just been ejected from the game. Dallas is falling apart. Now some jackass named Bell is trying to sock Bobby Jackson in the face. Jackson has a broken jaw and a fractured orbital bone above his eye. Incredible. How low do you have to sink in the slime of human stupidity to deliberately whack one of the classiest players in the league in the face when he has a cracked eye bone and a broken jaw?

That is unacceptable rudeness. Raja Bell is a knee-crawling, backstabbing punk with the soul of a Rat and the heart of a filthy virus. The NBA should have him committed to a state Mental Hospital and locked down with restraints until he gets his entire body dyed bright yellow, which will stay on his skin forever.

Excellent, eh? You bet. There is only One way to deal with a vicious Punk—and that way is viciously. Take my word for it. I know exactly how to deal with human scum. . . .

MORE THAN FORTY GAMES IN FORTY NIGHTS OF NBA PLAY-OFF BASKETBALL

"No. I am not a whore," said the bartender. "What do you mean by that?"

"Never mind the small talk," I said to her. "I came here to suck on your back."

She cried out with fear and tried to get away, but I slapped some plastic on her, then I locked the door. It was 2:06 a.m., and a freezing rain was falling. Beautiful, I thought. This is my kind of night.

ELSEWHERE IN THE WORLD OF SPORTS . . .

A gang of vicious fruitbags broke into the mosque yesterday and destroyed everything in it. Who knows what they will destroy tomorrow—maybe You, maybe Me. Something rotten is beginning to happen. I can feel it in my bones. Maybe we should steal a shipment of whiskey, just to be on the safe side.

I agree with you exactly, Mr. Ambassador. They laughed at Napoléon when he "gave away" the whole huge Louisiana Purchase for only fifteen million dollars, or less than six pennies an acre. Wow! Yes sir, we really robbed those French bastards this time. That is what we call an extremely high-yield real estate

investment. Ho ho ho. What fools these French turn
be, eh? Those pompous little suckers. Hell yes! W
those shameless perverts every day of the week. We own them.

I couldn't agree with you more, Mr. President. I have always
admired your freewheeling style of doing business. The French
suck.

Indeed, the French nation sucks! All of it. Look at all the
things we have fleeced them out of: the Statue of Liberty, two-
thirds of the western USA, all of what was once "Southeast
Asia"—Laos, Cambodia, Vietnam, etc. The list is long, if we
want to get weird about it: Hitler's gold, fellatio and cunnilin-
gus, two million magnums of elegant French Champagne, etc.,
etc.

But wait. There is another way to look at it. The prancing
little Emperor got his way in spades, when he dumped that
useless untamed wilderness. It meant nothing to him. He was
looking at Egypt for his next project, and for that he needed
real money immediately, not 200 years later—and 15 million
green dollars looked just about right to conquer all of Egypt in
those days, the star of the Middle East and all of its ancient
treasures: its Mystery; the immediate, in-hand Magic of owning Cairo; the pyramids; the Nile River; and the ghost of sweet
Cleopatra. The King, the emperor, the Pharaoh. Yes sir.

It was a big-time dream come true. Who needs some stupid
shack in Missouri? Napoléon was looking for instant, massive
gratification on a scale of the Gods and Goddesses, and he had
it right in front of his own greedy little eyes. Hot damn! Give me
that goddam fifteen million dollars right *now* in a clean brown
bag. I will soon be the Champion of Fun. Cazart.

So. What is the outlook for tomorrow, Doctor? What is the
gambling Prognosis? What is the score?

Well. . . . Who knows? Let me think on that, and I'll give
you an answer in the Morning. Ho ho. (Pause here for a spontaneous salute to Meatloaf, who has long been one of my heroes.)

What is happening now is a whole different game than it was yesterday. Both series in the West are tied 2–2, which is wonderful news for all those among us who are certified basketball junkies. We are seeing some strange and powerful games, and we *must* have every series go the full seven games. That is the law of nature.

I almost panicked last night, after that brutal and totally exhausting two-overtime game between the Kings and the once "unbeatable" brutes from Texas. I was beginning to see the gloomy prospect of an all-Texas Western final.

But no. Things changed, and now I see both series going seven wild games. Last year we had an all-California final. But so what? The mere possibility of Sacramento's actually winning the NBA championship without Chris Webber is so irresistible that I have to see it coming. That is all I know, and all I need to know. Good luck.

—*May 12, 2003*

The Good, the Bad, and the Vicious

Wow! This is incredible. We have just witnessed two consecutive good basketball plays in a single NBA Eastern Conference play-off game. It is 10:19 p.m. on a wet Tuesday night in America. The top-seed Detroit Pistons are more or less leading the quasi-dangerous New Jersey Nets, champions of the NBA East. Ho ho.

The score is 78–76, a repulsively low total for any NBA game with two minutes left in the fourth quarter. It is a shameless mockery of what the NBA used to look like at play-off time. These teams Suck. But do we really deserve five more minutes of Overtime in this ratbastard game? This is bad, bad, ugly, ugly basketball. Fuck overtime. We don't need any more of this brazen chickenshit. Get it over with.

Yes. Thud! There it goes, oozing away in the dimness of itself. The Nets win, by two, 88–86. And good riddance. The NBA East is a low-talent, low-rent tribe of carpetbaggers, and the TV moguls who foist this cheap, phony dung off on any sportswise TV audience should be killed. Yes, Virginia, there really is no Santa Claus—and things will never really turn out Right in the end.

What? One of these dumb yo-yos on TNT just compared the New Jersey Nets somehow to the showtime LA Lakers of 1985–88, etc. That is ridiculous. Only a fool would say a thing like that. Who was it?

Well, we know it was not Magic, because he was there on the set and laughing the insult off. And we know it was not Charles Barkley, because he is too smart to make such an ass of himself. . . . So that leaves Kenny Smith and Ernie Johnson, who both jabber and babble too much, so either one of them could have spit out something like that, without even being conscious of it. They are professional jabberers—while Magic and Charles are real-life heroes who are also real-life smart and quick and knowledgeable about the game. And Johnson shoots free throws at half-time.

Right. And so much for that, eh? The only truly shocking game of the play-offs so far was San Antonio's hopeless collapse against Dallas on Monday night, when the Mavericks came back from 18 points down to win the vitally important first game of the West finals by three little points, after trailing for all but the last seconds of the game. It was a disaster.

The last second was bad enough, but the last-second loss of the favored home team was utterly demoralizing to the proud and prancing Spurs, who self-destructed after Tim Duncan got his fifth foul. It was like watching the tortoise run down the hare, right in front of our eyes. Snap, crackle, POP. Even Jack Nicholson had to feel a twinge of sympathy for a first-class team like the Spurs—brought low by a seed of tragedy in themselves.

Tim Duncan is an agreeable, no-fun kind of guy who scored 40 points in a losing cause against a bone-tired Dallas team that had just finished playing 7 incredibly savage, draining games against Sacramento, obviously the best team in the NBA until they lost the best player, unanimous all-pro Chris Webber, to a season-ending injury about halfway through the play-offs. That was IT, once again, for the snakebitten Kings, who have been the best team in the league for the last two years but got bushwhacked both times by crippling injury or wretched hometown officiating.

I weep for Sacramento, but so what? It was like betting on a three-legged horse. And if San Antonio hadn't blown that game against Dallas on Monday, they would almost certainly have been the Champions of the NBA this year.

And they may still be—but things are different now, and the Spurs are suddenly looking a little weak, a little more vulnerable than they did after terminating the Lakers. . . . Hell, all Don Nelson and his conquering thugs had to do was deliberately and continually foul the worst free-throw shooter on San Antonio's play-off roster every time he touched the ball, and sometimes even sooner.

It was a crude and disgusting way to play the game, but it worked. The Spurs got rattled and taken rudely out of their game. They lost their rhythm, and that is usually fatal, especially in the play-offs. . . . Dallas is now the smart-money favorite. Suddenly this looks like a keenly competitive six- or seven-game series.

Good. That is the way it should be, according to my calculations and public predictions—except that I had the Spurs winning, if they could navigate the rest of the play-offs without major injuries.

I did not even think about the chance of one team's resort-ing to flat-out public thuggery as a secret winning strategy, and that makes me feel vaguely stupid. How could I have been so silly? So naïve?

Ah, but I am being hard on myself again. My overall predic-tions are looking pretty suave, so far. I even had Dallas plus nine in game One—which sounds a bit fishy, on the surface.

Indeed. How could any self-respecting gambler give Dallas plus 9, in a play-off game?

The answer is he doesn't—except maybe for halftime bets, like mine. So take a tip from a shameless hustler, folks. Make your most desperate bets at halftime, when one team is so far ahead that it looks like a certain massive beating. That is the time to pounce. That is the moment to sink your fangs into half-bright fans who are not really paying attention to this one-sided farce.

Yes. That is the moment to slip the dagger between their ribs. After that, it is only a matter of time before you will want to twist it. That is what a true gambler loves—the fleecing, the Whipping, the cruelty, the stabbing. They barely even feel it, until money changes hands and there is no escape from the sleazy truth. That is when you can physically feel their pain. That is what makes sports gambling so fun. It is wonderful.

—*May 21, 2003*

Rewarding
the Ugly

Somewhere men are laughing
Somewhere children play
But there is no Joy
in my house
The Pistons died Today
　　　—FX LEACH

That is a poem I wrote last week while I was locked up all night
in my own cistern. It was a nightmare, but it gave me time to
pay attention to Anything for more than nine consecutive seconds. And I had some hashish and a large brown bottle of 1982
Petrus, and even a Coleman lantern.

Very soon I was comfortable and thinking with great inten-
sity about the nature and fate of the Detroit Pistons, a team I
care nothing about and have never particularly liked.

But I am still vaguely irritated about the Pistons getting the
second overall pick in the NBA draft this year. It just doesn't
seem Right. How can the top-seed team in the NBA East be
picking at the top of the draft? Why are the Pistons being re-
warded for their Failure, so blatantly? Dallas, number two in
the West, is picking 27th. The Nets and the Spurs will pick 31st
and 32nd, just as they should.

But so what? Basketball season is over, and now it is
Summertime. Yes sir. Red Bull and grandma's apple pie. The
strange toxic smell of a freshly oiled baseball diamond. These
are the glories of summer, but things are different this year.
Now we have a gloomy sense of panic to include in our Summer
Schedule.

Summer has never been the same since the 2000 Presidential Election, when we still seemed to be a prosperous nation
at peace with the world, more or less. Two summers later we

were a dead-broke nation at war with all but three or four coun-
tries in the world, and three of those don't count. Spain and
Italy were flummoxed and England has allowed itself to be
taken over and stigmatized by some corrupt little shyster who
enjoys his slimy role as a pimp and a prostitute all at once—selling a once-proud nation of independent-thinking people down
the river and into a deadly swamp of slavery to the pimps who
love Jesus and George Bush and the war-crazed U.S. Pentagon.

But wait. I seem to be getting ahead of myself. The West
final will not be over until tonight, and the Nets–San Antonio
series hasn't even started yet.

But in truth, the crippled Dallas Mavericks will be badly
beaten tonight, perhaps viciously beaten. Dallas without
Nowitzki is like Sacramento without Chris Webber. Losers.
That is and always will be the fate of a team that loses a right
front wheel in the play-offs. A crippled team will never beat a
healthy team four times in 10 days. Never. So give the points in
this one, but also bet the Under. I suspect the Alamo boys will
not run up the score tonight, as a gesture of respect for those
gutsy little bastards from Dallas. They will be even harder to
beat next year.

As for the final championship series, it will be a drastic anticlimax to the closely matched and sometimes first-class
games we've been watching up to now. I will probably watch
the "finals" from my suite in the Palms Hotel in Las Vegas. I am
going there for some lengthy conversations with the Maloof
brothers, who own the Sacramento Kings as well as the Palms
Hotel. They seem to be high-end Sporting people, and they
plan to crown Anita the new Queen of Naked Bowling and give
her a new Mercedes 550E.

Gestures like that make me uneasy sometimes, but in this
case it seems entirely appropriate. Indeed, so enjoy your summer vacation this year, Bubba. It may be the last one you'll get
for the rest of your life. And please convey my deep and vivid
condolences to your family. *Mahalo.*

—May 27, 2003

Killed by a
Speeding Hummer

Whoever wins the championship this year will be the team that suffers the fewest injuries in the next 20 games. That is what it will take to survive these play-offs—and that team is probably San Antonio.

—HST, APRIL 30, 2003

Not everybody is happy with the NBA championship being decided in a showdown between New Jersey and San Antonio. It looks a little weak, for some reason—or maybe it's just me and these really are the two best basketball teams in the world.

Or maybe they are only the two toughest teams in the world—the only teams that made it this far in the Play-offs without crippling injuries to derail them and kill all their hopes. Consider that the East final and the West final were between a healthy team and a crippled team that simply couldn't compete.

Some people will tell you that surviving the NBA play-offs is the most difficult feat in Sports, and I think they are right. Surviving the NFL play-offs is like watering your lawn compared to the stark brutality of playing 28 savage basketball games in five weeks.

Have a look at what happened to Dallas, and Sacramento, and Detroit, etc., etc. They all failed because they were not the same team in the play-offs as they were at the end of the regular season.

It would be like playing in the Super Bowl without your all-pro running back, or the Stanley Cup finals with a 15-year-old substitute goalie. You are doomed to run out of gas before you get there.

On any given night, the Kings—with Chris Webber healthy—are simply a better, faster, and smarter team than

216

Dallas, or the Lakers, or even the powerful Spurs. They are definitely fun to watch and also the most reliable team to bet on—as long as you bet exactly like I do.

Dallas is the same way. They could no more whip the best teams in the league for five straight weeks without their leading scorer and rebounder than I could if I cut off my right hand.

Wow! That is an impossibly stupid thing to say at this point in time, isn't it? You bet it is, and I am now apologizing for it. Or maybe I am just too lazy to fix it, eh? How many players in the NBA worry constantly that they are simply too stupid to ever be a winner? I don't think Chris Webber feels that way—or Dirk Nowitzki. No. They are trying to play championship professional basketball on only one Leg, and that is impossible.

Ah, but I have said those things long before tonight, eh? Yes sir. It was somewhere back in April, as I recall, that I predicted, with great confidence and accuracy, that San Antonio would win it ALL, including an all-Texas final in the west.

But so what? The White House won again, and now it will be Texas against New Jersey for the big Kahuna, starting on Wednesday night on the Spurs' home court, with 30,000 whooping Texas people watching. Ho ho ho. Guess who will win, in five evil games—or 4–1 on the books, unless Tim Duncan gets hurt. And then it would be a whole different gig.

The Spurs are not going anywhere without Duncan. Period. If he got hurt, the Nets would probably reverse those numbers. They are too small to win legitimately. But remember that they are extremely fast, like water bugs, and they are definitely good enough to beat cripples—even Texas cripples.

It is horrible to think about Jason Kidd and Tim Duncan on the same team next year, and especially on the defending NBA champions. They would be unbeatable. Unless they get their legs broken, or get run over in some dark and lonely Parking facility by a speeding Hummer driven by a hit-and-run drunk who flees the scene and disappears forever.

Okay, okay, Yes, here it is. Send it. That is what I am saying to Anita, right now. She is getting aggressive about this deadline. So that's it for tonight—and beware of speeding Hummers in the darkness. The end.

—*June 2, 2003*

When in Doubt, Bet the Dark Side

We were just settling in for a frenzy of high-dollar horse racing on Saturday when the Sheriff was called away by news of a massive jailbreak in downtown Aspen. At least two dangerous Rapists had slithered out of Jail and were said to be heading our way. It was hideous news, but we paid no attention to it and continued to gamble feverishly. . . .

The Belmont was about to start, and a great roar of applause went up as Funny Cide appeared. He was the hometown hero, heavily favored to win easily. After winning the Kentucky Derby and the Preakness, he had become a national hero from coast to coast.

Funny Cide was "the people's favorite," they said. He represented "the little guy," the beer-drunk brute from Brooklyn who might run amok and kill his own children if Funny Cide lost, which seemed to be almost impossible. In New York City they seriously believed he was a Sure Thing.

The villain of this Triple Crown story was the thoroughbred racing establishment, the mint julep, pink lemonade crowd that had ruled the sport from the beginning of time. Known in the business as the dreaded Kentucky Mafia of horse breeders & trainers & money barons, they hated the sight of Funny Cide and "would do almost anything to keep him from winning this race." Rumors said they were Desperate—and the weapon they chose on this muddy Saturday morning was a finely bred 3-year-old colt from Churchill Downs named Empire Maker. He was the real thing.

The Belmont is always a big race, but this year it was gigantic. If Funny Cide won, he would pick up an additional $5,000,000 bonus from Visa for winning racing's Triple Crown, in addition to the $1.9 million he had already won, all in a single year. Funny Cide was on the brink of Immortality.

But not everybody saw it that way, including me. In my heart I was for the darling of New York, but my brain was telling me to bet on Empire Maker. He was a creature of the huge and sinister blue-blood racing establishment. I knew these people; I grew up with them, and I know they are capable of Anything.

Thoroughbred horses are extremely delicate animals. At three years old, they are like pimply teenagers just getting into the business. They are flaky and temperamental and bitchy, just like us, and most of them are flat-out useless. If they break a leg, which is common, you have to execute them, right there on the spot. Put a bullet through their brains and haul them away to a glue factory and keep a stiff upper lip. That is how it works in the horse-racing business life. It is a profoundly Darwinian world, where there are many losers and winners.

Betting the Belmont was a classic example of the "heart vs. head" syndrome that I have struggled with all my life. Funny Cide was the heaviest favorite to win the Belmont since Native Dancer and Secretariat, a solid 4–5 and falling. Funny Cide was America's horse.

Nevertheless, he got run down at the top of the stretch by Empire Maker and was never heard from again. He faded to a well-beaten third, and so did that $5,000,000 bonus from Visa. When in doubt, bet the dark side. It is the nature of this business we have chosen.

—*June 10, 2003*

Welcome to the
Big Darkness

Hi, folks, my name is still Thompson and I still drink gin with ER Nurses at night—but in one particular way I am a New Man, a different man, a more dangerous man than I was the last time we talked. And that was a few weeks ago, eh?

Indeed, I can walk again, and I like it, because last month I felt an acute spasmodic pain in my spine when I walked. There was nothing cute about it, no socially redeeming factor. It just plain sucked.

But I have just returned from an extremely intense few weeks at the world-renowned Steadman-Hawkins Clinic in Vail, Colorado (Yes, where Kobe Bryant . . .), where I had radical surgery to repair what was beginning to give me some pain. Great pain on some days, and I finally decided to get rid of it.

I am no stranger to organ replacement, and I always find it refreshing, always a happy improvement over Pain.

I hate pain, despite my ability to tolerate it beyond all known parameters, which is not necessarily a good thing. I once gouged about two-thirds of my hip socket into mush for five straight years, until I finally felt enough pain to have the bastard replaced.

And Titanium turned out to be far more comfortable and flexible than the human spine anyway, especially mine. It is lighter, stronger, and far more adaptable in every way than bone or steel or anything else in the human body—and I am installing it in my own body as rapidly as possible without doing anything stupid.

My alloy spine replacement is about 70 percent finished, and after it's completed, I will take a break. And maybe have a look at this weird and degrading Kobe Bryant story, which interests me. The more I learn about this case, the more I understand that this is not about Rape at all. It is about money, pure money, and nothing else. Nobody is going to jail in this case, but some people are going to Pay.

The downward spiral of Dumbness in America is about to hit a new low. You thought O. J. was bad? Wait until we get a taste of the K. B. scandal. It will be like a feeding frenzy and a long parade of whores and cannibals.

When I went into the clinic last April 30, George Bush was about 50 points ahead of his closest Democratic opponent in next year's Presidential Election—and when I finally escaped from the horrible place, less than three weeks later, Bush's job approval ratings had been cut in half—and even down into single digits, in some states—and the Republican Party was panicked and on the run. It was a staggering reversal in a very short time, even shorter than it took for his equally crooked father to drop from 93 percent approval down to as low as 43 percent and even 41 percent in the last doomed days of the first doomed Bush Administration. After that he was Bill Clinton's punching bag.

Richard Nixon could tell us a lot about peaking too early. He was a master of it; it beat him every time. He never learned and neither did Bush the Elder.

But wow! This goofy child-president we have on our hands now: he is demonstrably a fool and a failure, and this is only the summer of '03. By the summer of 2004 he may not even be living in the White House. Gone, gone, like the snows of yesteryear.

The Rumsfeld-Cheney axis has self-destructed right in front of our eyes, along with the once-proud Perle-Wolfowitz bund that is turning to wax. They somehow managed to blow it all, like a gang of kids on a looting spree, between January and July, or even faster. It is genuinely incredible. The U.S. Treasury is empty, we are losing that stupid, fraudulent, chickenshit War in Iraq, and every country in the world except a handful of Corrupt Brits despises us. We are losers, and that is the one unforgiveable sin in America.

Beyond that, we have lost the respect of the world and lost two disastrous wars in three years. Afghanistan is lost, Iraq is a permanent war Zone, our national Economy is crashing all around us, the Pentagon's "war strategy" has failed miserably, nobody has any money to spend, and our once-mighty America is paralyzed by Mutinies in Iraq and even Fort Bragg.

The American nation is in the worst condition I can remember in my lifetime, and our prospects for the immediate future are even worse. I am surprised and embarrassed to be a part of the first American generation to leave the country in far worse shape than it was when we first came into it. Our highway system is crumbling, our police are dishonest, our children are poor, our vaunted Social Security, once the envy of the world, has been looted and neglected and destroyed by the same gang of ignorant, greed-crazed bastards who brought us Vietnam, Afghanistan, the disastrous Gaza Strip, and ignominious defeat all over the world.

The Stock Market will never come back, our Armies will never again be Number One, and our children will drink filthy water for the rest of our lives.

The Bush family must be very proud of themselves today, but I am not. Big Darkness, soon come. Take my word for it.

—*July 21, 2003*

The Nation's Capital

ESPN Editor's Note: The opinions voiced below are those of the infamous Doctor Thompson and are absolutely not the views of this network or the editors. That is free journalism.

I know this is hard for some people to accept, but the fact is that Football season is right on top of us again. The first game on TV is scheduled for August 9, less than two weeks from now. It will not be real Football, of course, but it will look like real football, and it will sound like real football—and if you cross your eyes and blow on your thumb hard enough, it will almost be possible to bet on it.

Only a real addict can look forward to that kind of desperate scratching and sniffing, and I am one of them. I am a student of the NFL game. I have been with it since the very beginning, since the start of the modern TV era.

In any case, I had an extremely busy schedule last week. It combined the best and the worst of everything and led into a frenzy of involvements. I was still recovering from my alloy spine replacement procedure when the real world suddenly caught up with me and called me back into action. There was no way to avoid it. I had no choice.

The real shocker of the week, for me, was and remains the stunning collapse of the evil Bush administration, which I view with mixed feelings.

In truth, I could be a lot happier about the collapse of Bush and his people and his whole house of cards and everything he stands for, if it didn't also mean the certain collapse of the U.S. economy, and the vital infrastructure, and indeed the whole "American way of life."

It will not be anything like the collapse and Impeachment of Richard Nixon, which had little or no impact on day-to-day life in this country. Nothing really changed then, except Some people went to prison, of course, but that was to be expected, considering the crimes they committed and the shameful damage they caused. They were criminals, and the righteous American people punished them for it. Our system worked and we were all heroes.

Ah, but that was twenty-nine (29) years ago, Bubba, and many things have changed. The utter collapse of this Profoundly criminal Bush conspiracy will come none too soon for people like me, though it may already be too late. The massive plundering of the U.S. Treasury and all its resources has been almost on a scale that is criminally insane and has literally destroyed the lives of millions of American people and American families. Exactly. You and me, sport—we are the ones who are going to suffer, and suffer massively. This is going to be just like the Book of Revelation said it was going to be—the end of the world as we knew it.

Okay, Okay, don't get away from yourself, Doc. That was an extremely heavy riff. Not all sports fans are in perfect agreement with your aggressive political opinions, so let's try to tread lightly for a while. You are, after all, a professional sportswriter, and you have work to do. Ho ho ho.

Exactly, and that is only one of the reasons I was visited last week by the eminent Daniel Snyder, "new" owner of the Washington Redskins. Dan gave me a football and we exchanged many other impressive gifts, such as the world's best whiskey and the finest Davidoff cigars. I liked Snyder and I have vastly improved expectations for the Redskins this year. They are a team that has played a large part in my life. I still have friends who played for the Redskins—people like John Wilbur, whom I still see frequently in Hawaii, and Billy Kilmer, Sonny Jurgensen, Roy Jefferson, Charlie Taylor—players mainly from the Good old days of the 1970s, when the Skins were usually on the top of the NFL East, and I was living, for intensely political reasons, right smack in the middle of Washington, DC. Those were violent years for everyone, or at least everyone even faintly involved with either Football or Politics, and that was just about every person I knew.

I particularly remember Edward Bennett Williams, who was then the Owner of the Redskins. He had been a personal hero of mine long before I ever met him. Ed was arguably the Number-One Criminal Lawyer of his time or any other. Ed Williams was royalty, he was a living legend at all Law Schools, including Columbia, where I was spending a lot of my time in those years. Edward Bennett Williams was the Real Thing.

And so am I for that matter, but we will not dwell on that now. Time is running out on us. Alas, we will be forced to abbreviate or even chop off the many other things I was planning to discuss this week. I am still fatigued from my extremely successful, though tiring, spinal situation. I feel no pain (knock, knock), which is a beautiful improvement. That is all ye know and all ye need to know, for now. *Mahalo.*

—*July 28, 2003*

Speed Kills and Other Football Wisdom

It is never smart to bet money on "preseason" NFL football games, because they are utterly meaningless to anybody except the hundreds of players who may or may not be cut after each one. There are roughly 100 players out there for each team, competing desperately with each other for 53 roster jobs. Few of them even know each other's names.

Preseason games are like a death dance for most of them. They will never be a starting player on any NFL team, they will never even get to wear a legitimate team jersey or see themselves on TV, like they always wanted to.

Trying out is like a huge casting call for a major Johnny Depp or Benicio Del Toro movie about sex, death, and violence in a typical all-American family that gets caught up in a kidnapping plot to move terrorists from Korea to New Orleans during the summer monsoon season. The movie will be a hot one, requiring thousands of mob-scene extras.

There will inevitably be many psychotics among them, many flaming unregistered Perverts and supergroupies depending entirely on Steroids and Downers to make it through the first few dozen practices. Most of them are habitually unemployed anyway, and trying out as an inside linebacker for the Miami Dolphins might look like a good idea, to some people.

And besides, there is always that one in a million chance that you might be suddenly discovered, like Marlon Brando.

Most of these stories have horrible endings, but there are, of course, exceptions to that rule, and we saw one of the best of them in real life on Monday night. Michael Lewis, known as "Beer Man" to his teammates, was a 29-year-old, onetime beer truck driver when he got his final tryout for the New Orleans Saints.

The Beer Man averaged 25.8 yards per kickoff return last year and 14.2 on punts, second in the NFL. He also runs the 100 in 4.2, which means certain death for any defender who suddenly gets assigned to cover him. Many failed, and many were instantly cut and sent back to the Arena League or NFL Europe.

That is the way it goes in the NFL, no mercy and no second chances. Speed kills, in the famous words of ultimate Raider Al Davis. You can't teach speed, he said. Everything else in the game can be taught, but speed is a gift from God.

Right. And where was Al Davis when Michael Lewis came down the pipe? Who knows? And that is an unfair question anyway. Al can't be everywhere at once, and he will likely get his hands on Lewis sooner or later.

We got a chance to see Beer Man in action on Monday night, and he performed as advertised. He ran off a truly spectacular 102-yard kickoff early in the game that got called back on one of those blind, dumb calls that can derail a referee's career if it happens during the season, but this was just another one of those free-fall Exhibition games that nobody cares about.

In Michael Lewis's case, it was a high-speed spin move that hasn't been seen in the NFL since O. J. Simpson's best days. Lewis was whacked sideways and seemed to fall down on his right shoulder, ending the play. But No. The Beer Man whirled and kept himself upright with the use of a stiff right arm to the ground and a rare trick of balance that kept him on his feet and picking up speed toward the goal line, while all the others watched. BOOM. It was special.

It was the Play of the Day, and probably the play of the NFL preseason. They don't hardly make 'em like that anymore. It was the kind of play that O. J. Simpson himself would have recognized and admired, in the good old days, before his ruinous trials and eternal disgrace.

I was reminded of Gayle Sayers and Jim Brown, or even Barry Sanders at his best—so Michael Lewis is a hot one to watch, this season. He is a game breaker.

The Saints look a little iffy so far, but I expect them to level out and be a solid play-off team. At least they are wild and exciting.

My other predictions and selections, etc., will have to wait for next week. Fear not. We have a long strange season out there ahead of us. *Mahalo.*

—*August 12, 2003*

Nightmare in Hollywood

I had a truly horrible dream last night about how I blundered into a fight between Mike Tyson and Arnold Schwarzenegger on Sunset Boulevard in Los Angeles. I was sitting next to Arnold (current betting favorite to be the next Governor of California) in the back seat of a black stretch limousine. We were on our way to a TV studio for a debate about his longtime working friendship with the powerful Bush family from Texas and how it might affect the next Bush presidency when the Terminator seizes power in Sacramento and tries to hand over the state's 55 electoral votes by election day in 2004. That is the basic plan behind Schwarzenegger's running. He doesn't want to be Governor, he just wants the electoral votes to go to Bush this time.

It was a solemn subject and I didn't quite understand why Schwarzenegger had agreed to debate it in public, with me or anyone else except maybe Karl Rove. He was raving and snarling into his cell phone about something that had to do with Arianna Huffington, so we tried to ignore him as the limo crept along in a gridlocked traffic jam. Tempers were rising and there were no ice cubes and we were sure to be late for the TV debate. I was ready to jump out of the car at the next stoplight and hide out at the Polo Lounge.

Suddenly I felt the car stop, and brakes screeched as the limo rear-ended a big SUV right in front of us. BANG. It was not much, more like a nudge than a crash, not even a small fender bender—and then the violence began.

I was looking over the driver's shoulder when I saw what looked like a small, burly black man leap out of the SUV and come sprinting toward us, bellowing savagely. "You goddamn crazy honky bastard! I'll kill you for this!" There were desperate screaming sounds and then the awful smashing of window glass, and then the car began rocking crazily. There was something familiar about our attacker's face, but it was all happening so fast that I couldn't be sure.

Then, ye gods, I recognized the vicious, snarling face of Mike Tyson, former heavyweight champion of the world who had once seemed unbeatable forever, by anybody—until he went over to Tokyo for a low-rent, bum-of-the-month type, no interest, who cares "tune-up fight" against some unranked, oft-beaten challenger named Buster Douglas, who was such a hopeless underdog that the fight was actually taken off the board in Las Vegas when the odds reached 40–1.

I only watched it on HBO because I knew I had to write about it that week. Nobody else even wanted to watch it with me. We had all been Suckered once too often into paying big money to watch Tyson race across the ring and beat another terrified fighter half to death in 90 seconds, or 85 seconds, and that was it. There was no more.

Mike Tyson took all the fun out of boxing—especially for those of us who grew up on Muhammad Ali and Joe Frazier.

I remember two minor details from the slow days leading up to the fight in Tokyo. One was a flippant reply by Tyson when Larry Merchant asked him if there was any possible way that he might lose this waltz with Douglas.

"Only if they have a sharpshooter in the crowd," said Iron Mike with a confident leer.

The other memorable detail from that week was that Tyson had traveled himself all the way to Japan, 15,000 miles RT, 36 hours on a commercial airliner, because he was publicly crazed and distressed by the breakup of his first marriage, to superpopular TV actress Robin Givens, which was driving him nuts.

I noticed this and made a mental note of it. Mike Tyson, as history now shows us, has an extremely fragile ego when it comes to being rejected by women. There is no record of his doing anything but flipping out and spiraling into violence.

Back in 1990 those episodes seemed vaguely quaint or goofy, clearly driven by passions beyond his control. What the hell? Aren't all violent high-strung athletes that way?

And that was my situation when the fight began. I was certain that it would end quickly, like all the others. Why shouldn't it?

Why indeed? But now, in long retrospect, that first and only Tyson-Douglas fight appears as a wild and crazy thing. Buster Douglas literally beat the living piss out of the champ. It was one of the best and most shocking upsets in the history of professional boxing. Scheduled for 12 rounds, it ended with a TKO by Douglas after only 10.

I still watch that fight on tape from time to time, just for the wild excitement of it, the sheer impossibility. It ranks right up there with some of Ali's finest hours.

There was no joy in Atlanta, or anywhere else in the NFL last week, for Michael Vick went down with a broken leg on the first offensive series of a meaningless preseason game. I was watching the play when it happened, and there was nothing particularly brutal or vicious about the tackle. It looked to me like a broken play that left Vick caught in his own backfield for a minor loss. So what?

But then, when he didn't get up for too many minutes, the crowd began to rumble and groan. And then they brought on that evil yellow cart that always signals something ugly—but never with a hot young superstar like Michael Vick, who was thought to be invincible, too tough to hurt and too fast to catch. Vick was perfectly on track to become the Michael Jordan of his time. It was impossible for him to be crippled and put out for the season.

But it was true. The Falcons' big Super Bowl dreams and high expectations went up in smoke when Vick went down. Their spectacular off-season trade for Buffalo's all-pro wideout Peerless Price was a sure bet to hook up with Vick and produce instant Joe Montana/Jerry Rice–type results. But it suddenly looked like just another stupid personal mistake for both parties. Buffalo gave up its finest and most productive receiver (1,252 yards, 9 TDs, 94 catches last year), leaving Drew Bledsoe nobody special to throw to and Price with nobody special throwing passes to him—and the NFL without its hottest box-office attraction.

As for my horrible dream about Tyson and the Terminator beating each other to death on a crowded street in the middle of Hollywood, I woke up before it ended and I can't remember who prevailed. It was just another small tragedy in the world of sports.

Okay. That's it for now. Banzie.

—*August 18, 2003*

Speed Will Rule the NFL This Year

The football season is creeping along to a violent official start now, and I am starting to feel cranked up again. The summer has been strange and quick, as it usually is when you are 8,000 feet up in the mountains. Between getting married and having half my spine replaced, there has been a lot of leisure time for healing other people's puncture wounds. The world of sports has many of them.

But so what? Puncture wounds come with the territory

in this business. Look at Michael Vick. Look at the Atlanta Falcons. Look at Kobe Bryant. They are all facing nasty seasons.

The Denver Broncos are expected to be a force in the AFC West again this year, but I doubt it. The Broncos never quite recovered from the loss of John Elway, arguably the greatest quarterback of all time. He retired at the peak of his glory, after winning two straight Super Bowls, and the Broncos have never been the same without him, despite the heavy presence of alleged supercoach Mike Shanahan. His winning percentage since Elway's departure has hovered just a bit over .500.

The Oakland Raiders' W-L record since then has been .644, tops in the NFL. But that will not happen again this year. The San Diego Chargers are ranked in the bottom third of the league this year, and they will probably stay there.

Actually, there is nobody in the West of either conference who looks like a Super Bowl contender. I hope Oakland will get there and get even for last year's freakish defeat, but I am not real optimistic. This is not going to be a good year for feel-good stories, in sports or anywhere else. Big darkness, soon come.

Tennessee's rookie wide receiver Tyrone Calico is the most exciting wideout in the NFL to see on TV, but on paper he is a useless dunce and a sure bet to be cut before Labor Day.

Speaking, as always, as a Gambler, I'd have to say that Tyrone is a lock—if only because he is going to sell tickets. And take my word for it, Bubba, Tyrone Calico is going to be big this year.

Is that clear? Good. I see a lot of Speed coming into the league—and thank you again, Al Davis—which always means Action, and that is highly desirable. Teams like Philadelphia and Tennessee, and also the Washington Redskins, in the East are going to turn some serious Speed loose on the league in September.

Darrell Green has long been one of my personal heroes. He is what the best people in sports call a class act. For 21 years he has been the smartest, fastest, and meanest defensive back in a league where Fast and Smart and Mean are not especially rare commodities. No sir. You want speed? We got plenty of speed. Let's see what you have.

Tyrone Calico runs the 40 in 4.3 seconds, which is Fast, but not red-hot fast, if you know what I mean. We have tall linebackers in this league who are at least as fast as that. Four point two is hot, 4.1 is real hot, and Dan Snyder told me about a Redskins undrafted rookie who regularly clocks four seconds flat. That is 4.0 over 40 yards.

Tyrone Calico weighs 222 pounds and stands six feet four inches tall. That is a speeding mass that nobody sane wants to get in front of, and definitely not more than once. Hell, look what happened to Michael Vick, and he barely got Hit at all.

And then there is Jets QB Chad Pennington, who went down and out on Sunday with his wrist broken in seven places. WHACKO! Now, 40-year-old Vinny Testaverde is all that stands between the Jets and a 3–13 finish this season.

I also like Miami and New Orleans for early-season wildness, and I have always had a special fondness for Jim Irsay's high-speed, high-precision Indianapolis Colts. I have never believed that Tony Dungy really enjoys coaching Offense anyway. Defense is supposed to be his specialty, and the time has come for him to live up to that rep.

Nobody in the NFL has three individual players better than Peyton Manning, Edgerrin James, and Marvin Harrison. They are all very close to being the best in their business, and I wish them good luck this season.

I like the Colts' wide-open, quick-strike-anytime offensive style. They are always fun to watch, but I can't honestly recommend betting on them, not even with Points. It has something to do with the Curse of Baltimore that came down on the Colts when Irsay's father raped them away in the dead of night to a curious new home in Indianapolis 33 years ago.

It was an ugly deed, and the Colts have never won anything since then. Football fans have long memories. . . .

What? Anita tells me that I am being unacceptably cruel to our friend James Irsay, current owner of the Colts, who is a very different man from the beast that his father was.

"Why are you holding a grudge against his Father?" Anita screams. "His father is dead. What can James do about it now—take the Colts back to Baltimore?"

I hesitated. She was right. It was like expecting me to stand trial for the sins of Jack Kennedy. They could do that, "but it would be wrong."

Richard Nixon said that, and I always get mushy about Nixon when football season rolls around. He was the Real Thing, a genuinely educated football fan.

I miss Nixon. Compared to these Nazis we have in the White House now, Richard Nixon was a flaming Liberal. Dr. Thompson said That. *Mahalo.*

P.S. It would not be fair to end this rant without answering your many questions about the final ending of that Tyson-Schwarzenegger fight I was telling you about last week. It never happened, because Arnold ran away. Iron Mike tried to chase him down, but he ran into a moving Police car and got arrested again.

There is a school of thought among sportswriters that believes Mike Tyson should be put to sleep for the greater good, and I am beginning to think they are right. We have enough to be terrified about these days without having to worry about accidentally running into that monster Tyson in the middle of a routine traffic jam.

—*August 25, 2003*

The Bush League

Why are we seeing George Bush on TV every two hours for nine or ten days at a time, like some kind of mutated Mr. Rogers clone? Something is dangerously wrong in any country where a monumentally Failed backwoods politician can scare our national TV networks so totally that they will give him anything he wants.

The answer to that one comes in two parts. One is that Bush will have to run for reelection next year, which three months ago seemed like a harmless waltz—but which is now looking like a dangerous gang fight that Bush might not win, because his overall game plan for Iraq was so hopelessly flawed that it could never have been successful. It was arrogant and ignorant and stupid, and now the vultures are coming home to roost.

Tragic, eh? No. In fact it couldn't have happened to a nicer guy. I believe very strongly that George Bush can and shall be beaten like a gong in next year's extremely important election, where he won't be the only jackass politician running for his life.

Who gave George Bush permission to preempt and butt into NFL football games and turn pregame ceremonies into some half-bright rave about rebuilding a nation that we just bombed back into the Stone Age? What kind of cowardly swine would freely give $25,000,000 worth of commercial time to any political candidate in a presidential election year?

How about the greed-blind Commissioner of the National Football League? Does that sound right? You bet it does, Bubba. It was Paul Tagliabue who let the egg-sucking weasel from Texas into the henhouse, because he thought it was necessary at the time.

*   *   *

My darkest fear right now is that we will be seeing George W. Bush on NFL TV every Sunday for the rest of this year and far into the winter and maybe all year long next year until election day rolls around, constantly jabbering about how his jackass war on a nation of Muslims is joined at the hip with the nature of football in America and especially the NFL. If you love to watch anything that looks like professional American football, you will also love the brutal culture of War and all the murderous violence that goes right along with it. Right. In war you do 200 push-ups a day, and in pro football you do about 50. In war you carry a nine-pound full-auto assault rifle at all times, and in football you carry a pointed leather ball.

They are both profoundly violent and cruel and utterly unforgiving, and they both require public brutality by people wearing elaborate uniforms. I have tried them both for long periods of time, and I frankly see no basic similarity at all, beyond the powerful desire to hurt people.

—September 8, 2003

Boxing Sucks

The time has come, the suckfish said, to get rid of professional Boxing in America. It has been a horrible traveling hoax since Muhammad Ali's retirement, and now it has turned itself into a bag of Poison scum. Those crooked bastards have finally gone too far. The U.S. Congress should immediately pass a special Criminal Fraud law to permanently Banish professional boxing spectacles like Saturday night's Moseley–De La Hoya fight from all public airwaves in America. There is some shit we won't eat.

That is strong language, in some circles, but when you start talking about the ugly, evil nature of boxing today, no language is strong enough. Like "Wait a minute, whoreface! That's my airspace that your hired swine are stealing and using up there! That space belongs to me. That is public property, and I am part of the public. You're trespassing! You are a brazen shit-eating criminal, and it is legal for me to kill people like you!"

You want to be vaguely careful when you start screaming about killing people. It can be a touchy subject. Never threaten to kill people in front of witnesses. Take my word for it.

Ah, but never mind that. Let's get back to some pure sport, like professional football in the USA. It may be fixed, but at least it is Artfully fixed, compared to the out-front, in-your-face, screw-you kind of cheap-ass shuck that boxing is.

I can say that with a straight face because I have a special knowledge of boxing that comes with growing up with Muhammad Ali as our champion—which is sort of like living in a time when toys like Acid and Marijuana were legal. It was a very different time.

Indeed, and so much for that craziness. The Denver Broncos looked tough in a whole new way on Sunday, as "new" quarterback Jake the Snake Plummer finally came to life. It was a nice surprise to see him throwing and diving for first downs, in the style of John Elway. If Plummer has finally meshed with his Offensive line, Denver could ambush a few people later in the season. Clinton Portis is a major new running back, and second-year wide receiver Ashley Lelie will go to many Pro Bowls. I watched him when he played college ball in Hawaii. I never cease to be amazed at Coach Shanahan's eye for raw talent. Denver keeps rolling along.

Hell, I am full of sports news and judgmental opinions today. Boxing sucks, the Raiders look maybe a full step slower this season, George Bush is looking weaker, Wes Clark looks Interesting, and it looks from up here that Washington and Indianapolis will meet in the Super Bowl next year.

How's that for looking ahead? Why not? It is always safe to

say the Yankees will win the World Series. Big money works wonders in America . . . but apparently not in Iraq, where we are spending 2 billion dollars a week just to keep from being humiliated in the eyes of the world, which is no longer all in our corner.

Which reminds me somehow of the Philadelphia Eagles, who have lost more than just a step since last season. One of the most basic factors in sports is that Winning becomes a Habit and Losing is the same way. When Failure starts to feel Normal in your life or your work or even your darkest vices, you won't have to go looking for trouble, because trouble will find You. Count on it.

Our dangerously goofy child-president from Texas is a squalid example of trouble coming home to roost. He is like a half-bright football coach who goes into a big game without a Game Plan. BOOM! Shame and failure will follow you for all the days of your life. *Selah.*

The Bush family reeks of fraud and bad karma. But even worse than our wretched gibbling president are the cowardly whores in Hollywood who are currently smearing film stars and music people like Johnny Depp by calling them unpatriotic Americans for righteously questioning the wisdom of invading a whole nation of Muslims—which is a dangerously stupid idea. Disagreeing with Donald Rumsfeld about bombing any-body who gets in our way is not a crime in this country. It is a wise and honorable idea that George Washington and Ben-jamin Franklin risked their lives for.

These thieves in the White House are so crazy with greed and power, and they are causing so much drastic damage to the world we live in, that they are the ones who should be put on trial for treason.

Okay. I am getting a little excited here, so I think I'll wrap this up quick, before I spiral out and burst into flames. I am widely known as a bedrock, natural-born patriot and a lover of what this country used to stand for. The Statue of Liberty wasn't out there for nothing. Beware of Warmongers. They don't give a hoot in hell if you live or die. They are in this racket strictly for themselves. *Mahalo.*

—*September 15, 2003*

George Plimpton

Earth receive an honored guest;
William Yeats is laid to rest:
Let the Irish vessel lie
Emptied of its poetry.

Time that is intolerant
Of the brave and innocent,
And indifferent in a week
To a beautiful physique,

Worships language and forgives
Everyone by whom it lives;
Pardons cowardice, conceit,
Lays its honors at their feet.

Time that with this strange excuse
Pardoned Kipling and his views,
And will pardon Paul Claudel,
Pardons him for writing well.

—W. H. AUDEN, FROM
"IN MEMORY OF W. B. YEATS"

George Plimpton was an elegant man. He was an aristocrat of the spirit and one of my finest friends. Being a friend of his carried a special responsibility for behaving in a style that he would be proud of. You didn't want to let him down, and George had extremely high standards. Every moment of being in his company was part of my Education. It was a proud moment when I first introduced my son Juan to "my friend George Plimpton." There was no need to explain anything extra about George: you didn't have to know him to realize that he was genuine American Royalty and that it was a privilege to be in the same room with him.

I loved George, and he has been a gigantic influence in my life. When I think of him, I see a tall, loose-walking man strolling through the lobby of the Carlyle Hotel with an armload of fresh Calla Lilies.

George Plimpton was about as good a friend as a man can have in this world. He lived his life like a work of fine art. George Plimpton was a winner. He was comfortable with everything, from reading Plato in the original Greek to sparring with Muhammad Ali and courting Jackie Kennedy. He was an athlete and a scholar. He played touch football with Bobby Kennedy on the lawn of Hickory Hill and built some of the most dangerous and colossal firebombs ever seen in the American Century. He was absolutely fearless.

There are so many wild and beautiful stories I could tell you about being with George, having savage and unnatural adventures all over the world, that I am feeling dumb and paralyzed when I try to write them down. He was the highest and truest authority on American literature of his time, a genuine Man of Letters.

George Plimpton kicked ass. He was a champion in everything he did. He was the finest advertisement for Harvard University since LSD-25, and he loved Calla Lilies, along with beautiful women and Bob Dylan and the finest Afghani hashish.

Whoops. Enough of that mushy stuff. My real reason for writing tonight is that I think the friends of George Plimpton should and must create a permanent white monument to him.

It should be built in the little plaza next to his home and the offices of the elegant *Paris Review*, at the end of 72nd Street in Manhattan, overlooking the East River. I don't know much about building or creating monuments to people in any neighborhood, but I have a powerful feeling that this one is the right idea at the right time and is absolutely doable immediately.

Okay. This is just a start, so let's get rolling on it. Who knows what it will look like? Not me, but I have some suave and aggressive ideas. Give me a ring. Thanks.

HUNTER
—*September 29, 2003*

Victory

Monday was another bad night for watching football. We had rain, violence, fraud, and scenes of miserable failure. If I had to pick a Super Bowl winner right now, it would have to be Kansas City. The Chiefs have that smart, speedy kind of confidence that has always been the mark of Dick Vermeil's best teams.

Now he has the Chiefs, looking big and fast and cool. If it is true that speed kills, then Kansas City will win the whole thing. Priest Holmes will kill you all by himself. He follows his blockers better than any other running back in the League, and Dante Hall is so quick that he barely needs blockers.

Even a retread like quarterback Trent Green can look great in Vermeil's Gotcha! offense, which is way too smart to be a failure in this Here today, Gone tomorrow, free agent league where nobody hangs around long enough to become a legend. My wicked old friend Max McGee wouldn't last three weeks in the NFL today. He didn't have enough respect for the Rules.

And so much for that, eh? The time has come to move beyond simple football predictions. What the hell? Let's try Baseball. That looks easy. So why not predict that the musty Chicago Cubs will win the World Series this year? They are long overdue, and the times are right for it.

George W. Bush is a baseball man, so I wonder about who he'll choose to win the Series this year, if only to know who to stay away from.

I have never had much faith in our embattled child-president's decision-making powers. He comes from a long line of Losers. . . . I know that is not what you want to hear/read at this time, especially if you happen to be serving in the doomsday mess that is currently the U.S. Army.

I take no pleasure in being Right in my dark predictions about the fate of our military intervention in the heart of the Muslim world. It is immensely depressing to me. Nobody likes to be betting against the Home team, no matter how hopeless they are.

I have done that, from time to time, and it never fails to leave me feeling guilty and confused, even if I win. Winning is vitally important in the gambling business, but it is better not to publicize your most shameful and predatory bets. How many red-blooded Americans really want to go down in history having voted for George Bush and Military disaster in 2000?

Not me, Bubba—but I feel the pain anyway. Any failure of this magnitude is a shared experience, like it or not. Not every passenger on the good ship *Titanic* voted to hit that iceberg. Of course not; it was the Captain's decision—and the Captain went down with it, just like his father.

It is up to the rest of us to make sure this fool of a President doesn't take us all down with him. . . . WHACK! And that's it for realpolitik, eh? That evil crap can take all the fun out of Football.

But I have learned, in my life and work as a sportswriter, that big-time Sports and big-time Politics are not so far apart in America. They are both a means to the same end, which is Victory. . . . And why not? Victory is good for you and don't let anybody tell you different.

—*October 13, 2003*

"POLITICS IS THE ART OF CONTROLLING YOUR ENVIRONMENT"

BY HST

That is one of the key things I learned in these years, and I learned it the hard way. Anybody who thinks that "it doesn't matter who's President" has never been Drafted and sent off to fight and die in a vicious, stupid War on the other side of the World—or been beaten and gassed by Police for trespassing on public property—or been hounded by the IRS for purely political reasons—or locked up in the Cook County Jail with a broken nose and no phone access and twelve perverts wanting to stomp your ass in the shower. That is when it matters who is President or Governor or Police Chief. That is when you will wish you had voted.

Honor Roll

Muhammad Ali
David Amram
Jeff Armstrong
Lisl Auman
Tracy Avedisian
Doc Barahal
Bob Beattie
Sandy Berger
Steve Bornstein
Ed Bradley
Sheriff Bob Braudis
Doug Brinkley
Lucy Brown
Kobe Bryant
George W. Bush
Senator Byrd
Tyrone Calico
Sue Carrolan
Graydon Carter
Fidel Castro
Dick Cheney
Rick Clark
Michael Cleverly
Donald Corenman
Alice Cotton
Louisa Davidson
Al Davis
Morris Dees
Johnny Depp
Evan Dobelle
Bob Dylan
Tara Eggert
Wayne Ewing

Tim Ferris
Flor Flores
Deborah Fuller
Gerald Goldstein, Esq.
Al Gore
Hal Haddon, Esq.
Dante Hall
Marvin Harrison
Josh Hartnett
Hugh Hefner
Abe Hutt
Jim Irsay
Kevin Jackson
Doris Kearns
Senator John Kerry
Michael Kinsley
Emily Laroque
Wayne Lawson
Gerald Lefcourt, Esq.
Kathleen Lord
Bob Love
Lyle Lovett
Jay Lovinger
Marilyn Manson
Terry McDonnel
Norm Mueller, Esq.
Laila Nabulsi
Damon Oliver
Prince Omar
Princess Omin
Dolly Parton
Sean Penn
Alison Petterson

Ed Podolak
Marysue Rucci
Christina Santiago
Mark Seal
Chloe Sells
George Sells
Daniel Snyder
Ralph Steadman
Michael Stepanian, Esq.
George & Patti Stranahan
Jennifer Stroup

Anita Thompson
Davison Thompson
Juan & Jennifer Thompson
Robin Thompson
George Tobia
Dita Von Teese
Dick Vermeil
John Walsh
Jane Wenner
John Wilbur

About the Author

HUNTER S. THOMPSON was born and raised in Louisville, Kentucky. His books include *Hell's Angels, Fear and Loathing in Las Vegas, Fear and Loathing: On the Campaign Trail '72, The Curse of Lono, Songs of the Doomed, Better Than Sex, The Proud Highway,* and *Kingdom of Fear.* He is a regular contributor to various national and international publications. He now lives in a fortified compound in Colorado.